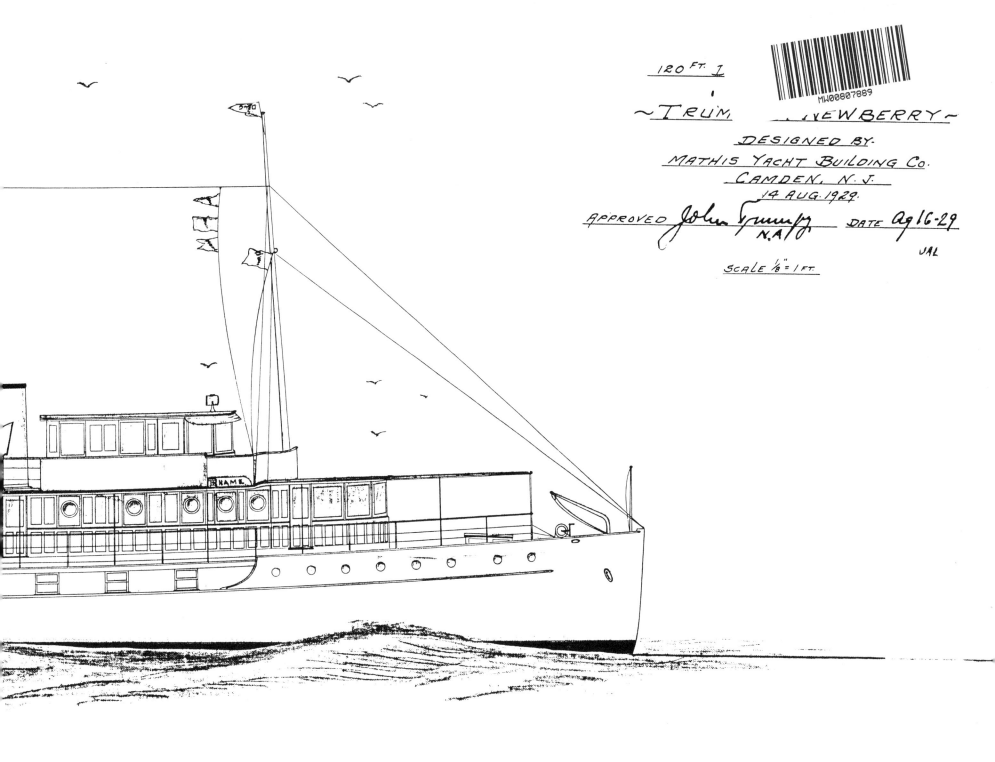

120 FT. 1

~TRUM ___EWBERRY~

DESIGNED BY-
MATHIS YACHT BUILDING Co.
CAMDEN, N.J.
14 AUG. 1929.

APPROVED John Trump
N.A.   DATE Ag 16-29

JAL

SCALE 1/8" = 1 FT.

TRUMPY

Robert Picardat, Illustrator   Robert Tolf, Author

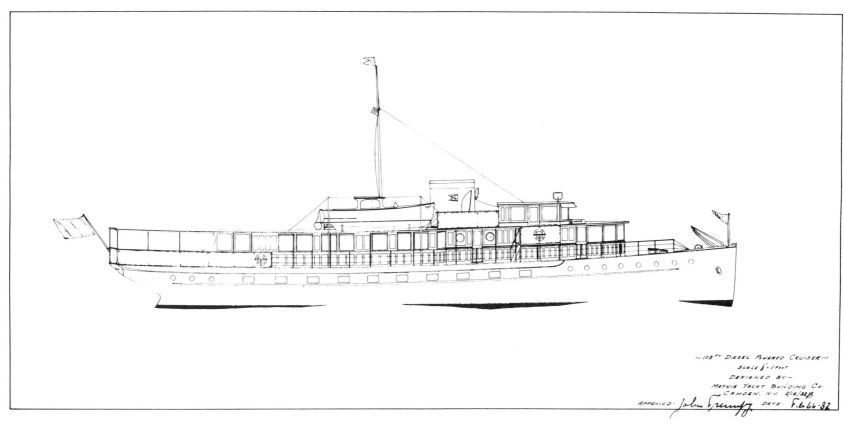

~100'' Diesel Powered Cruiser~
Scale ⅜=1 Foot
Designed by—
Mathis Yacht Building Co.
Camden, N.J. 2/16/32 B
Approved: John Trumpy   Date: Feb 66-32

Tiller Publishing

Tiller Publishing
P. O. Box 447
St. Michaels, MD 21663
Voice: 410-745-3750
Fax: 410-745-9743

85' *Luneta*, contract number 118, built in 1921 for Col. S. L. H. Slocum

~~~❦ PREFACE ❦~~~

TRUMPY was born aboard a Trumpy—in Fort Lauderdale on Fred Ruffner's *Mary Ann*, a 76-footer built in 1939 as the *Drifter*.

Author and artist met for the first time, one commissioned to paint a portrait of the beautifully restored classic and the other invited on board to consider a new project.

The initial conception was a cocktail table collector's book but interviews with the principal players, research and on-scene reconnaissance revealed a far more complex subject than originally considered.

There were Swiss origins to check out, a century-and-a-half of Italian Trumpy family marine-related achievements, three generations of Norwegian ship-builders, plus review of all the surviving company records made available through the trusting kindness of Johan Trumpy, direct lineal descendant of great-great grandfather Hans Jacob Trumpy (who built his first boats in the 1820s) and current Director of the Daytona Beach Boat Works.

Sigrid Trumpy of Annapolis generously provided a variety of clippings and her brother, Donald, offered valuable insights into the workings of the company. In Bergen, Norway, Hans Jacob and Britt Trumpy had vital information on the history and business activities of the family; and in Genoa, Oskar and Walter Trumpy extended every courtesy as they filled my head,

heart and notebook with valuable information on the many accomplishments of their family in Italy. On this side of the great waters, Trudi Rossi provided translations and interpretations of those accomplishments, vital to a full understanding of the Trumpy presence.

What a great pleasure it was to track Trumpys across Western Europe and the eastern United States, recording the saga of ship design and construction of the country's premier yacht houseboats; unfurling the banner saluting another American Dream, not one of those Scandinavian "Giants in the Earth" who struggled and survived in the plains of the Midwest, but a Norwegian giant who strode and sailed to greatness in eastern shipyards.

Fair winds took us to many homes and museums, shipyards, marinas and yacht clubs, where we found safe harbor with Trumpy aficionados and a fleet of experts to whom we are grateful for support, advice and information. Late in the voyage we discovered Jerry Foster, a Trumpy nut if ever there was one, and compiler of the list included as Appendix B.

I am grateful to Mrs. Pat Bausell, President of the Eastport Historical Committee for going way beyond the call of duty to provide a wealth of information; John Dulany, Fort Lauderdale yacht broker who handled 50 to 60 Trumpys over the years and 400 other vessels, shared his love of the classics, as did Carolyn

Weaver, owner of two Trumpys. Carroll Bjornson, yachtsman, collector, experienced marine expert and heir to a Norwegian nautical tradition, offered beacon-bright guidance and the advice that "Mankind has never devised a more effective vehicle for the transfer of wealth from the affluent to the less affluent than the ownership of a yacht."

A special debt of gratitude is due the Bergens Sjøfartsmuseum, the Bergen Maritime Museum, which opened to me its invaluable collection of period paintings, models, publications and pertinent archival material.

Other maritime museums which generously provided data of use were the Maine Maritime Museum in Bath; the Penobscot Marine Museum in Searsport, Maine; Mystic Seaport in Connecticut; the Mariners' Museum in Newport News, Virginia; and Southport Museum in New York City. Thanks are also due to the New York Yacht Club and the New York City Historical Society; to Bill Anderson of Oslo for his constant attention to Trumpy-Norwegian ties; to Doris B. Littlefield, Assistant Director for Collections and Exhibits at Vizcaya, for vital information on James Deering and his Trumpy; and to Professor Robert Johnson of the University of Alabama for insights on the Trumpy "six-bitters" built for the U. S. Coast Guard.

A final word of thanks to Karen Holcomb who ably navigated manuscript and appendixes through a maze of scribbles, rewrites and revisions.

*85' **Sequoia**, contract 140, built in 1924 for Richard M. Cadwalader*

TABLE OF CONTENTS

*95' **Nahmeoka**, contract 17, built in 1911 for H. N. Baruch*

Chapter 1
BEGINNINGS

Trumpy, the family name so intimately identified with the grace and elegance of American yachting, is a Swiss name, originating in Glarus, one of the thirteen cantons which formed the Swiss Confederation in the seventeenth century. Snuggled into the vastness of the Glarner Alpen, the rural and sparsely settled 267 square miles of Glarus is bordered by St. Gallen to the north and east, Gräubunden (Grisons) to the south, and in the west by two of the most ancient cantons, Uri and Schwyz.

The first record documenting the name Trümpy occurred in the early seventeenth century, a few years before the Swiss Confederation was recognized by the Treaty of Westphalia, which ended the infamous Thirty Years' War.

Heinrich Trümpy was governor of Sargans in the Rhein valley, close to the border with Liechtenstein—a disputed county which eventually became part of the canton of St. Gallen. Heinrich died in 1638 leaving a son, also named Heinrich, who was the father of Caspar Trümpy von Schwanden.

Caspar, born in 1642, had the honor of being the official flag-bearer of the canton of Glarus from 1683 to 1688. He bore the banner at the head of the Glarus militia and during important civil ceremonies, when cantonal colors were shown. He was elected to this important position at the annual Landsgemeinde, a popular assembly of all adult male citizens executing the practices of a pure, direct democracy. For nine years, 1701 to 1709, the founder of the family also served as a judge, and in 1704 was elected governor of the Glarus settlement of Werdenberg. Previously Caspar had been a member of the cantonal judicial review council.

During this period the Trümpy coat of arms displayed a turned-down horseshoe on a blue background under an eight-point star of gold. Atop the shield was a round crown hat with three ostrich feathers. A turned-down horseshoe is unusual in heraldry—elsewhere it was believed luck would run out if not turned up. At the Battle of Trafalgar, Lord Nelson nailed a horseshoe to the main mast of his flagship, with the tips pointing up.

Trumpy Coat Of Arms

Schwanden, a small town on the Linth River in the heart of the canton a few miles south of the capital city of Glarus, was the home of the Swiss Trümpys. Like most of their countrymen they were caught up in the turmoil of the time.

From the beginning of the seventeenth century, Switzerland, once so united and powerful, was hopelessly dismembered, struggling through civil and religious conflicts. Glarus had been Protestant since the early 1500s, thanks to the reforming zeal and conversion skill of its chief priest, the redoubtable Ulrich Zwingli. There were wars, civil disturbances and revolts in between peace treaties, and while Glarus managed to stay out of the fiercest of the fighting, the effect on the economies of both urban and rural areas was severe—as Catholic France and Protestant Germany fought for the loyalty and alliance of Swiss cantons. Throughout much of the eighteenth century Switzerland was regarded by those two countries and others as mainly a recruiting ground for mercenaries. Thousands of Swiss served in the armies of France, Holland, Spain, Italy and in the service of the Pope.

But there was also an awakening of manufacturing and basic improvements in agriculture and animal husbandry. In Glarus, where the dairy industry, export of cheese and slate had been mainstays of the economy, cotton spinning began to take hold as well as other home industries. Swiss trading companies were established all across the continent.

Yet the old ways died hard. In the mid-eighteenth century there were still trials for witchcraft. Glarus had the dubious distinction of staging the last witch trial in Switzerland—indeed in all of Europe—in 1782, when a serving girl was tortured on the rack and beheaded, a century after the Salem trials in New England.

The wars of Napoleon reduced much of the land of Glarus and surrounding cantons to a gigantic battlefield, with Austrians and their Russian allies contesting French hegemony, and the French dunning the Swiss for material and monetary support to pay and provision their thousands of troops.

In Glarus and the forest cantons conditions were desperate as entire herds were confiscated or slaughtered by the occupying French. Farms were decimated by forced provisioning and quartering. Many of the leading citizens of Glarus, pre-war prosperous and holding important municipal and cantonal positions, were forced to beg for basic necessities in cities not as crippled by the ravages of war. Thousands of children were sent down from mountain villages to the towns to escape starvation.

But by that time at least one member of the Trümpy family was safely out of the country, escaping all the way to Norway and settling in the important west coast trading port of Bergen. Hans Jacob Trümpy von Schwanden, grandson of Caspar and bearer of his father's name, made the move in the 1750s. He was the founder of the Norwegian Trümpy dynasty, fathering nine children before his death in 1792 at the age of 68.

How does a Swiss make it all the way to Bergen? Why does an ambitious young man select such a seemingly isolated city?

Bergen—founded in 1070, two centuries before the first Swiss Federation of Cantons—was as well known as any other port in the Baltic by the middle of the eighteenth century, having been "colonized" in the fourteenth century by that all-important trading monopoly known as the Hanseatic League.

It was certainly a long trip, taking the adventurous Trümpy, then in his mid-twenties, through several countries, presumably traveling north through the valley where the mountains did not block passage, sailing the water route on the River Linth to Lake Wallen and then connecting to the German river system to the Elbe River, flowing to Hamburg. Bergen was an significant city for the Hanseatic League and for Hans Jacob who worked and married there.

By the time he arrived in Bergen in the 1750s, the beautifully situated city was beginning to spread along its seven green hills and the azure fjords that pocket the coastlands. It was the largest city in Norway, the third most important port in the north. Bergen offered a good deal of opportunity to ambitious, capable and hard-working immigrants. The city had freed itself from the iron grip of the Hanse, but their warehouses, offices and traditions, the infrastructure and impelling necessity of trade still remained strong.

Europe's first seaborne empire, the Hanseatic League, was also its first Common Market, a federation of a couple hundred cities stretching from Bergen in the north across the all-important German entrepôts of Hamburg, Lubeck, Rostock and Danzig and as far east as Novgorod in Russia. The simple broad-beam vessels of the League, the ubiquitous cogs, were stacked high with salted and dried codfish from northern Norwegian waters. In Bergen, some cargoes were transshipped while other cogs sailed regular sea routes to unload their precious harvests of stockfish and cod liver oil, and to take on new goods for selling and trading in other ports—textiles, grains, beer, salt, wax for church candles, furs.

Bergen was not a full-fledged Hanseatic League town but a Kontor, one of four main trading outposts along with Bruges, London and Novgorod. Traders in Bergen did their business from waterfront warehouses, three-story structures which served as offices as well as living quarters. Erected in long rows, one behind the other at right angles to the shoreline. They survive beautifully today as Bryggen or Tyskebryggen, the German Quay, with a fascinating Hanse Museum, shops and galleries. Bergen merchants and those trading with the men of Brygga, however, did not rank very high on the Hanseatic power scale as their trade was never more than modestly prosperous.

During the seventeenth century, Hanse power waned. Europe was laid low by the ravages of the Thirty Years' War and the emerging power of Dutch maritime expansion humbled the Hansards who were forced to accept the disruption and destruction of their Common Market.

In a period of rising nationalism, economic interests were fragmented but the trading patterns established by the Hanse did not disappear. Europe still needed stockfish and cod liver oil as well as products from Norway's forests. Bergen became more active than ever as a central harbor and collecting point for Norwegian ships bringing harvests from sea and land for transshipment to eager European consumers.

Bergen was not only the country's most international port, it was, for all practical purposes, Norway's only international port. Captains and crews from the far corners of the earth traded in its marketplace alongside the Norwegian merchants who were being encouraged to develop craft guilds and companies independent of the Hanse Kontor. There was a steady stream of non-Norwegian, non-Hanse businessmen eager to compete in the open market free from Hanseatic restrictions, and with the blessings of the government.

Skilled craftsmen and tradesmen from England and Scotland, Flanders and the newly liberated Dutch provinces, German cities and states, the Baltic countries and Russia—even Switzerland—were attracted to the city, swelling the population of 13,000. They were not Norwegian by birth but they became Norwegians and Bergensers, welcomed by an expansion-minded civil authority that granted citizenship if their talents and potential profits merited such recognition.

Hans Jacob Trümpy von Schwanden certainly qualified and, in 1757, the 33-year-old businessman took the oath of citizenship in Bergen. He was therefore entitled to the full privileges of a merchant trading with the local population and its many visitors, buying and selling during the annual trade fairs, the so-called stevne, held in spring and summer when more than a hundred boats from the north sailed into the Bergen harbor. They were laden with butter and cheese, eider down, skins, furs and the delicate cloudberries, picked in the northern wilderness and bringing premium prices for centuries. And of course the all-important stockfish, stacked as high as five yards above the gunwales.

The ship of choice for the north Norwegians was the jekt, a combination of the Hanse cog with its cuddy aft, and the medieval Norwegian high prow cargo vessels. An open boat with only a small half deck fore and aft, the jekt originally had a single, square sail but later a topsail was added.

After the precious cargoes were unloaded along Brygga and at the marketplace, payments made and credit given, the men of the north could run the gauntlet of wooden stalls manned by hucksters hawking their wares, tempting the northerners with coffee, porridge and pastries and the staples they needed in the isolated north for another year—grain and flour, rope and hemp, cloth, salt, spirits, fishing gear.

Hans Jacob was survived at his death by his second wife and six children. One of his four sons, Johannes, followed his father in business as did his own son and son-in-law. Two emigrated, Hans Jacob to Copenhagen where he was a tinsmith, and Christian to Livorno where he started an Italian Trumpy dynasty. A daughter, Magdalena Christina, married a Norwegian ship captain.

Caspar remained but only when he was not at sea. He worked his way up to merchant captain, taking Bergen boats to many of the same ports that were so vital to the economic power of the Hanseatic League.

Caspar's sons were as adventurous as their uncles Christian and Hans Jacob. Only one decided to stay in Bergen. Caspar's other sons were impelled to seek brighter futures abroad by the same kind of economic conditions that were still motivating Trümpys to leave Switzerland for as distant a country as Russia, where Johan Trümpy of Glarus founded a trading company—the Handelsgesellschaft Jenny, Trümpy & Company—in Odessa after the end of the Napoleonic Wars.

Caspar's son Jens Kobro became a successful merchant in New Orleans. Johan followed his father to sea and became a ship captain, living in Antwerp until his death in 1855. Caspar took an entirely different route, becoming a master baker and pastry chef and moving to New York. He liked his country of adoption so much he named his son Benjamin Franklin Trumpy.

It seems inevitable that one or another Trumpy would get

involved in shipbuilding, as so many other families did in this seaside city where the forests of land swept down to the forests of masts in the harbor. Bergen lived by the sea and it lived on the sea, its sons sailing the world's waters and working the wood, sail and rope in the yards at water's edge.

But then all of Norway lived by the sea, clumped in clusters along the rugged, rocky coasts, stretching out to deep waters in narrow peninsulas of inhospitable soil, walled by perpendicular precipices of crag-filled fjords joined by only one life line since the time of the earliest settlers—the sea.

There was no communication by land, no roads pushed over mountains or cut through flood-threatened valleys. Only by sea, the frigid waters of the North Sea, Norwegian Sea and the Skagerrak—seldom warmed unless trapped in bays and inlets along the long fingers of the fjords— could daily life be sustained. With well over 80% of the population clustered along 2000 miles of coastline, water-borne transport and water-borne exploitation of the riches of the sea were the only means of contact and survival.

When the harvest from the sea was unusually rich, the surplus had to be sold somewhere beyond the confines of the central community, and when there were excess harvests from the land, scratched from barren soil and cut from stone quarries, or sawed and sized in forest mills, markets had to be found far removed from the immediate region.

Water transport was the only answer and if the fleet was too small the Norwegians had to build more ships and boats as they had been doing for centuries. Shipbuilding and seafaring had become a way of life.

Caspar's number three son, Hans Jacob, decided he would join them. He sailed from Bergen in 1825, the year the first Norwegian immigrant ship, **Restauration**, a 54-foot sloop sailed from Bergen for the New World, with the first trickle—fifty-two passengers—of the floods of thousands during the next hundred years.

He was twenty years old and heading for New York City to learn how to build world-class, ocean-going ships.

95' *Nahmeoka*, contract 17, built in 1911 for H. N. Baruch

*95' **Nahmeoka**, contract 17, built in 1911 for H. N. Baruch*

Chapter 2
NORWEGIAN SHIPBUILDERS

From the ninth to twelfth centuries Norwegian boat builders were creating some of the most remarkable vessels the world has ever seen. Light, strong and perfectly shaped to glide through the water, they carried Viking raiders, traders and settlers seeking fame and fortune, plunder, profit, and new opportunities far beyond their own coastal villages.

The sagas called the ships "ocean-riding bison," "surf dragons," "fjord elks," and they were solid enough to withstand threatening waves, powerful enough to cross—in open boats—the ice-cold waters of the North Atlantic. Their sleek shape kept them from swamping and with a single square sail they were slim and fast enough to outrace enemies, broad and deep enough to carry trading provisions and settlers' supplies—the worldly goods of entire families, cattle and all—and yet with a shallow enough draft to enable them to navigate rivers, fjords and low-lying bays. They were light enough to be dragged in portages across headlands as their masters, builders and sailors traveled the water routes of Eastern Europe and hop-scotched lands to the west—the Shetlands, Orkneys and Britain, the Faroes, Ireland and Iceland, then to Greenland and finally

Vinland—Newfoundland.

Clinker-built with each plank of the 75x16-foot hull lapped over the plank below and perfectly shaped to fit the curves of the hull, with cleats hewn on the inside face of each plank lashed tightly to the ribs, the supremely seaworthy Viking ships

had a single rudder, on the right side—the steer-board or starboard side.

Double-ended with a high stern and high stern post, Viking ships had no rival on the high seas. Not until the clippers, "downeasters" and whaleboats of the 1800s were ocean-going vessels so well-designed with faultless form and function built into every plank and rib.

By the time that young Hans Jacob was making plans to learn the craft of designing boats, the Viking vessels were long gone. Other lands and other yards had taken the lead in designing the ships demanded by newer times. Bergen, handicapped to some extent by not having a ready supply of forest land close at hand, and forced to import wood from other Norwegian coastal villages, had only a couple of shipyards. The oldest dated from 1602. That was the year shipper Giert Evertsen got the whole-hearted approval of city authorities to extend his dock with a bulwark at Bradbenken alongside Bryggen so he could accommodate ships in need of bottom repairs and mast replacement.

Not much more than those basics were performed at Bradbenken over the next two centuries and by 1800, there were only two real shipyards in the city, small yards owned by Rasmus Rolfsen who had Elsesro out in Sandviken and Herman Brunchorst in charge of Georgernes Shipyard. The first employed 70 to 80 carpenters and the second 40 to 60, a total of 10% of the city's craftsmen. In 1805, another was established, the Gran Yards at Laksevaag.

In the ten years before Hans Jacob went to America, 87 ships were built in Bergen, but they were all small ships, sloops and pinnaces, ketches, single-masted jekts and 60-foot coastal vessels called galeas. In 1823 almost a quarter of all the tonnage built in Norway came from Bergen but two years later that share had fallen to eleven percent.

Hans Jacob, who preferred the name Jacob, could have apprenticed himself to Elsesro, Gran or Georgernes if he wanted to learn how to design and build small boats but he had to go abroad to learn how to build the larger and longer vessels, those that billowed across the trade routes of the world in the great age of sail.

Bergen shipbuilders Rolfsen and Brunchorst also went abroad to study, to Copenhagen and Fredriksvern, and in later years Norwegians apprenticed in the yards of England, Germany, and Holland.

Hans Jacob Trumpy headed for New York where the first settlers had been shipbuilders and where the city's great shipbuilding era was already underway.

He arrived when the first marine railway was being built. The 300-foot line, financed jointly by a conglomerate of shipbuilders, was located at the foot of 10th Street and initially used horsepower to pull boats out of the water. Later, steam provided the power.

In 1826 new ship tonnage, built on 23 slips in New York City yards, totaled 29,137 tons—68 sloops, 49 schooners, 19 canal boats, 15 towboats and 12 starboats, many of them by the individual who would later become the wealthiest shipbuilder in the city in the years before the War Between the States, Jacob Aaron Westervelt. He was to be the teacher of Trumpy.

Westervelt, from Bergen County in New Jersey, had been on his own since age 14 when his father, a dock contractor, died. He signed on a ship as an ordinary seaman and then apprenticed himself to the shipbuilding firm of Christian Bergh, a seminal force in the industry. Westervelt went to Charleston after his period of apprenticeship but returned a short time later to become a partner with Bergh and Robert Carnley. By the time Bergh retired in 1837, the firm had built 247 vessels, the second largest tonnage in the city. The William Webb company was first, but Bergh-Carnley-Westervelt was number one in the construction of packets, those fleet little ships that carried passengers and mail on regularly scheduled runs between New York and Le Havre, London and Liverpool.

Christian Bergh had started his career in 1804 with the building of the 400 ton *North America*, active for years in the British and Russian trade. During the War of 1812 he built warships on the Great Lakes under the most primitive conditions. His yard where South Street meets Corlear's Hook was infinitely more modern and efficient, remarkable among the fourteen shipyards that extended side by side from just below Corlear's Hook to Fourth Street. Of the 400 shipyard workers there, 244 were foreign-born.

The giant Bergh, six feet, six inches in his stocking feet, established an enviable reputation. In the words of notable contemporary diarist, Philip Toner, he was the father of that great system of naval architecture which made New York City famous across the globe, "the first to raise the character of Yankee packet ships to a height unmatched in the world." Bergh was also a superintendent of construction at the Brooklyn Navy Yard.

Bergh and Westervelt were masters of their craft and provided Hans Jacob with a thorough grounding in the most up-to-date methods of ship construction and design. He was already a good draftsman and had displayed a fine hand when sketching scenes of life in Bergen—a man and woman from

Trumpy Yard, Bergen, Norway

Hedemark and a farmer from Opdal going to market are typical of his talent.

When he returned to Norway in the early 1830s, he worked for a time at Rolfsen's Elsesro shipyards, then being run by founder Rasmus' son, Tønnes, who had not only learned his profession from his father, but also from visits to various yards in Denmark, Sweden and northern Germany. His son, Rasmus, who studied nautical engineering and architecture at Karlskrona in southern Sweden, returned to the family firm about the same time Hans Jacob Trumpy was ready to start his Norwegian career. The two joined forces at Bradbenken, which became for the first time an actual shipyard, and not just a place where ships could be brought to undergo that thoroughly inelegant, awkward, almost embarrassing act of being careened. Hull bottoms had to be scraped clean of barnacles, checked for worms and other damage and recaulked—with hot pitch cooked by fires that always posed a threat to the wooden buildings of Brygga. Masts had to be lashed and anything movable secured or taken off to prevent damage as the ship hove down.

In 1836 Trumpy took over sole control of the yard and started building ships of all sizes. Bradbenken became a company the competition and the country had to take seriously. The setting was a super one, right at the eastern entrance to the inner harbor with Brygga to the south. To the north, and still remaining, are the historic landmarks of King Haakon's Hall from the thirteenth century and the Rosenkrantz Tower from the sixteenth. Close by is the twelfth century St. Mary's Church. There was no finer location for a shipyard anywhere in the country if not all of Scandinavia.

Hans Jacob dove right in, negotiating contracts and setting his shipwrights, caulkers and sail makers to work on his first ship, the 156 ton brig, *Preciosa*, a two-master square-rigged both fore and aft, intended for the coastal trade. She was launched in 1837.

In accord with the practice of the time, when ships were ordered, usually by shippers and merchants owning other vessels, only the desired length, beam and draft were agreed upon. Few, if any, other specifics were discussed. The precise price was set after all costs were considered and the construction completed. As a guarantee that the shipbuilder would perform satisfactorily and deliver a well-built ship, he usually had to retain a certain percentage of the ship. Performance would then mean as much to the builder as it did to the owner or the shareholders.

The next two ships Trumpy completed were schooners, the 123 ton *Eidsvold* and the 110 ton *Den 11te April*. The names commemorated the date and place of the constituent assembly which adopted the Norwegian Constitution in 1814. The local newspaper, *Den Bergenske Merkur*, praised *Den 11th April* as "one of the most beautiful ships that has ever been built here," and they described with similar glowing words the exciting launching of the *Eidsvold* three months later, on the Fourth of July, 1838.

It was quite an event at Bradbenken as thousands gathered in the evening for the festivities, with Norwegian and American flags everywhere. Everyone in town knew that Jacob Trumpy had learned his craft in New York at the famous Westervelt Yards, and he was proud to use the occasion of the launching of a schooner with such a significant name as a very visible way to show his gratitude to both nations.

Slipping off the ways in the following years were the barks *Johan Gerhard Ameln*, *Peder Schrøder* and *Augusta*, along with the *Newcastle Pacquet*, *Henrik Wergeland*, *Hans Holmbo*, *Olav Kyrre*, *Dronning Victoria*, *Professor Schweigaard*, *Czar* and *Christopher Hansteen*; brigs and brigantines, schooners, sloops and schooner-brigs named for their primary owners, national heroes, statesmen, royalty or literary figures.

In the 1840s he built a totally different kind of vessel, a bath boat. He converted an old schooner into a floating bath, a place where the public could take a warm or cold salt water soak.

She was anchored where the public salt water baths were later built (now a huge freezer-cooling warehouse complex) at Bontelabo. Masterbuilder Trumpy advertised the season opening in the town registry office in April, 1845:

"The bathship at Bontelabo opens the morning of May 1 and welcomes women from 8 in the morning until 1 p.m., and men from 6 to 8 a.m. and from 1 to 9 in the afternoons. The facilities have been improved in a variety of ways, e.g., there are now six warm and eight cold baths. Season tickets can be picked up in the afternoons at my office. Tickets from the previous years are not valid."

In 1856 it was time for another Trumpy to make the trip to New York City and learn the trade. Caspar was the only one of Hans' six sons who wanted to follow his father's chosen profession and in 1856 at the age of 20, he sailed to the land of nopportunity and an apprentice position with the same Westervelt who had been such a positive influence on the first Trumpy.

During the twenty-odd years from the departure of Hans Jacob and the arrival of Caspar, Westervelt had continued to be a prominent player in the New York shipbuilding profession, and was well on his way to becoming the city's wealthiest shipowner.

Christian Bergh had retired in 1837 and four years later Westervelt teamed with George Mackey to form the firm of Westervelt and Mackey, still competing with the Webbs who at the time were building more tonnage than any other shipyard in the country.

Jacob Aaron had just finished a term as mayor of the city which then numbered just over half a million inhabitants. He was a Tammany Hall democrat but a reform one, bound and determined to clean up corruption and stop bribery and

Presiden Harbitz built by Trumpy in Bergen, Norway

kickbacks. Against great opposition he forced the police department to put on uniforms.

It was New York's boom period of shipbuilding. When Caspar arrived, there were 31 shipyards with a payroll exceeding 2,300. And there were another 68 companies serving as suppliers—of sails and spars, windlasses, rigging and all the other gear needed to sail a ship in those days.

Westervelt and Mackey were wooden boat builders but they were not slow to realize the value of steam power. They built the first steam-powered vessel in the city, the 1700 ton *Washington*, a paddle-wheeler which made her maiden voyage in 1847.

Westervelt and Mackey also built clipper ships, joining the competition in fulfilling the demands for ever-increasing speed, turning out ever sleeker ships with limited cargo space, dependent on hard-driving captains and indefatigable crews. Their *Kathay*, *Sweepstakes* and *N. B. Palmer* were built for the China–Australia–California trade and they proved so popular that several more were built on speculation. The *N. B. Palmer*, named for the contemporary captain of the sloop *Hero* who discovered Palmer's Land, then thought to be part of Antarctica, was a 1399 ton (202.5' x 38.5' x 21') racer that took 107 days from New York to San Francisco and 100 from Hong Kong to New York.

The same year *Kathay* was launched, the *Great Republic* slid down the ways. She was the largest clipper ever built—334.5 feet long, 53.5' in the beam with a 38' draft. The designer was the legendary Donald McKay.

A Bergenser was at his side, learning all about clipper ship construction. 21-year-old Annanias Dekke, an apprentice from the Georgernes Yard, had been studying with the McKay team and when he returned to Norway he too put the knowledge gained to good use. The first ship he designed was the 1856 505 ton clipper-frigate *Hebe*, which attracted great attention for her graceful lines—more like a yacht than a merchant ship—and speed—10 knots downwind and 8 to 9 knots close-hauled.

His later ships attracted equally favorable notice. Worthy of special mention is the 1867 *Lina*, which at 874 tons was the largest sailing ship built in Norway up to that time. During the nearly forty years Dekke was in charge of Georgernes, the yard built 41 sailing ships and 15 wooden steamships, a combined total tonnage of 30,000. In addition, his plans were used by several other shipyards in Norway and abroad.

The total number built by the Trumpys at Bradbenken was 47—all but three with sail. After Caspar returned to the yards the average size increased considerably. He had learned how to design and build the big ones, as well as those powered by steam.

One of his surviving New York drawings is a fine piece of art for a steam-sailer named *Brooklyn*, a fitting name inasmuch as Brooklyn, especially the Bay Ridge area, was where many of the Norwegian immigrants congregated. Another set of his detailed plans was for a clipper ship.

Caspar left Westervelt and the U.S. the year before the outbreak of the Civil War. His "formal" education, apprenticeship and on-the-job training were over. He would not have learned much more had he remained during the five years of war. Westervelt prospered building gunboats for the Union Navy, but Confederate raiders sunk or severely damaged so many of his own ships he was forced to the wall. Increasing labor costs and inflated real estate prices put him in a position where he had to declare bankruptcy. By the time he was appointed Dock Commissioner in 1870, the concentration of wooden shipbuilding along the eastern seaboard had shifted from New York to Maine.

In the last three decades of the century, fully 70% of the 702 barks, brigantines and ships and almost half of the 1522 three-masted schooners built in Atlantic coast yards were made in Maine. They were not only the proud producers of the "downeasters," fullriggers superior to the clippers in strength and cargo capacity, but also of large, multi-masted coasting schooners, four-, five- and six-masters carrying coal from mid-Atlantic ports to New England. The largest was the 3401 ton *Eleanor A. Percy*, 323.5 feet long with a 50-foot beam and depth of 24.8 feet.

No one at Westervelt was thinking along those long lines when they built their sleek and speedy packet ships and Caspar certainly had no intention of trying to compete with those giants when he returned to Norway. But his first year back in Bergen he did work on the second largest vessel built at Bradbenken up to that time, the 358 ton bark *President Harbitz*, built for the China trade where, at the time, about ten Norwegian ships were actively engaged, sailing between Chinese and other foreign ports or along the China coast.

Only three of the two dozen Bradbenken boats built up to that time had been over 312 tons, the barks *Laura*, 327 tons, and *Dronning Victoria*, 372 tons. The Queen and the Professor represented a trend of the time in Bergen and accounted for the dramatic increase in gross tonnage of the Bergen fleet.

Two years later the Trumpys built the 434 ton bark, *Kong Carl*, and that was followed by the 292 ton bark *Eliezer*, and the 499 ton bark *Harald Haarfager*, named for the first king of Norway who ruled in the tenth century. They were launched in 1864.

The *Eliezer* was a mission ship, built by subscription to ease and expedite passage of Norwegian missionaries traveling to South Africa, Madagascar and other distant lands. But she was also a cargo ship, one that was intended to be completely self-supporting, paying expenses from the proceeds of trade. Any profits were returned to the mission. She was one of the few ships of the time that sailed off into the blue uninsured. There was a general belief that the Lord would provide the insurance.

More typical of the time was the insurance taken out on the *Professor Schweigaard* which cost 20,800 spesidaler on delivery to the owners, who insured her for 18,500 spesidaler, which was roughly equivalent in value to the same amount in U.S. dollars.

In the next four years a schooner-brig and three more large barks were built, the 526 ton *Ceres*, the 413 ton *Ludvig Holberg*, named for the immensely popular and influential liberal playwright and historian, and the 565 ton *Valkyrien*, launched in 1868 and setting another record as the largest Trumpy had ever built.

The *Valkyrien* appeared on the banner of the Bradbenken Carpenters Association, pictured during her launching behind the work sheds and dock where a boat was careened and workers were putting hot pitch into the caulking. The bark was put on the New York run but in 1872 ran into trouble there when her entire crew jumped ship. Two other Trumpy-built vessels, *Eidsvold* and *Kong Sverre*, had similar problems when several seamen simply walked off and disappeared or were enticed by runners from nearby seamen's boarding houses. The captains and the owners complained bitterly to the authorities about the lack of support they received from New York port officials and police and requested that stiffer penalties be placed on those who desert their posts. It was a far more prevalent problem in New York ports than elsewhere in the world and the causes are not too difficult to comprehend given the rugged conditions and the back-breaking labor aboard ships of the time.

The Trumpy length record was not bested until 1873 when the 783 ton bark *Johan Irgens* was launched, followed two years later with the 973 ton frigate *Professor Mohn*. They were constructed not by one, but two, masterbuilders. In 1869 Hans Jacob Trumpy had made his son a partner and he changed the name of the company to J. Trumpy & Son.

The new partner had earned the promotion and he continued to earn it as he proceeded to design and supervise construction of the first Trumpy steamship, something similar to the *Brooklyn* he had designed for Westervelt.

Steam power was not a novelty in Norway. In 1852 the Bergen Steamship Company put its first steam-operated vessel in operation, the *Bergen,* built in Newcastle and used for the Bergen–Hamburg run and later Bergen–Hammerfest and Bergen–Christiania. Steamships and steam-sailers were not unusual sights in the Bergen harbor.

The first contract for a steamship in Bergen was signed in 1870 and in the next three years the city's four shipyards built nine of them, three at Bradbenken. The first was Trumpy's aptly-named *D/S Alpha*, 272 tons, followed by her sister ship *D/S Idraet*, 172 tons and the *D/S Zaritza*, 314 tons. The cost of the first two delivered with all necessary machinery was 18,000 spesidaler, or some 25% more expensive than a sailing ship of the same size. The larger *D/S Zaritza* cost 30,000 spesidaler including 13,500 spesidaler for the steam engine.

Nine years would elapse before another wooden steamship would be built in Bergen, but there was no slowdown in laying of iron bottoms.

Steamships became the preferred vessels of trade for Bergen's all-important grain trade from the Black Sea. They maneuvered more easily and faster through Gibraltar and the Dardanelles than the schooners and fullriggers.

To accommodate the larger ships somewhere other than the Customs Pier, the city expanded the Ludwig Holberg Dock, originally built as a jetty across from Bradbenken in 1874. It served as the city's ceremonial dock, the site of Bergen's most "festive" burial. In 1880 the Trumpy-built *Kong Sverre* brought the coffin of one of Norway's most famous sons, the internationally acclaimed violinist Ole Bull, into port. On board as well were two other equally famous Norwegians, composer Edvard Grieg and writer Bjornstjerne Bjornson along with other dignitaries.

But the Trumpys did not watch the event from their shipyard across the harbor. By that time they had vacated Bradbenken and had moved their sheds and shops from the most historic shipbuilding site in town south to a new location, around Nordnes Park and the Seamen's School, past Georgernes Yards to Jekteviken.

In the early 1870s the city had decided to strike some kind of arrangement with J. Trumpy & Son to take over the Bradbenken yards in order to expand dockage space in the main harbor. In the fall of 1875 the city council received the necessary approvals to construct a stone pier along Bradbenken past the old fortress to a point beyond the Rosenkrantz Tower and Haakon's Hall. In 1879 the deal with Trumpy was made. The city took over Trumpy's obligatory payments to the seamen's poor house and exchanged Bradbenken for a portion of Jekteviken and permission to operate a shipyard there.

Trumpy quickly set up in his new site and in the next 15 years his old yard was transformed into the most modern dock in the city with new warehouses, several cranes, even public restrooms—the first in town—necessitated by increased harbor traffic and the number of pedestrians who were then able to stroll along the harborfront.

The property Trumpy received in exchange had only recently been purchased from the Blaauw family. From the beginning of the nineteenth century the land and shoreline had belonged to Jacob Blaauw, known locally as Jacob Hollender, descendent of an old Dutch Hanseatic Kontor merchant. The city paid him 100,000 kroner for the extensive property. The Blaauw mansion alone was worth that much money.

The last ships built in the Bradbenken yards—which had been a fixture of the city's landscape since 1602—were the 265 ton schooner-brig *Italia*, initiated perhaps by that branch of the Trumpy family prospering as ship brokers in Genoa and Livorno; the 973 ton frigate *Professor Mohn*; the 371 ton schooner *Sirius*; and the largest ship the yards ever built, the 921 ton frigate *Jacob Trumpy*. The name honored Hans Jacob who died in 1874.

In 1877, while the negotiations were going on for the land exchange, construction was started on the last major Trumpy vessel to be built in Norway, the 491 ton bark *Carl Konow*. She was launched in 1878 and towed to Jekteviken where she

was completed while Caspar worked on improvements to their new home, adding a gazebo to the lovely gardens and overseeing the several careening and repair jobs that came to

Trumpy Ferry in Bergen, Norway

the new shipyard.

Carl Konow was a wooden vessel just as all the others had been, but the days of wooden sailing ships were numbered. Not everyone agreed with this, however—certainly not Rasmus Olsen, the shipowner who put together the group of investors paying for the *Carl Konow* and then took over as managing director of eight of the last great wooden schooners to be built in Bergen yards. But eight years after *Carl Konow* set sail, Olsen put together a syndicate with 31 others to order an iron bark from the new yard in town, Martens, Olsen & Company at Laksevaag which replaced the old Gran Yards. The 1232 tons of iron was christened *Australia* and she was the last large Norwegian sailing ship, of wood or iron, to operate in foreign waters.

Two years before *Carl Konow* was launched, the first Norwegian registered iron bark had been delivered to her

Norwegian owner, the 1110 ton *Europa*, built in Glasgow for the East Indies and California trade.

Iron was becoming the building material of choice. The Great Age of Sail, the glory years of the clippers and schooners, was coming to an end. In the 1870s Bergen had the most modern sailing fleet in the country, competing on an even keel with the giants flying out of other ports in Scandinavia, Germany, Holland and America. But Britain was demonstrating conclusively the new power of steam and steel. Less romantic and certainly not as pleasing to the eye as they chugged and smoked across the horizon or sailed out of harbor at sunset, but more efficient, reliable, and providing a greater return on investment.

The days of wood, sail and rope were numbered, just as Trumpy's had been at Bradbenken, then at Jekteviken. There continued to be a little activity however, at the dock and in the work sheds, some of it generated by Caspar's son, Jacob, an engineer who in a show of Trumpy entrepreneurial energy started the Bergen Electric Ferry Company in 1894.

Jacob wisely perceived the practicality and potential profitability of taking passengers from the Brygga side of the main harbor across the water, to the Ludwig Holberg Dock and to other destinations. But the city did not have an electric plant at that time, so Jacob had to take his ferries on round-trips to Jekteviken to recharge the batteries.

He had eight boats which were quickly dubbed BEFs or BEFFENs—from the letters of Bergen Electric Ferry Company, Bergens Elektriske Faergeselskap—and the public lined up to use them. The first year of operation 620,000 passengers used the service and the second year that figure jumped to 700,000.

A century later there were over 2,150,000 passengers annually.

His father did not live to see the success, to smile down on the new generation still taking goods and people across water in a new kind of boat. Caspar died in 1894, the same year as Jens Gran. Gran had closed his shipyard while Trumpy was moving to Jekteviken. The company he leased the yards to, Martens, Olsen & Company, wasn't interested in wood, only iron and steel.

The ever-resourceful Annanias Dekke had died two years earlier and his Georgernes Yards built its last ship in 1900, but as early as the mid-1870s he had recognized that the age of sail and wood was in its last stages and was making plans to convert his company to iron ship construction. He brought in a specialist, Adolph Tidemand, and had a dry dock built. But his new expert died shortly thereafter in the midst of one of those cyclical collapses in the chartering market. Annanias' son, Kristian, took up the challenge a decade later but the plans were abandoned when the father-founder died in 1892.

Caspar left ten children. His namesake did not follow his father's footsteps, but became an agronomist. Son Georg had a distinguished army career. First-born Jacob had the ferry company and his younger brother, Johan, born in 1879, also wanted to get involved in some kind of nautical career.

Johan was an avid boatsman from an early age, and was not only weaned on the lore and lure of the sea but the practical aspects of building wooden boats. He was not raised at Bradbenken with all its hectic activity during the heydays, but at Jekteviken. He was born when the yard was finishing its last ship. But the sheds were still filled with fine shipbuilding woods as he grew older, and Caspar and his remaining crew of carpenters worked them into marvelous scale model miniature sailboats. Johan no doubt built a few himself and he could certainly study all the half models, the paintings, the photographs of the many ships proudly bearing the Trumpy hallmark.

But there was no J. Trumpy & Son to join as apprentice and no other firm in Bergen or elsewhere in Norway that appealed to his particular needs and desires. There wasn't even a shell of a Trumpy shipyard anymore. The city had been interested in buying back the Jekteviken property as early as 1880 and in 1894 the Trumpys offered to sell it all, the large house and all the surrounding acreage, for 400,000 kroner. The price was considered a bit steep. However, in the seemingly inevitable ways and wisdom of city officials, when they again got serious about the purchase five years later, they had to pay 800,000 kroner. The city built its new gas works on the site and used the mansion as the main office building.

Johan wanted to be a nautical architect, a designer of boats, just as his father and grandfather before him, but there was no Westervelt in New York to do the teaching. He would have to begin his studies at home, at Bergen's Technical College which "really gave you an education," he proudly explained years later. "You could go out and get a job doing almost anything when you graduated." But before he started working, he wanted more formal education and a period of apprenticeship outside of Norway, so he headed for Germany. To perfect his German, he worked for a short time in a Bremen shipyard. There were precious few yards or institutions where he could receive the kind of training he desired.

Johan Trumpy and his family decided Germany would provide the kind of education and training he was seeking and five years after his father's death he went to the capital of Germany to study in Berlin, in suburban Charlottenburg with its highly regarded technical academy, the Technische Hochschule. There the young Trumpy received a thorough and disciplined training in the craft of designing ships of all sizes, but yachts were his special interest and his final examination

Trumpy Home in Bergen, Norway

paper was Entwurf einer Sonderklassen Yacht, Design of a Special Class Yacht, signed by J. Trumpy, December 19, 1900. The boat was 10 meters long, 1.2 meters in the beam with a 1.25 meter draft and a weight of 2.1 tons. The woods specified were pitch pine and yellow pine, cedar and oak.

The drawing is a work of art, a striking visual confirmation of the fact that the young Trumpy had learned his lessons well and that he had inherited the same sure genius for ship design displayed by his father and grandfather. He had also inherited the same eagerness to perfect his skills in the New World.

After a term as apprentice in the Kiel shipbuilding yards of Howaldts Werke, working on a yacht, he was ready to face new challenges, to find his career in the New World.

In 1902 Johan sailed for the United States.

Artwork by Hugo Trumpy

Chapter 3
THE ITALIAN CONNECTION

Caspar Trumpy had prospered as a Bergen ship captain early in the nineteenth century, but he was captured three times by British men-of-war during the Neopolitan Wars. When peace was restored he continued his career sailing from Bergen to Mediterranean and Baltic ports. But his 33-year-old brother, Christian, decided to depart permanently, leaving for Livorno, Italy's third most important commercial port and the first free port in the Mediterranean. He became a very successful ship broker, representing the major shipping companies transiting Livorno and selling Italian-built warships to Norway, Sweden and the Baltic countries. Livorno yards produced war ships for the Italian Navy and the city was the home of the Royal Marine Academy as well as the Royal Commercial Marine Institute.

Christian Trumpy also had a factory there, one of the first in the country to utilize steam power, and he made important contributions to local navigational needs, cutting channels through island passages outside the city harbor.

Captain Caspar's son, 15-year-old Hans Christen, followed his uncle to Livorno where he worked for a time as an assistant in the main office of the company, but the two did not get along and Hans moved to Genoa where he organized Stub, Trumpy and Company, ship brokers. It was a short-lived partnership. Hans died young, at 25.

Two years later, the youngest son of Caspar, Valerius Nilsen York—also age 15—moved to Livorno. He worked in his uncle Christian's company, The Society of Northern Relations. Twenty years later, in 1846, Valerius became an independent broker, representing some of the largest merchant ships in the world and founding the A. Bastogi firm which took over the direction of the Northern company. In a career of 22 years Valerius made

Hugo Trumpy Plaque

millions, but lost it all in 1866 when the Italian government, encouraged by French Emperor Napoleon III, joined with Prussia in a war against Austria. The Italians lost on land and at sea gaining control of Venice and Veneto, but not Trieste, Istria or Trentino. Financial ruin led to Valerius' death in 1868 but his surviving thirty-year-old son, Gaspero David Valerio, was destined to bring even greater glory to the Trumpy name.

He entered the Bastogi Company as an apprentice when he was 18 years old, but during the war of independence and unification he left the world of commerce and volunteered in the Italian Alpine forces. He transferred to the famous Bersaglieri where he was first a non-commissioned and then commissioned officer, taking part in the war which ruined his father, the struggle against Austria to liberate Venice and the neighboring provinces.

Gaspero was promoted to Major of the Italian Eighth Corps in 1895 and when he retired ten years later, he did so with the permanent rank of colonel, wearing proudly the four medals he had been awarded for bravery in three different campaigns and for his efforts during a cholera outbreak emergency in 1867.

Three of Gaspero's sons distinguished themselves in different careers. Luciano Ernesto pursued a commercial course and went to South America at the turn of the century, settling in Buenos Aires where he prospered among the multitude of Italians there.

Younger brother Federico Eraldo became a naval officer, serving as chief of the Naval Police and then as ship commander during the 1894 Abyssinian campaign and the 1912 war against the Turks for the conquest of Libya. He traveled the world's oceans and visited ports from China and Japan to North America, throughout the Mediterranean and into the Red Sea. He too was awarded medals for bravery, receiving a citation and medallion with cross for his aid to the victims of the December 1908 earthquake in Medina and Reggio-Calabria.

The youngest of Gaspero's sons, Rodolfo Umberto, born in 1884, was also in the Italian Navy. Educated as an electro-technician he served as a non-commissioned officer and section chief during World War I. At the end of that war he was named head of the Italian Society of Engineers and was recognized by the Society of the Ministry of Industry and Commerce, winning its gold medal for his innovations in electrical engineering.

Rodolfo attracted the attention of another Italian "electro-technician," one who had also completed his education in Livorno, one who was to become one of the most famous inventors in the world, Guglielmo Marconi.

Marconi, the "Father of Wireless," was also a pioneer in the formulation and foundation of multi-national business enterprises. Marconi offices and officials were found all over the world, and the Nobel Prize-winning phenomenon was front page news wherever he went.

Shortly after Rodolfo Trumpy met the genius, he joined Marconi's Wireless Telegraph Co. Ltd., incorporated in 1897. One of his first assignments was at the company's radio-telegraph station in Sicily, a new installation transmitting to other Italian cities; and he opened the office in Genoa where Marconi transmitters were in contact with ships in Italian coastal waters and as far distant as Greece.

One of Rodolfo's most important responsibilities in the company was the 1911 organization and construction of the most powerful wireless station the world had ever seen. It was built for the Italian government at Coltano near Pisa. They wanted to have instantaneous communication with the wireless station at Massowah in the Red Sea and with Buénos Aires, 7,000 miles away, home of a huge Italian émigré population.

The signals were so strong from Coltano they reached Glace Bay in Nova Scotia. When Marconi heard that news he sent his first message direct to Glace Bay, more than a thousand miles longer than the previously used Clifden–Glace Bay routing. It was on November 19, 1911 and directed to the editor of the *New York Times*.

The sudden and sensational success of the Coltano station prompted the Italian government to send special citations to Marconi and his "Director and Collaborator," Rodolfo Trumpy. There were other commendations for the war efforts of Trumpy, made a "Cavaliere de la Republica," and Marconi, who was put in charge of all military wireless operations. Trumpy was instrumental in setting up the first formal school in the country for shipboard radio operators, several of whom were of course on board Marconi's own ship.

After the war, when Marconi could return to peace-time pursuits, he converted a ship of the British Royal Navy for use as a private yacht. Or rather, re-converted, because the 220-foot, 730 ton vessel built by Ramage and Ferguson of Leith, Scotland, had been the private yacht of Archduke Stefan and Archduchess Maria Theresa of Austria. She was commandeered by the British at the outbreak of war and made to serve as a rather luxurious flagship for the Admiral directing minesweeping operations in the North Sea.

The British re-outfitted the yacht to Marconi's specifications and he gave her the very appropriate name of

Elettra. Italian poet Gabriele D'Annunzio called her, "The shining ship that works miracles, penetrating the silences of the air."

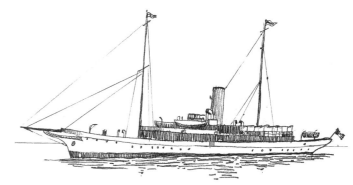

Marconi's Yacht

Elettra did work miracles, for she was a floating laboratory, one in which Marconi could work uninterrupted in solitude for long periods of time. The largest Italian yacht ever to cross the Atlantic, the sleek, elegant, white and gold *Elettra* carried a crew of 31, most of them Italian.

A pair of special masts were mounted to provide antenna supports for Marconi to flash and receive his globe-spanning messages as he worked ceaselessly to improve his inventions and search for new horizons. Short waves and microwaves, which he believed held the secret of television, fascinated him as did a series of experiments conducted in the waters off the Italian port of Santa Margherita.

A Trumpy was there. Walter Trumpy, son of Rodolfo, had joined the Marconi Company in 1931 at the age of 21. He was assigned to ship and shore duty supporting the inventor's latest efforts to extend the boundaries of short wave radio transmission, developing microwaves with wave lengths of less than a yard and exploring certain phenomena associated with them.

During one of his frequent trips to the U.S.—the *Elettra* made nearly a hundred trans-Atlantic crossings—the Italian genius explained his experiments to a New York City meeting of the American Institute of Electrical Engineers:

"It seems to me that it should be possible to design apparatus by means of which a ship could radiate or project a divergent beam of these rays in any desired direction which rays, if coming across a metallic obstacle, such as another steamer or ship, would be reflected back to a receiver screened from the local transmitter on the sending ship, and thereby immediately reveal the presence and bearing of the other ship in fog or thick weather."

Marconi knew that if he could perfect the application of those waves, it would be of great value to navigators. To prove his point, he outfitted the *Elettra* with a pair of short-wave radios, each sending a different beam to reflect off two buoys in the harbor of Sestri Levante south of Genoa and again in the nearby port of Santa Margherita, where Walter Trumpy and other technicians had checked into a top floor room of the Miramar Hotel to monitor the progress of the ship and to man the transmitter they had installed on the hotel roof. They proved that microwaves could be transmitted to distances two to three times beyond visual range, and demonstrated that a ship could navigate completely blind. The crew had put blankets over the windows on the bridge, removing the possibility of

anyone in the pilothouse being influenced by the sighting of familiar installations in the harbor. The *Elettra* was beamed safely to an anchorage alongside the dock.

The experiments were expanded to include the microwave detection of other objects at a distance, objects that could be a navigational hazard to the ship, or for that matter a plane.

Radar was in the process of being born and the military implications of these experiments were obvious to Marconi. In his capacity as President of the National Scientific Research Council, he convinced the government to continue them.

A team of British observers had been present at Sestri Levante and Santa Margherita but by 1935 Mussolini decreed that the work should be secret and carried out exclusively by Italians.

Strangely enough, when Marconi died two years later, official Italian interest waned and they obviously believed they had better uses for the yacht, the technicians and the money.

But the British remained interested. They had been the first to recognize the wartime potential of wireless to locate enemy forces. At the World War I Battle of Jutland, they used radio direction finding devices to locate the German fleet.

As explained in Georgia's Robins Air Force Base Museum of Aviation exhibit entitled "Electronic Warfare-What's It All About?"—next to a portrait of Marconi—the wireless, "like most new techniques, was quickly put to military use."

Five years after the British witnessed the initial *Elettra* blind navigation they developed the magnetron, which made radar practical. Their debt to Marconi was acknowledged after the war when they put up a plaque at the Miramar Hotel where Trumpy had been during the experiments. Shortly after they were completed and the *Elettra* headed out to sea again, Walter left the Marconi Company and pursued a different course, graduating from architectural school with honors. His brother, Oskar, became a distinguished doctor in Genoa.

Two other Bergen Trumpys—making a total of five—emigrated to Italy. Herman changed countries in 1862 at the age of 25, going directly to Livorno, as did all the emigrating members of the family. His uncle, Valerius, gave him a position in his company, banking on the nephew's intimate knowledge of ships and shipbuilding. Herman had worked in a Bergen shipyard for several years.

After a few years, Herman organized his own firm, Compania Commerciale Noleggi, a maritime commercial concern that soon had branches in Genoa, Savona and Spezia. He worked closely with Norwegian and Swedish shipping firms and was officially named Cavaliere.

In 1875 Herman asked his brother, Hugo, 19 years his junior, to join his company and work closely with his son, Eugenio. Hugo remained in Livorno only a short time before moving to Genoa to represent Herman's company there. In the beginning Hugo's chief clients were Scandinavian shippers moving cargoes of stockfish to Genoa and Savona.

Hugo was an ambitious young man, capable and confident, even though in his first years he had only a small desk and chair in a corner of the offices of a Genoese friend, Cavaliere Francesco Giordano, a customs broker. The office was strategically located near the harbor which at that time was undergoing major expansion and improvement.

Not since the eleventh century when the first piers were built, and 1638 when Molo Vecchio, the Old Pier, was constructed had there been such activity in the harbor. From 1877 to 1888 the Giano Pier, a pair of dry docks and the giant breakwater, Duca di Galliera, were built.

Genoa became more attractive as a port of call and the expanded ship traffic was valuable raw material for Hugo Trumpy. He soon had his own offices with branches in Savona, Spezia, Naples and Livorno.

Hugo, Herman and later, Herman's son, Eugenio, served as Vice Consuls for Sweden and Norway in the days of union and as Vice Consuls for Norway after their native country's total independence from Sweden in 1905. Eugenio's brother, Enrico, was Consul of Belgium in Livorno.

Independence was enthusiastically welcomed by the shipowners of Bergen who for years had protested the lack of concern by Stockholm (and earlier Copenhagen) representing Norwegian shipping and trade interests abroad.

Three of Hugo Trumpy's chief clients were Nordisk Skibsrederforening, the Northern Shipowners Association, shipper Otto Thoresen and Bergens Assuranceforening, the Bergen Insurance Association. In addition to his brokerage activities—he was the biggest in all of Italy—Hugo was also a very active shipowner himself, owning all or part of some twenty ships that transited Genoa.

He was also an accomplished artist. He painted a series of splendid watercolors and made a series of sketches of life in the Bergen area, ships and sailboats, including those in the family. It's obvious when looking at his works that the artistic genius displayed earlier by his father passed on to Hugo as well as brother Caspar, who used the skills to good advantage when designing ships.

Hugo died in Genoa in 1917 at age 61 and in accordance with the terms of his will, the Hugo Trumpy firm was turned over to the employees, led by a 25-year-old Dane, who was later joined by a prominent, experienced Norwegian shipbroker. The firm continued its profitable representation of Scandinavian shippers. Hugo's widow was paid 30,000 Italian lira.

Hugo Trumpy SPA, Agenzia Maritime Brokers, thrives today at 10 v. San Siro in Genoa. In Livorno the Herman Trumpy Agenzia Marittima Brokers, controlled by a French holding company, is at 21 v. del Lanzi. The Livorno branch office of Hugo Trumpy SPA is at 183 via Italia.

There are no longer any members of the Trumpy family involved in either company. After three generations of ship agents, brokers, and even builders—Valerius Trumpy's grandson, Ermanno, was a foreman in the Livorno Navy Shipyard—the Italian Trumpys were land-locked.

*120' passenger ferry **Palisades**, contract number 56, built in 1915 for Bessey*

Chapter 4
IMMIGRANT ENTREPRENEUR

When Johan Trumpy boarded ship for the New World he was one of thousands of Norwegians who were making the decision to leave land and loved ones on one side of the Atlantic in favor of the unknown on the other. That first trickle of immigration had been in 1825, the year the first Trumpy traveled to New York. The real waves began 40 years later, after the Civil War. From 1866 to 1915 close to three-quarters of a million Norwegians emigrated to the U.S. In the peak year, 1882, when economic conditions were at their worst, 30,000 Norwegians arrived in the United States seeking new lands and new lives.

Most of them headed for fresh farm lands in the Middle West, especially to Wisconsin, Minnesota and the Dakotas, but many made it all the way to the green forests of Washington.

Thousands more never got past the seaports and shipyards of the east coast. Reared in sea-going, shipbuilding families, they had no trouble finding work, and easily adjusted to new jobs in the many shipyards along the Atlantic, hired by fellow Norwegians and working alongside fellow Norwegians. In the Long Island firm of Brewer Dry Dock at Mariner's Harbor for example, Norwegian was the language of choice among a good many of the 500 employees, including the foremen of construction, model-making, repair and special projects. At the Brewer Shipyards on Long Island the superintendent was Norwegian and he hired quite a few fellow Vikings.

Most of the boat builders in New York were Scandinavians, a high percentage Norwegian, a fact that came as no surprise to the local Norwegian language newspaper, *Nordisk Tidende*, writing on August 20, 1925 about the prevalence of their countrymen in the yards from the turn of the century right through the 1920s:

"It is not an accident that the shipyards along the harbor of New York employ so many Norwegians. Aside from the fact that the Norwegians are a seafaring people and have a larger percentage of able seamen than any other nation, and that because of this they have a natural interest in everything connected with seafaring, there are other features which attract them. If we visit the shipyards on Staten Island, we are struck by the strong resemblance between these places and the small seacoast towns in Norway. We feel the smell of the fresh, salt sea, we see the big piles of planks, we pass large heaps of old scrap-iron, a broken propeller, an old discarded boat, rusty abandoned machines, small offices, sheds for machines and materials, scattered about in perfect disorder. It is just like visiting an old shipbuilding establishment at Selvik or Arendal, or in any other small Norwegian seacoast town. The young man coming from Norway often seeks employment in the shipyards in order to have something to do until something better can be found, but often, very often, he has to stick to the job until he is old and gray-haired and sees a son or sons engaged in the same occupation. How many Norwegians are employed in the shipyards on Staten Island cannot be stated definitely, but there are hundreds of them, and many who are now working in the building trades received their first training in some American shipbuilding establishment."

Johan Trumpy was not just another Norwegian workman who knew how to build boats. He had a degree in naval architecture, an apprenticeship in an internationally recognized shipyard, and was the heir-apparent of a distinguished family tradition of hand crafting quality ships. The 23-year-old presumably had no difficulty finding employment in his new country. Boat building was in his bones. And his heart and soul.

Shipbuilding is the oldest industry in the U.S. and when Johan Trumpy arrived in 1902, east coast yards were in the midst of a building boom. Shipyards in the Delaware Valley, from the New Jersey towns of Bordentown in the north, to Dorchester and Leesburg in the south, and across Delaware Bay to the Vinyard Shipbuilding Company in Milford, had been building ships for the navy since the Revolution. One hundred and thirty years later, after the Spanish-American War resulted in our gaining colonies, coaling stations and two-ocean ambitions, the yards in the valley were busier than ever.

One of the most successful was also the most recent arrival, New York Shipbuilding, organized by Henry G. Morse, former president of the Wilmington shipyard, Harlan & Hollingsworth, which was bought by Bethlehem Steel in 1904. He had wanted to build a yard on Staten Island but could not negotiate the real estate. However, he kept the original name, no doubt puzzling geographers.

With the important backing of Pittsburgh's industrial powerhouse, Andrew Mellon, Morse bought a parcel of farm land south of Camden and north of Newton Creek. His ambition to put up the most modern of yards to build the biggest boats in the valley was quickly realized, and by the time Johan Trumpy arrived to take up his post at one of Morse's drawing boards, New York Shipbuilding was working on a pair of battleships, the 16,000 ton *Kansas* and *New Hampshire*, and a 14,500 ton armored cruiser, *Washington*.

Morse was a trailblazer, an inspiring leader determined to make his new yard the most modern in the country. He introduced a mold loft template system to replace the old method of cut and try, and established a continuous flow of structural raw materials throughout the plant, working them into large sub-assemblies. Overhead cranes, capable of lifting 100 tons, were part of a comprehensive system serving ships and shipways, all five of which were under one roof. There was maximum utilization of machinery.

Trumpy was impressed if not overwhelmed as the orders kept coming in. In 1906 there was another 16,000 ton battleship, *Michigan*, the 21,825 ton *Utah* and a giant 27,940 ton *Moreno* for the Argentine Navy. In 1908 the drawing boards were covered with plans for a quartet of destroyers, the 700 ton **Lamson** and **Preston**, and the 742 ton **Burrows** and **McCall**.

But when work was progressing on the new, larger battleships, the 26,000 ton **Arkansas**, the 27,500 ton **Oklahoma**, and 32,000 ton **Idaho**, Trumpy was busy designing other kinds of vessels, promoting far more peaceful pursuits.

He was still thinking about yachts, but not the giants that were built for royalty. Every head of state had a yacht, even the Pope—the **Immacolata Concezione**—and they cruised the circuit, from the Riviera in the winter to the Baltic and the Isle of Wight in the summer, joined by the American yachting captains of the Gilded Age—the Vanderbilts, J. P. Morgan, Jay Gould, Carnegie, who had their own rallies at Newport. Their vessels of choice were long, sleek, steam-powered and with only vestigial masts but with enclaves of interior elegance every bit as ostentatious as their mansions on New York's Fifth Avenue.

Working to build larger and larger yachts was not what Johan Trumpy wanted to do. He might as well stay at New York Shipbuilding and continue to work on destroyers and battleships. He wanted to work on more modest yachts. But only those with some other reason for being than winning races. He was thinking of yachts which could serve as cruising homes for passengers and crew sailing internal waterways of the country and in protected bays and inlets.

There were any number of boatyards building racing yachts to compete in the major regattas, and Trumpy was familiar with the names, aware of the fact that it was his countrymen who made up the crews for the most important American racing boats. The year before he arrived in the U.S. the America's Cup was successfully defended by the **Columbia** against another challenge by Sir Thomas Lipton. The **Columbia** crew consisted of 34 Norwegians, two Swedes, a Dane and a German. Lipton's challenge two years later was beaten by the **Reliance** whose 51-man crew consisted of 44 Norwegians plus Norwegian first, second and third mates. Lipton called them "the smartest sailors I ever saw in my life."

The American yacht, **Vivian II,** with a crew of Norwegians won the trophy races for the Atlantic Yacht Club in 1905, and in 1909 the **Susie** with an all Norwegian crew won the major cup at the Jamestown Exposition.

But in 1909 Johan Trumpy was not thinking about designing faster and faster racing yachts. Nor was he intending to appeal to those strenuous yachtsmen who always had to challenge the sea. He was convinced that there was room for another kind of yacht, one that would capture a market that was only beginning to be exploited.

That market was the yacht houseboat, and he was ready to change jobs, move out of a giant company building giant ships into something more manageable. He had learned all he could at New York Shipbuilding and had spent the years since his arrival perfecting his English, discovering other shipyards in the Delaware Valley, getting adjusted to the American way of life and finding a bride, also an immigrant but not Norwegian or even Scandinavian. Margaret Trotman was English—her father was a British banker in Atlanta—and they were married in 1905. A son, Johan, was born in 1906. Donald came along in 1912 and daughter Dorothy two years later.

1905 was an auspicious year for Norwegians on both sides

of the Atlantic, for it marked the end of the union with Sweden and the declaration of total independence. The reception of the new king, Haakon VII, in Bergen—across from the old Trumpy yards at Bradbenken—was described with great enthusiasm in a letter from Johan's brother. He also informed the expatriate about the latest news in Bergen's shipbuilding circles, the newest launchings, the feelings about the future. Johan followed events back home as closely as he could and in future years would make regular trips to the old country. He probably told his family about his new plans and ideas.

In the preface to his 1905 volume **Houseboats and Houseboating**, editor Albert Bradlee Hunt explained at the outset that it was "devoted to a field entirely new in the literature of the day," although he had learned in the process of compiling the contributions for the book that, "The houseboat already has a place on many waters of the United States from Casco Bay to the Golden Gate, from the St. Lawrence to Lake Worth."

Houseboats and shantyboats were used on American rivers to carry new settlers to the frontier, and they served as base camps for fishermen, hunters, trappers, and living quarters for families who liked being on the water even though in many cases the boat had no independent means of propulsion and had to be towed to her anchorage.

In England, houseboating had been popular for years and had developed into a fine art with fleets of houseboats lining the Thames, providing supreme viewing platforms for such sporting and social events as the Henley Regatta. The Oxford College houseboats were like royal barges and others were lavishly decorated with a profusion of blooming flowers in windowboxes along the railings. Almost all of them had to be towed into place, the larger ones staffed by the same retinue of retainers, butlers and grooms as found in a country estate. They sported spacious salons, dining and drawing rooms.

The Chinese, the Dutch and Belgians all had houseboats and the French have been mooring vacation houseboats along the Seine as long as the English on the Thames, but in Hunt's survey of the scene he came to the conclusion "that Florida is about the only region in America where houseboats are used to any extent." But then Florida had all the conditions for ideal houseboating, "the sluggish waters of the rivers and bayous and the wide stretches of the lakes and lagoons, with the dense overhanging foliage of the tropical forest . . . a wondrously pleasant place in which to enjoy an outdoor life."

Hunt found that Florida's Indian River had a flourishing houseboat colony with a society which came closer to houseboat life on the Thames than any other spot in the country, and he praised those who spent the entire season cruising the Florida coast from St. Augustine to the Keys.

One of those houseboats in the pack was the *Savanilla*, an 84'6" sailing vessel built in 1903 in New Jersey by the Greenwich Piers Marine Railway Company. The designer was the noted Renaissance man of Coconut Grove, Florida, Ralph Middleton Munroe who, for 22 years, was commodore of the Biscayne Bay Yacht Club which he founded. He was famous for his shallow draft, seaworthy little sailboats, ideal for cruising the reef-filled shallow waters of Biscayne Bay.

In designing the *Savanilla*, Munroe faithfully followed the instructions of the owner, John Price Wetherill of Philadelphia, who wanted no engine. The boat's 47-foot tender with a ten horsepower engine provided the only power. When the wind failed, the tender could tow her mother ship—and also take her through the narrow inland channels and canals. The *Savanilla* was really an oversize sharpie with a skeg aft and two centerboards to stabilize steering but she had four staterooms and ample space for crew. She was designed specifically for cruising the shallow waters of Florida and while the rig was that of a top-sail schooner her draft was only 2'6".

For sailors who thought first about the boat and then the cabin, Munroe's design might have seemed to be the best of both possible worlds but no matter how simple the rig and how convenient it might be to handle, such compromises could well be dismissed as the worst of both possible worlds.

There had to be a better solution for Florida and those other areas of the country that provided hospitable conditions for houseboating: Gardiner's and Great South Bays, Orient Point in Long Island Sound, Sheepshead and Jamaica Bay and one of the best areas where there were miles of landlocked water with innumerable little creeks and inlets for anchorage, Barnegat Bay in New Jersey—a picturesque piece of New Jersey shore that Johan Trumpy already liked as a summer destination. He eventually bought a cottage there for family summer holidays.

It was one thing to have an idea but to convert it into reality, to convince others of the wisdom and potential of it, was the challenge. However, Johan Trumpy had already demonstrated the Viking spirit of adventure and individuality when he made the decisions to get his education in Germany and cross the Atlantic for a new life. He was certainly not lacking in confidence, nor some of the other characteristics singled out by the editor of the 1904 classic, **History of the**

Scandinavians and Successful Scandinavians in the United States. O. N. Anderson regarded the Norwegians as possessing a determination that bordered on stubbornness, but also a powerful sense of daring, with a passion for freedom and personal independence. He quoted Bjornstjerne Bjornson's evaluation of the Norwegian spirit: "The condition of conditions is the right to self-determination in order that it may concentrate its bias for adventure and its talents in forming new things and, if possible, in making these an example for others."

Johan, or John as he now called himself, proved the point when he moved up river to the city of Camden where he found a position with the John H. Mathis Company, builders of ocean-going freighters and a variety of other vessels for industrial and commercial use, but not yachts. At least not until Trumpy arrived.

It wasn't too long before the idea was put on paper and commitments made. On the 27th day of January, 1910, the Mathis Yacht Building Company was incorporated in the state of New Jersey with the registered office at 417-419 Market Street, Camden and with the New Jersey Corporation Guarantee & Trust Company designated as statutory agent. The purpose for which the corporation was established was primarily:

"To build, construct, repair, alter, buy, sell, trade, deal in and with yachts, ships, motor boats & boats of all kinds and description and to acquire by purchase, lease, construction, manufacture or otherwise any buildings, machinery, materials or articles used in any way in connection therewith."

Twenty thousand dollars of capital stock was issued, divided into 400 shares with par value of $50 each. The capital stock with which the new corporation commenced business was subscribed by John H. Mathis of Camden, William W. Robinson, a businessman from Lansdowne, Pennsylvania, each with nine shares for a total of $900, and John Trumpy with two shares for a total of $100.

Mathis Builder's Plaque

For $100 the 31-year old Norwegian immigrant was a director of a company that he had conceived. He was elected at the first annual meeting the day after incorporation, on January 28, 1910. The other directors were those who put up the money, Mathis the president and Robinson the secretary. Together they adopted a set of bylaws and set the date of the annual meeting as the last Thursday in January, and the monthly meetings of the Board of Directors the first Thursday in the month.

Also approved at the first meeting was the purchase for $10,000 in shares of the new company from John H. Mathis & Company:

"A certain frame building or Boat Shop with the right to remove the same, together with a lease for one year at $1,000 per year on the land upon which it is located, viz.: a certain lot of ground situated on the Delaware River, containing in front about 50 feet and extending in depth about 200 feet at a distance about half way between Point and Front Street in the City of Camden, N.J.,

"And also the machinery, stock on hand, materials, tools and the good will and existing yacht building business carried on by them at said shop."

This agreement was made between the Board of Directors and Mathis and Robinson, trading as "vendors" for John H. Mathis & Company.

The next order of business, once the real estate question was resolved and Mathis Yacht Building Company actually had a work shed, slip and necessary equipment to commence construction, was for the three directors to vote a waiver of notice of assessment of the subscription shares pledged at the meeting of incorporation. It was decided the money would be called for "in such amounts and at such time or times as the Board of Directors may require."

In other words, no one had to pay up but after the transfer of property was completed, Mathis and Robinson each received 70 shares of the new company and Trumpy was awarded 60. They then elected a new slate of officers: Robinson as president, John Trumpy vice-president and Mathis secretary-treasurer. The First National Bank of Camden was selected as their central depository and clearinghouse and it was agreed that an office be opened at the new shop on Point and Erie Streets.

At a special meeting of the board a week later, it was unanimously agreed to accept the charges of John Mathis & Company for steam, air, telephone and gas, and to empower Trumpy to accept bids for electric lights in the shop and to award the contract. At another special meeting in May, the board voted (and the stockholders—one and the same—agreed) to increase the capital stock of the company from $20,000 to $50,000, to be divided into a thousand shares with par value of $50 each. They also voted to pay president Robinson $2100 a year for the next two years, retroactive to January 1, 1910.

Salaries for Trumpy as vice-president and Mathis as secretary-treasurer were set at $1300 and $1500 with the same provisions. The board voted to pay the sums in capital stock at six-month intervals.

The Board of Directors voted on December 19, 1912, to pay president Robinson $100 a month and Mathis as secretary-treasurer $75 a month and to increase the salary of Trumpy $5 per week. There were no other board meetings recorded in the minutes, it being reported for each month that only Mathis was present and there was no quorum.

The same situation persisted throughout the following year, but then only Robinson was recorded as being present. In June, 1914, however, there was a meeting with quorum. It was called to accept the resignation of Mathis as secretary-treasurer and his replacement with Cornell R. Finney. Robinson was re-elected president and Trumpy vice-president. Finney was replaced in 1918 by W. F. Eddleman. Neither Finney nor Eddleman received capital stock payment for their services, and at the meeting on November 3, 1916, it was decided to move Trumpy's salary from a monthly basis to yearly, in the amount of $3000, retroactive to the first of the year.

The May, 1917 monthly meeting of the board increased Trumpy's annual salary to $15,000 and Robinson's to $18,000. The tremendous increases were a result of government contracts to build submarine chasers. Trumpy proposed at the meeting that a percentage of the profits be paid to their parent company, in view of their "assisting in every way possible" in the building of those naval vessels. Mathis & Company had also made additional land and sheds available to its now-independent offspring, receiving in return $10,000 annually for

rental of the entire yacht building company complex.

War profits were not the only reason for the success of the

MATHIS YARD - CAMDEN, N.J.

spin-off from Mathis. By the time the first naval vessel was on Trumpy's drawing boards, he had already designed and supervised construction of 49 yacht houseboats plus a couple of yacht tenders, a dredge hull for the city of Philadelphia, tugboats and a special houseboat for the Boy Scouts called *Young America*.

John Trumpy demonstrated that he had the idea whose time had definitely come and it didn't take long for the yachting public to realize it. He had the first contract in hand the year before Mathis Yacht Building Company was incorporated. It was from Philadelphian M. B. Brigham for a 65-foot motor yacht christened *Caliph*.

It was a proud moment for John Trumpy and the 40

employees of the new company when the *Caliph* took top prize in the first long distance motor boat race between Philadelphia and Havana, Cuba.

As important as that achievement was to attract the attention of the boating world looking at a new product from a new company, the order in 1910 from William Disston was destined to be more significant for the future of Mathis Yacht Building Company.

A socially prominent Philadelphian, Disston was president of the Keystone Saw Company, the Henry Disston & Sons File Company and Disston Steel Works. His brother, Hamilton, had single-handedly restored faith in Florida bonds and gave the state a reliable financial reputation. In 1881 he guaranteed the interest payment on $14 million worth of bonds with a million dollar pledge—but when the time came to pay it took only $200,000 to settle the deal. In the process, Disston bought a total of four million acres, 1/9th of the state, for 25 cents an acre and he spent heavily on internal improvements believing, unlike Henry Flagler on the east coast and Henry Plant on the west, that the future of Florida was dependent on steamboats, not railroads.

Disston dredged canals, drained lands, experimented with subtropical agriculture and at the Disston Shipyards in Kissimmee, built dredges and steamboats. By the time William ordered his Trumpy, Hamilton had been dead more than a decade but the Disston presence was still a vital one and he was an important booster of the state. He wanted a class yacht that could take him into the shallow waters of the inlets, the canals and the Keys. His *Cocopomelo* which drew only 18" of water, did just that and the next year he ordered another yacht

houseboat, the *Pauline*. William Disston proved to be a terrific promoter of Mathis/Trumpy yachts. He apparently convinced A. H. Disston to order the *Alela* in 1913.

Hartwig "Harty" N. Baruch was another prominent contemporary who recognized the graceful sturdiness of a Trumpy-designed yacht. In 1911 he signed a contract for the *Nahmeoka*, and two years later for the second *Nahmeoka*. Harty's brother Herman ordered his Trumpy in 1919, the *Riposo II*, and brother Sailing, the *Donaldo* in 1920. Harty had originally pursued a theatrical career but when brother Bernard offered to give him his seat on the New York Stock Exchange if he would give up the stage, Harty joined the already famous Bernard on Wall Street. Herman, a medical doctor, gave up his practice in favor of high finance. Brother Sailing also signed on.

Wall Street wizard Bernard got them to join his company but they could not convince him to buy a yacht, or even to sail on theirs unless really pushed to it despite the fact that he had the perfect waters around his 17,000-acre escape, Hobcaw Barony in South Carolina. Hobcaw is an Indian word meaning "between the waters," and it's a fitting name with the rivers Black, Peedee, Sampit and Waccamaw all flowing into Winyah Bay. The Intracoastal Waterway goes into and out of the Waccamaw.

Bernard Baruch was a terrible sailor, one who had a frightful experience during an early childhood voyage on a stern-wheeler from Charleston to Georgetown, and he was not ashamed to admit that "the terrors of the ocean have remained with me from that day to this."

But his brothers' yachts were popular with the many movers

and shakers who frequented Hobcaw during the season—bankers, brokers, generals, statesmen. Harty Baruch usually brought a bunch on his *Nahmeoka* but others, such as Harry and Payne Whitney, arrived on their own yacht for a weekend of hunting at Hobcaw.

President Roosevelt didn't hunt during his visits; he preferred fishing and never failed to try to convince Bernard to join him. "He knows I get seasick easily," Baruch complained to an aide, but in his philosophical approach to the rigors of making money he penned what is an insightful explanation of one of the joys of owning a boat, if we substitute boat deck for park bench:

"In this hectic Age of Distraction, all of us need to pause every now and then in what we are doing to examine where the rush of the world and of our own activities is taking us. Even an hour or two spent in such detached contemplation on a park bench will prove rewarding."

John Trumpy could have used the statement in his advertising, although in that department he proved so adept he didn't really need any help. An article he wrote for the mass-circulation *Leslie's Weekly* in 1912 entitled "Uses and Delights of the Power Houseboat," puts forth his philosophy of boat building and the reasons he was convinced he had an idea that was not only workable, viable, but also potentially profitable:

"When one hears the word houseboat, he involuntarily has in mind something more or less like a floating house - a barge or scow type of a hull, with deckhouses giving living quarters for the owners, the boat being anchored in some protected bay or harbor, and only able to move around with the assistance of a tugboat."

That judgment was true enough before the advent of the internal combustion engine and the impact it was having on marine propulsion. The development and perfection of gasoline motors made it possible for Trumpy to design and build houseboats which met all the requirements for a boat or yacht, adding to the advantages "home comfort to the owner and family, without the necessity of building a large yacht," which was much more expensive and resulted in a vessel that could not navigate the shallow waters of America's inland waterways.

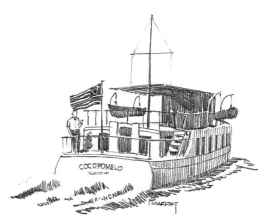

Cocopomelo

Trumpy explained that the kind of modern houseboats he was building provided the home comfort of a large yacht but costs much less to build and maintain, and there was ample room for owner, crew and guests. In a houseboat he had just completed for A. J. Quakenbush, the *Lunaria*, fully seventy percent of the overall length was devoted to the owner's quarters. There were three large staterooms, each fitted with a lower berth and an upper (folding) berth, en suite bathrooms and rows of windows allowing for light as well as ventilation. Each window was equipped with storm shutters for use in heavy weather.

An open stairway led from the dining room to the

pilothouse and the long deck which was entirely covered with an awning. The 3'6" draft allowed for cruising in shallow waters. Trumpy acknowledged that larger draft vessels had better seagoing qualities, but "It is the opinion and experience of the writer that these boats can be built on a draft that will give them all seagoing qualities necessary to take the outside runs encountered cruising along the Atlantic with perfect safety."

In the *Lodona* built for E. J. Graecen of New York in 1911, the 77' x 18'6" yacht was able to cruise outside as well as in with her draft of 2'6". The 70-foot *Ibis,* built the following year, had the same advantages.

The *Ibis* has had eight different owners since 1912 and she is currently seeking her ninth—she's on the market for $150,000 by her latest captain, Jeff Siben, who discovered the Trumpy in a Maine boatyard in 1983. He did most of the restoration himself and had to replace only six planks in the hull—the long leaf yellow pine was rock hard. He also replaced the original gasoline-burning Chrysler engines, installing Isuzu diesels.

When we first went aboard the *Ibis* in 1988, she was with Fred H. Gordon, Jr. of Rochester, New York, who had his own Trumpy, the 63-foot *Sinbad* built for him in 1970. Gordon led us directly to one of the staterooms and pointed out the bunk he had used at the age of eight when he was on board with his father, a friend of the owner, F. F. Christie. They were there in the slow and easy days before World War I to do a little serious fishing and were docked at the pier of Henry Flagler's six-story Royal Palm Hotel, a 450-room giant in the shape of the letter "F" where the Miami River flows into Biscayne Bay. Flagler

had cut a channel across the bay so guests could bring their yachts directly to the hotel. He was the railroad king but he knew how to please the boaters and in season, the docks were crowded with the finest private yachts in existence, including, as the years rolled by, more and more stellar examples of the artistry of Mathis Yacht Building Company.

The inventory included the **Black Duck** for Alexander Sellers, **Ruffled Grouse** for J. H. Carstairs and the *Georgena*, the next boat built after *Ibis* and one of eleven whose contracts were signed in 1912. She was ordered by Frederick Francis Proctor, a one-time professional acrobat who controlled a couple dozen theaters and road shows in New York City, Albany, Troy and other eastern centers. His 70-foot yacht houseboat was named for his wife.

In 1913 there were two tugboat deck houses and a tugboat built in addition to five yacht houseboats. The following year there were three tugs built, the *Okisko*, *Perry* and *Skycock* for U.S.E.D., the Underwater Sound Explosive Devices Branch of the Naval Weapons Stations in Norfolk, Jacksonville and Yorktown. It was the company's first government contract and proved to be an important precedent, one which established lines of communication and convinced the Navy that Mathis and John Trumpy were skilled, reliable suppliers.

In 1915 the *Mifflin* was built for U.S.E.D., *the Lady Baltimore* for the Hall-Seeley Motor Company, a couple of boats, *Akbar* and *Ace* for G. W. C. Drexel and the *Adios* for prominent Philadelphian L. L. Biddle, along with a yacht houseboat for the publisher of the *Philadelphia Inquirer*, christened to no one's surprise, the *Inquirer*.

The 1912 *Lanai*, a 76-foot tender for the giant, 218-foot

ocean-going bark *Aloha* of super rich Arthur Curtiss James, had to be built with more attention to ocean-going capabilities and thus had a draft of 3'6".

In 1981 the former *Lanai* was extensively rebuilt, refastened and restructured in Thomaston, Maine. A third of the long leaf yellow pine carvel planking was replaced, the interior insulated and rewired. A pair of Detroit 4-71 diesels, 130 hp, were installed and the accommodations for five were reworked. She was given a second life, a second good life, re-christened *Argo*, but when she was originally built and made her maiden voyage to Florida she served, along with the Trumpy-designed yachts that William Matheson was enjoying in South Florida, as an outstanding model for other would-be yachters and houseboaters who wanted to explore the off shore islands and Florida Keys. With 1,350 miles of Atlantic and Gulf coastline and 4,470 square miles of inland waters there was a lot to investigate.

The Trumpy-designed boats sailing off the slips of the Mathis Yacht Building Company were attracting serious attention, not only for the purpose-built practicality of shallow water navigation but also for the Swiss watchmaker approach to workmanship, the persistent attention to the smallest detail without a hint of cutting corners or utilizing anything but top quality raw materials. Yachtsmen discovering the joys of houseboating appreciated the yachty feeling, the sleek lines, solidity of construction and careful craftsmanship.

John Trumpy, yacht houseboat designer and builder, was establishing quite a reputation.

Photo of yard dated 2-27-19

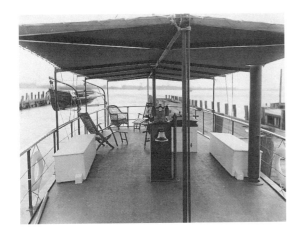

Note that even this small houseboat has a light, airy and spacious feeling aboard.

*43' **Alice**, contract number 43 built in 1914 for J. J. Smith and Mary Scofield*

Chapter 5
A TRUMPY AT VIZCAYA

On May 22, 1916, John Trumpy's Mathis Yacht Building Company signed a contract with yet another international industrialist who was having a tremendous impact on South Florida, James Deering.

The bachelor vice-president of the International Harvester Company of Chicago—a company created in 1902 when J. P. Morgan power-brokered a merger of the Portland, Maine, based Deering Harvester giant and Chicago's Cyrus McCormick Harvesting Machine Company—was in the process of completing what would become one of the great homes of the country, if not the world, Vizcaya. Nearly 10 percent of Miami's population of 10,500 were employed in the project.

Set on 180 acres of shoreline, hammock and piney woods in what was previously the jungle of Coconut Grove, an early settlement four miles south of Miami and close to a hundred miles safely removed from the social scene of Palm Beach, the many-splendored mansion was filled with reminders of Florida's rich Spanish conquistador and maritime history. The name chosen for the estate, Vizcaya, was inspired by the Basque name for Biscayne but Deering liked to tell his guests that the smallest ship on Columbus' fourth and last voyage, was named *Viscaino*, and that a Viscaino was master of the ship Ponce de Leon took on his voyage of discovery to Florida in 1513. Deering named the three little artificial islands created by the dredging of channels at the bayfront of the villa Nina, Pinta and Santa Maria.

A beautifully built model—over five feet long—of Ponce's ship *San Cristoval*, one of the three caravels he sailed to La Florida, which he careened somewhere in the Florida Keys, hangs from the high ceiling of the east loggia in a manner suggesting votive ships dangling from chains in churches whose congregations regularly gather to pray for, or mourn, those that go down to the sea in ships.

The loggia leads to the deck with an inlaid compass, stairs to the dock and the sensational surprise of a giant stone barge decorated with a crew of sculptures by Alexander Stirling Calder depicting the delights and terrors of the sea. The 175-foot barge serves as breakwater and has become a symbol of the estate.

Above the center door in the tea room, leading out to the gardens, surely among the finest in the land, is a carefully executed stained glass caravel, the official emblem of the estate.

Deering had it engraved on his stationery and commissioned Tiffany to create caravel scarf pins for presenting as thank you gifts to key personnel involved in the massive and challenging two-year building project.

NEPENTHE

The rooms of Vizcaya's main guest suite were called Caravel and Galleon and Deering's official burgee pictured a caravel with yellow background on a red swallowtail.

It would fly proudly on the yacht John Trumpy was designing for him and would be crossed with the blue background, white star pennant of the New York Yacht Club— Deering was a member, of course—on the French crystal and silver-rimmed English Cauldron bone china he commissioned for the yacht.

The name chosen for the 48th yacht designed by Trumpy (contract number 67) was *Nepenthe*, meaning forgetfulness of sorrow. An 80-foot twin screw of 65 tons with a beam of 17'4" and draft of 2'6", she had three staterooms, each of them carpeted, and a like number of baths, each with inlaid linoleum, which was also used in the deck house. There were twenty-nine sets of curtains, including fourteen for the deck house, a large shade for the skylight in the state room forward and roller spring shades with guides for all the deck house windows.

The upholstery was specified as a box spring seat and back with end cushions along with box spring and mattress for the owner's portside stateroom. Seat and back cushions were also ordered for the other staterooms, starboard and forward, one with a single coil spring and mattress bed and one with twin beds.

Three white enameled stools were ordered for the bathrooms and the deckhouse, along with a mahogany extension table and a dozen narrow dining chairs with leather backs and seats. Deering wanted to be able to entertain twelve guests at table bedecked with his monogrammed gleaming crystal, bone china, Gorham silver plate flatware and serving pieces.

One wicker table and eight wicker chairs were placed on the canvas-canopied afterdeck and there were also twelve folding camp chairs as well as one small wicker chair for Deering's stateroom. On the wall of his quarters were Japanese prints, selected by Deering's interior designer and resident entrepreneurial artist, Paul Chalfin, who had served for a time as Curator of Asiatic Art at the Boston Museum of Fine Art.

Chalfin lived on his own houseboat, **The Blue Dog**, while working on Vizcaya. She was a local sensation docked on Miami's bayfront, resembling with her fireplace, walls of windows, spacious canopied upperdeck, flowering window boxes and awnings an English houseboat permanently parked on the Thames.

Deering had asked Chalfin to help with selection of furnishings for the new *Nepenthe*, specifying that he wanted an electric phonograph and an electric player piano, the model made by the same manufacturers who built the pipe organ in the house, Welte-Mignon, armed with thirty rolls.

The cost of the phonograph was $250 and the piano $1500. The total cost of all furnishings, including china, glassware, silver for the dining salon, silver ashtrays and matchbox holders, thermometers and brass clocks in each of the staterooms, was $16,576. The cost of the yacht, with a motorized tender delivered to Vizcaya in February 1917, was $37,650.

It took a crew of seven to run *Nepenthe*, a captain and engineer, two seamen, chef, messman and messboy. All were in uniform and the caps had a specially designed insignia. The first captain, Cloyd B. Hewes, was on board only a few months before being succeeded by Captain Joseph Santini who remained until 1924, the year before Deering's death—which occurred on board another ship, the trans-Atlantic liner, *S.S. Paris*. Deering was en route from Le Havre to New York.

Whenever Deering was in residence, usually throughout the four-month winter season, Santini and his crew were on standby duty and the housekeeper kept linens, galley supplies and provisions always ready for instant use. Sometimes the *Nepenthe* would merely go on a luncheon cruise around the bay, but on other occasions, Deering would take guests on longer cruises through the Keys, along the Florida coast or into the islands.

Itineraries were planned in advance at Vizcaya with Deering taking his voyagers to one of the north arcade walls of the courtyard where huge brass and glass frames held sea charts. On the other wall flanking the grand staircase were rolls of maps he could pull down to show his guests precisely where they would be cruising. Details could be discussed over

breakfast, ideally in the second floor Breakfast Room with its magnificent 18th century harbor murals executed in the manner

VIZCAYA, MIAMI.

Viscaya, Miami, Florida, Home of James Deering,
owner of Nepenthe

of French master Claude Joseph Vernat.

If less ambitious boating was desired, guests could take one of the electric launches which glided along the canals and waterways of the formal gardens, or they could join a fishing expedition going after the big ones aboard Deering's other boat, the 45-foot, twin screw *Psyche*, built by Gas Engine & Power and Seabury Company in Morris Heights, New York. She was launched the year before *Nepenthe*, and remained at Vizcaya year-round. Captain Santini took *Nepenthe* north at season's end, docking her near Atlantic City for his employer's use when residing in his New York City apartment.

Nepenthe's log, had it survived, would make fascinating reading, a roll call of the rich, well-born and able who enjoyed the luxury of cruising on her—politicians such as William Jennings Bryan who had his own mansion in Coconut Grove, capitalists like William Vanderbilt who could give vivid accounts of his own cruises and races as America's premier yachtsman, and artists like John Singer Sargent, who painted a fine portrait of his host and scenes of the gardens before embarking on *Nepenthe* to catch a 120-pound tarpon.

Deering knew he had a fine yacht for such purposes, even though he did from time to time talk about getting something bigger than 80 feet. But how did he know about John Trumpy and the Mathis Yacht Company? Where did he learn about the yacht houseboats so ideal for cruising Florida waters?

Deering had considered the desirability of getting a houseboat early on during the construction of Vizcaya, discussing it with Paul Chalfin to whom he wrote on August 3, 1915, explaining that there were two classes of boats currently in use in Florida. One, he wrote, was like the Everglades which draws "considerable water," and can go only where there's a deep enough channel. They cannot go in and out of the Keys nor "land at many of the most charming and attractive places."

The other class Deering had observed, "is well typified by the two boats belonging to Matheson and James. These draw only 27 inches of water and can go almost anywhere they please to go in Florida waters." After discussion with his friends Matheson and James, and trips aboard their boats, Deering decided he definitely should have the second class of boats, the kind they were enjoying, "yacht houseboats; at least, that's what the builder calls them. They are made to look like a small

steamboat rather than like the typical houseboat."

Matheson and James both had Trumpys. Arthur Curtis James, an important landowner in Coconut Grove, was considered by many of his neighbors to be one of the wealthiest men in the world. He had the 14th yacht houseboat designed and built by Trumpy, the *Lanai*, whose keel was laid in 1911. Her voyage south was described in Trumpy's article in *Leslie's Weekly* the following year.

James took possession of *Lanai* the year after he returned from a round-the-world cruise on his giant yacht, *Aloha*, one of the all steam-driven yachts replacing the fully rigged sail-steam yachts. The first diesel yacht was still a year away.

James was president of Curtiss Southwestern Corporation, director of Phelps Dodge, U.S. Trust Company and various railways, and a trustee of the Metropolitan Museum of Art as well as Amherst College. In Coconut Grove he had built a hunting lodge not far from The Barnacle, the unique waterfront home of Grove pioneer artist, naturalist, photographer, and boat designer Commodore Ralph Middleton Munroe. James had built a lookout tower of native coquina stone nearby on the shore. Similar stone was used for the restoration of the Grove's Spanish mission landmark, Plymouth Congregational Church. James and Deering split the expenses for that important preservation project.

Two other products of Mathis Yacht Company which Deering knew well were the 1912 *Calabash* and the 1915 *Marpessa*, the yacht houseboats of Dr. William J. Matheson. A Wisconsin native who made his fortune in New York's chemical industry, Matheson had purchased extensive acreage in the Grove, some of it close to the properties of both James Deering and his brother, Charles, who was creating his own jungle estate in the area. Both brothers had known Matheson for years, ever since they first wintered in the modest Coconut Grove home built by their parents after the merger of the family business with McCormick of Chicago.

Matheson was a pioneer developer in Greater Miami, especially Coconut Grove and Key Biscayne, most of which he and Deering owned. Until they arrived on the scene, the island was mainly a haven for salvagers eager to plunge on wrecks floundering on the treacherous Florida reef. Matheson drained swamps and built 18 miles of roads, an extensive coconut plantation, and yacht basins for his and other Trumpys. He was commodore of the Biscayne Bay Yacht Club. The membership rolls included names immediately recognizable as among the power brokers of the land—Armour, Flagler, Grosvenor, Mellon, Vanderbilt and James Deering.

The commodore and James Deering financed the rescue, shoring up and strengthening of another local landmark of note, one that could clearly be seen from Vizcaya, the 95-foot Cape Florida Lighthouse, built in 1825 at the tip of Key Biscayne.

Deering, James and Matheson were generous contributors to such causes and when the U.S. entered the war two months

after the *Nepenthe* was put into service at Vizcaya, International Harvester's vice-president offered her to the Navy—just as many yacht owners were doing. She was taken to the Key West Naval Base where she was not armed and converted to some kind of patrol duty, but utilized as officers' quarters.

It was a short-lived tour of duty and in November, 1917, *Nepenthe* was returned to Vizcaya, her owner commended by Secretary of the Navy Josephus Daniels for his patriotism.

106' Leonie, contract number 69, built in 1916 for Murry Guggenheim

John Trumpy and Mathis Yacht would soon be getting their own commendations as all efforts were directed toward the war. Norway was able to remain neutral during World War I, but not John Trumpy. He was in the thick of it, designing and building for the military and not the millionaires. The last boats that came off his drawing boards in 1916 before war was declared, were the *Chieftan* for meat baron A. Watson Armour, a neighbor of Deering's on Chicago's Lake Shore Drive, and *Leonie*, built for Murry Guggenheim, a director of Guggenheim Brothers in New York.

*106' **Leonie**, contract number 69, built in 1916 for Murry Guggenheim*

Chapter 6
WORLD WAR I

When James Deering patriotically offered his brand new yacht houseboat to the Navy he was responding to their urgent need for vessels to patrol the shipping lanes then under constant attack from a new and powerful German weapon, the submarine.

At the beginning of hostilities in August, 1914, the Kaiser's underwater fleet numbered 30. By February 1, 1917, when the Germans declared unrestricted submarine warfare, they had nearly four times that number to enforce their declaration that in the waters of the Eastern Mediterranean, Italy, France and Great Britain, all shipping regardless of country of origin or neutrality of carrier, would be "attacked with every available weapon and without further notice."

When asking for a declaration of war two months later, President Wilson denounced "the recent course of the Imperial German Government to be in fact nothing less than war against the government and people of the United States," and he promised that the nation would "exert all its power and employ all its resources to bring the Government of the German Empire to terms and to end the war."

At the time, German U-boats were sinking 37 merchant ships a month; by February 1918, 105 and by April, 127, one out of every four ships that left British ports.

New ships had to be built as quickly as possible to keep open the life line shipping lanes from the arsenals, granaries and factories of the U.S. New ships were also needed to transport the troops, and to carry the raw materials needed in U.S. industries—chrome ore from New Caledonia, manganese and nitrates from South America, pyrites from Spain, wool from Australia, hemp from the Philippines, and many other vital imports.

In 1917 destroyers were the only weapon in the U.S. Navy's arsenal of anti-submarine warfare. But destroyers were expensive and took too long to produce. A different kind of ship was needed and naval procurement officers were soon calling for hundreds of wooden boats. There was a sudden revival, a boom in wooden shipbuilding. Idle yards, made obsolete by the advent of steam-powered steel ships, were revitalized and reborn and many others established. For Mathis Yacht with its seven years' experience building wooden luxury houseboats, the switchover to wooden naval craft was a natural.

To replace the losses of merchant ships, to ensure an

uninterrupted flow of foodstuffs and military materiel, and then to build the transports to ferry our own troops and all their

U. S. Navy Tugboat No. 76

necessary supplies, as well as a navy to protect the valuable cargoes, the U.S. government launched an incredibly ambitious shipbuilding program. Sixty new shipyards were established and an army of more than 625,000 recruited to work in those yards and related industries involved in the manufacture of marine machinery and fittings.

As Charles M. Schwab, Director-General of the U.S. Shipping Board's Emergency Fleet Corporation, put it, "When the need arose and it looked as though the war might be lost through inability to get American men and supplies to the battlefront, there were few shipyards of any productive capacity in the U.S. Almost overnight vast plants began to appear along the three coasts and on the shores of rivers and lakes."

Largest of all the 203 shipyards was the giant Hog Island plant near Philadelphia. It took over $50 million to transform, practically overnight, a muddy swamp into the largest shipbuilding facility the world had ever seen. The American International Shipbuilding Corporation stretched its 50 shipways for a mile along the Delaware River and employed some 28,000 workers. They were producing standardized ships, not the kind John Trumpy had been working on.

U.S. shipyards were building 15 times as much tonnage as they were before the war and on one glorious day, July 4, 1918, nearly a hundred ships were launched—an incredible, unprecedented achievement in the history of shipbuilding.

Norwegian shipbuilders and shipowners made a sizable contribution to the tonnage totals and the number of new shipbuilding firms. In New York alone there were a dozen including Hallbjorn Navigation Company, Kristiansand Navigation Corporation, Skjold, Viking and Stolt Nielsen Steamship Companies. The enterprising Christoffer Hannevik organized in Gloucester City, New Jersey—near the site of a future Trumpy shipyard—the Pennsylvania Shipbuilding Company and the New Jersey Shipbuilding Company for the production of vessels five thousand tons and over. To house his workers, many of whom were Norwegian, he laid out a town he called Noreg Village housing some six thousand people.

The majority of steamships launched by American shipyards between August, 1914, and January, 1917, were built for Norwegian firms, but on August 3, 1917, the U.S. government requisitioned all vessels over 2500 tons built in the U.S. for foreign companies and then ran the shipyards which built them. Suitable compensation was to be paid after the end of hostilities.

As the British High Commissioner, Lord Northcliffe, stated in a speech reported in the September 1918 *National Marine*: "Norway has done more to put the United States in a position to combat Germany and her consorts than all our measures of preparedness together. Without the ships that Norway has ordered and the yards that have been built because of those orders and with capital actually advanced on those orders, the United States, with all her wealth of natural resources, would have been practically helpless to aid our allies across the seas."

The statistics are as incredible as those documenting the number of new shipyards established and the number of workers. Lord Northcliffe drove the point home by stating that "Norwegian orders at American yards, Norwegian tonnage building in addition to the original contracts that made the majority of American yards of today possible, on conservative estimate, constitute 75 per cent of all the shipbuilding that has been done in the United States for the past two years, and nearly all that can be done in the next two."

The only known Norwegian hands in wartime airplane production were those of John Trumpy who helped design the bodies of certain kinds of aircraft. Not fighters or bombers but reconnaissance planes providing another means of protecting our shores and ships from the submarine threat. Hydroplanes and flying boats provided aerial surveillance of surface and underwater enemy vessels, although range and adequate attack armament were severely limited. Two wars later, a different kind of aircraft, the helicopter, proved to be an invaluable, integral component of minesweeping forces, partnering with the Trumpy-built minesweepers that served in Korean waters.

Although World War I air power was considerably more primitive, the Naval Aircraft Factory in Philadelphia, across the

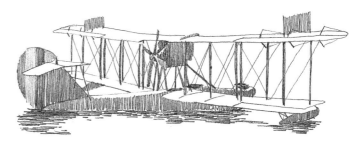

Flying Boat, 1918

river from Mathis yards, was building fifty twin-engine flying boats a year, planes with 103'9" wingspan and an overall length of 49'3". In 1918 the company ordered ten hulls from Mathis. What more logical producer of flying boat body fuselages—hulls in fact—than a wooden shipbuilding yard?

Mathis also built 75 hulls for Standard Aircraft Corporation in Elizabeth, New Jersey, second largest manufacturer of airplanes in the country. It had produced the first aircraft designed specifically to carry mail as well as a wartime trainer craft and the DH-4A two-seater fighter. Its Handley-Page Type 0-400 bomber was the most popular aircraft in both the U.S. and Great Britain for bombing runs over enemy territory.

Mathis provided the hulls for Standard's HS 2L flying boats, biplanes with engine propeller reversed and mounted between the wings. It was the smallest in the naval air force with a wingspan of 74', and overall length of 38'6". The Curtiss H 16 was 95' x 46' and its giant NC 1 was 126' x 68'.

The Standard-Mathis flying boats were powered by a single Liberty 12 engine, manufactured in every automobile plant in

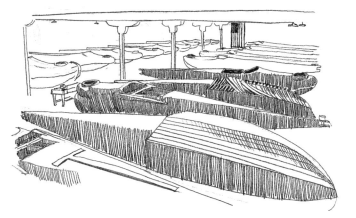

Airplane hulls, 1918

the country, and, in the words of the Secretary of War in 1917, "the main reliance of the United States in the rapid production in large numbers of high-powered battle planes for service in the war." That production in the 21 months of U.S. involvement in the war totaled 15,000 planes.

Sky-high reconnaissance patrols were useful, but surface vessels had to be the main means of defense for the convoys. To fill the need, the Navy considered several patrol vessels already in production, starting with the 75-foot anti-submarine launches built for the British by the Electric Launch & Navigation Company (ELCO) of Bayonne, New Jersey. The forerunner of giant General Dynamics Corporation, ELCO had its beginning by successfully bidding to build electric-powered launches that glided along the canals of Chicago's famous Columbian Exposition in 1894. That was the same year John

Trumpy's brother, Jacob, established his electric ferryboat company in Bergen.

ELCO's first government contract had been signed in 1906, four years before the founding of Mathis Yacht Building Company, and it was for six U. S. Life Saving Service boats.

When that ripple was not followed by a wave of orders, ELCO turned to producing luxury yachts until 1915 when the British Royal Navy gave them an order for fifty 75-foot motor launches, and then for 500 more, 80 feet in length. ELCO, using super-efficient mass production methods, sped through the production—500 boats in 488 days.

They added another 152 for the Royal Navy as well as the French and Italians and were hoping to repeat the feat for the U.S. Navy. But the Navy wasn't buying. They knew that the British were having difficulties with the small boats maneuvering in rough coastal waters, and they wanted larger, better-armed boats, vessels 100 to 120 feet long. They definitely had to be built in wood—to save iron and steel for naval warships, freighters and military armaments. And they had to be built by the private sector.

The U.S. Naval Bureau of Construction and Repair Preliminary Design Department decided, after a period of study and competition, to order 110-foot vessels armed with a 6-pounder and a Y gun aft and powered by 220 horsepower Standard Motor gasoline engines with a speed of 17 knots.

As the first subchasers came down the ways and were put through their trial runs on the Delaware River, British Prime Minister Lloyd George was overcoming the opposition of his admirals and forcing the adoption, finally, of the policy of sending ships in convoy formation, not as inviting, defenseless singletons.

Designed for mass production, the new 110-foot, 85 ton subchasers were launched in record numbers, from a couple dozen different yards including three in the Delaware Valley, the Jackson & Sharp plant of American Car & Foundry in Wilmington, Vinyard Shipbuilding of Milford and Mathis Yacht Building of Camden.

But before the Navy Department could sign a contract with Mathis, Johan Trumpy the Norwegian had to become John Trumpy the naturalized American. He had been planning to become a U.S. citizen for years. The war and the government conditions for contracts speeded up his decision.

One of the first vessels ready for sea duty was Mathis' SC 65 completed January 11, 1917, three months before the U.S. declaration of war. Another nine, SC 66–74, were completed by March 28 the following year.

Mathis SC 209–213 were finished from March through November, 1918, and the third series, SC 381–385 from June to October of that year. The final five, SC 426–430, were finished between December 28, 1918, seven weeks after the Armistice, and January 15, 1919.

Only one of the 25 Mathis subchasers, SC 209, was destroyed by enemy gunfire. Disposition of the others after the war varied: SC 65–67 were transferred to France where they were renamed C 13, C 14 and C 22; SC 68 and SC 70 were transferred to the U.S. Coast Guard. The others were sold in 1921 and 1922.

SC 210–213 were sold, SC 210 as late as April, 1930.

All the third group, SC 381–385 were transferred to the French Navy and renamed C 64, C 69, C 76, C 77 and C 80.

Four of the final five Mathis subchasers were put up for sale in 1921 and 1922. SC 428 was transferred to the City of Baltimore in May 1921.

Of the 440 subchasers built for the U.S. and French Navy, only two survived until World War II, SC 421 from Clayton Ship and Boat Building and SC 437 from Rocky River Dry Dock. We entered World War II as bare of

Subchasers, 1917

coastal patrol boats and subchasers as we did the war a quarter century and 116 Mathis-Trumpy luxury yachts, houseboats, cruisers and cutters earlier.

The poetic tribute in the *Boston Herald* by historian Mark A. DeWolfe Howe could be applied to both wars—

So arm ye, who may not bleed in France
With tongs and hammers and saws:
These by your weapons—aye, these your lance
To break in the holy cause!
For they that go down to the sea in ships,
With food for the gasping, hungering lips,
With armies that cry for a squadron vast,
These, these shall bring peace at last!

1918 production of airplane hulls (above) and subchasers (below)

Chapter 7
POST WAR BOOM

Other yards and other industries had difficulties in adjusting to the post-war economy, one in which government contracts were canceled and seemingly unlimited payments from Washington dried up. But Mathis Yacht Building Company moved into peacetime with a backlog of orders for their luxury yacht houseboats, and with a crew of workmen who had benefited from the continuing experience of working with wood.

John Trumpy's standards had not been lowered during the war and his joiners and shipwrights took the same careful approach to building subchasers as they did in constructing vessels for an affluent audience that did not worry about being blown out of the water.

Trumpy had used his free moments during the company's production of naval vessels and airplane hulls to plan for the future and design a new line of yachts, 52-footers.

The first customer who signed up—making a milestone for the company, their 100th contract—was William G. Selby, formerly of Tulsa, Oklahoma, but then living in Sarasota, Florida. His Selby Oil Company had merged with Texas Oil to form Texaco. He wanted a shallow draft yacht to live on comfortably while exploring the Keys, the Ten Thousand Islands and other coastlines of his new state. The 52-foot *Bilma II* fit his requirements and she was a handsome addition on the dock of his eight-acre estate on Sarasota Bay, the present-day site of the only gardens in the world devoted almost exclusively to epiphytes, air plants.

Selby Botanical Gardens serve as the world's Bromeliad and Orchid Identification Center, a jungle paradise filled with aroids, cattleyas, gesneriads and dendrobiums. Selby's mansion no longer has a Trumpy docked on the bay, but for years they were there as stellar advertisements, the 52-foot *Bilma II* in 1919, the 70-foot *Bilma III* in 1923 and the 46-foot *Bilma IV* in 1927. The boats are gone but Selby's philanthropy survives— his foundation financed the library, football stadium, symphony hall and awarded hundreds of scholarships to college students.

Seven more 52-footers followed *Bilma II* in 1919, the *Loafalong* for John C. King of New York City, *Riette II* for George G. Shelton of Ridgefield, Connecticut, *Scarus* for John H. Eastwood of Bayshore, New York, *Zigan* for Edward S. Moore of Chicago, the *Helen Louise* for V. B. Hubbel, and a pair for the Baruch brothers, *Donaldo* for Sailing and *Riposo II* for Herman. Brother Harty ordered his third *Nahmeoka* in 1921.

In 1919 the company also contracted for 80-footers, the *Kingfisher* for E. L. King of Daytona Beach, Florida, the *Nadesah* for H. D. H. Carstairs of Philadelphia and *Osana* for Clayton G. Dixon of the same city. They were close enough to the Mathis Yards they no doubt went across the river several times to check the progress on their new boats.

Mathis Yacht publicists pushed the Florida theme and in the trade publications, such as *MoToR BoatinG* in February, 1920, they listed the three 80-footers and the first six 52-footers in full page ads under the bold headline "IN FLORIDA," encouraging the reader "On to the Sunny Southland" and advising that "The ideal Winter is that spent cruising along the picturesque inland streams of Florida in a Mathis-built houseboat, of the latest 1920 perfected type. Go anywhere—and have comfort and cruising pleasures with you wherever you go."

By the end of 1920 Mathis was taking out another series of full page ads announcing "A SIGNAL ACHIEVEMENT . . . THE NEW 61-ft. MATHIS-BUILT HOUSEBOAT . . . newest product of the Mathis yards . . . a master combination of our 80-ft. and 52-ft. houseboats of last year, with every advantage of the former retained with Lower Operating Cost as in the smaller boat . . . 16 feet in beam . . . Draws but 42 Inches of Water."

Built with enclosed steering stands, a large deckhouse and afterdeck, the "Signal Achievement" would be "able to go anywhere, in shallow, tortuous inland streams." The ad proudly pointed out the "trim yachtiness of all her lines," and the company's belief that "We have never turned out a more

seaworthy model."

The power plant consisted of a six-cylinder, 70–90 horsepower Standard Engine, capable of making eleven to twelve miles an hour. The Standard engine was installed on all Trumpys of the time and the Jersey City Standard Motor Construction Company was happy to point out that after trying and testing many engines over the years, Mathis Yacht had made the Standard its standard. In an ad in *MoToR BoatinG*, Standard had these words of praise:

"A good many years ago The Mathis Company originated their now well-known Semi-House Boat type in which they have specialized so successfully and standardized into a stock boat. Their's has been a consistent, persistent development of an idea meriting success."

Mathis built a half dozen 61-footers but soon found there was more of a market for larger houseboat yachts, even if only four feet longer, like the 65-footers *Emeska* and *Minken* for John L. Kemmerera of the New York Yacht Club and Paul A. Schoelkopf. *Ocoee*, built for W. S. Milne of Chattanooga was 70 feet and so too was the second boat for Selby, *Bilma III*.

For Dr. George D. Rosengarten, a Philadelphian who was vice-president of Powers-Weightman-Rosengarten, predecessors of Merck Pharmaceutical Corporation, Trumpy designed the 70-foot *Jane VI* in 1916 and in 1923 the 80-foot *Mariposa* and four years later, in 1927, the 98-foot *Mariposa*. With a Ph.D. in chemistry from the University of Jena, received the year Johan Trumpy completed his studies in Berlin, Rosengarten could have negotiated the contracts with Trumpy in German.

In the roaring twenties, with a Bull Market Damn-the-

Expense mentality, there was more demand than ever before for large luxury houseboat yachts as exhibited by Rosengarten, the 85-footers built for Matheson in Miami, *Sequoia* for Richard M. Cadwalader of Philadelphia and the *Zenithia* for A. J. Fay of Lowell, Massachusetts. Fay replaced that yacht with the 103-foot cruiser *Freedom* in 1927.

Other yards had post-war slowdowns and other designers retired from the front lines. The great racing yacht designer Nathaniel Herreshoff, who had lived on houseboats when Trumpy was still at New York Shipbuilding, retired and spent his winters in Miami with Commodore Munroe, building model yachts and sailing them outside Munroe's unique home on the bay, The Barnacle.

Trumpy and the Mathis team were not only working to full capacity in 1924 they had to put their main business on hold and devote considerable talents and energies to another priority government order.

John Trumpy, veteran naval constructor, was called upon by the U.S. Coast Guard to design a new class of cutter, one built for inshore patrol duty intercepting rumrunners, a new class of American entrepreneur created by the passage of the Eighteenth Amendment to the Constitution, forbidding the manufacture, sale, import or export of intoxicating beverages after January 16, 1920. The coastal waters of Florida, which Trumpy and his yachts knew so well, were natural havens for smugglers arriving on high speed motor boats bringing in the "real stuff," off-loaded from larger vessels anchored safely off shore, or coming directly from ports in Canada, Bermuda, the Bahamas, West Indies, Belize, Cuba and other supply bases in the Caribbean.

Other yards couldn't resist the inflated prices and fast cash

tendered by mobsters and their minions who suddenly saw huge profits in building revved-up boats. But not John Trumpy and Mathis Yacht. They wanted to make their money the old-fashioned way—designing and building quality products for legitimate customers.

To combat the smuggling from liquor-loaded ships moored in "Rum Rows" just beyond the three-mile limit along New York and New Jersey coasts as well as the Chesapeake and Delaware Bays, the Florida coast and cities from Boston to New Orleans, Congress in April, 1924, appropriated nearly $14 million for the restoration and adaptation of Navy destroyers and minesweepers and the new construction of cruisers, cutters and smaller boats.

Secretary of The Treasury Andrew Mellon had requested $28,500,000 for his eight-year-old Coast Guard, but had to settle for less than half as the orders were issued for rapid expansion of the anti-smuggling fleet, and the recruitment and training of some 4300 officers and men. While twenty of the Navy's oldest destroyers were being reconditioned in the Philadelphia Navy Yard, Coast Guard officers across the river were working with Trumpy to design a new kind of cutter.

Similar in outline and hull line to the subchasers Mathis Yacht built during the war, the cutters were 75-footers with gasoline engines capable of 13.5 knots (15.7 knots during the 1924 trial runs). Armed with a mounted one pounder and a .30 caliber machine gun, the sturdily built wooden vessels carried a crew of eight commanded by a warrant officer or chief petty officer.

The new Coast Guard was also supplied with a mini-fleet of 30- and 36-foot picket boats, 103 of them, but they were restricted to daytime use and carried only small arms.

Two hundred and three of the 75-footers were ordered, and were quickly dubbed "six-bitters" by the workmen in the Mathis Yards, where thirty of that number, including the first of the class, were built—CG 100–CG 114 in 1924 and CG 278–292 the following year.

The "six-bitters" were reliable performers. In the spring of 1925 a specially assembled task force of ten cutters with a converted minesweeper in the lead managed to disperse the fleet of smuggling ships lurking on Rum Row off the coasts of New York and New Jersey.

All the "six-bitters" had radios on board and one of them was specially equipped to intercept the radio traffic of the smugglers they were surveilling. On board was a cryptanalyst to break the codes the Rum Runners were using. Four of the 75-footers had high-frequency radios installed with experimental radio direction scanners to intercept that traffic, and to pinpoint the locations of the liquor-laden boats as well as their shore stations and destinations.

The Nineteenth Amendment ending prohibition in 1933 changed all that, however, and the "six-bitters" were gradually transferred to the Navy. By the time of Pearl Harbor all but 36 of the 203 built were officially in the Navy, given new designations of YP.

After the 15th "six-bitter" slid down the ways, Trumpy signed a contract for a 98-foot cruiser houseboat for Mrs. Sticker Coles of Bryn Mawr, Pennsylvania; and when the 30th, the last, was completed, the company was practically swamped with large yacht orders.

Starting with Coles' *Alscotia*, Mathis Yachts built 31 yacht houseboats over 90 feet from 1925 through 1931. Five were between 80 and 85 feet; one, the *Burlington*, was for the New Jersey Fish and Game Commission and was 70 feet overall. Selby's 46-foot *Bilma IV* was the midget of the golden era which didn't end until the impact of the Great Depression finally hit the luxury yacht market.

One of the better-known customers of the time was Walter P. Chrysler, the motor mogul who had started as a railroad machinist's apprentice and rose to the summit as one of the country's last rugged, willing to risk it all, industrialists. He used his 75-foot Trumpy cruiser, *Frolic*, in the waters off his Long Island estate at Great Neck. After his death in 1940 the property was bought for a bargain price to become the U.S. Merchant Marine Academy at Kings Point.

Another industrialist who made a fortune in the automobile industry was DeWitt Page of Connecticut, top executive of General Motors and head of a company that produced more than half the ball bearings in the world. An avid sportsman who raised and raced thoroughbreds, he also was an enthusiastic yachtsman, a member of the New York Yacht Club. His 110-foot Trumpy, *Maemere*, built in 1929, bore the same name as his stables.

George Codrington was another General Motors executive who had to have a Trumpy, but he had infinitely more experience in the marine world than the other automobile executives, or most of the other movers and shakers who were ordering Trumpys. Codrington started as an engineer with the Jacksonville Ferry Company and after going to sea for a spell and working as a marine engineer and yard superintendent, he worked his way up to general manager and president of General

Motors Diesel Engine Division. He was a director of the Shipbuilders Council of America, member of the Society of American Naval Architects and American Society of Naval Engineers, member of the Annapolis, Larchmont and New York Yacht Clubs. When someone with those credentials had a Trumpy—it was an 80-foot yacht houseboat christened *All Alone*—it served as a significant role model.

Diesels were replacing gasoline engines as the preferred means of marine propulsion. The first in the world had been the 1913 *Pioneer* built by Camper and Nicholsons on the south coast of England for American millionaire Paris Singer. His 163' x 24'6" yacht had 250 horsepower Atlas Polar Diesels.

After the war Singer concentrated his winter yachting and socializing energies on Palm Beach, that 14-mile long and half-mile wide sandbar which first Flagler made attractive to the winter-weary wealthy and then, in the 1920s, Addison Mizner, that Alladin of architects who built magnificent mansions for the super rich, creating the Everglades Club and Worth Avenue out of a swampy alligator farm.

The spirit and substance of Palm Beach were perfectly captured a few years later by *Sports Illustrated*: "At the peak of its season, Palm Beach can boast the greatest concentration of inch-square diamonds, block-long yachts, beautifully dressed women and heavily bankrolled men."

The Palm Beach Marina was the rallying point for the block-long yachts from New York and Philadelphia, Maryland and Massachusetts. Many of them were too large to dock at the marina and were anchored out in the wide expanse of water off Flagler's mansion, Whitehall.

The boats rallied in Palm Beach and they rallied on the pages of *MoToR BoatinG*. In the July, 1926, issue of the New York magazine there was a center spread emblazoned "WHY DO THEY COME AGAIN?" and asking "Why do men who know—men of national prominence, experienced judges of values—who once learn by experience what a MATHIS-BUILT HOUSEBOAT offers in comfort, yachtiness, seaworthiness and ability to go anywhere, come back to the Mathis yards to have their new boats built?"

The two boats pictured in the ad, each framed with a scroll that could serve as precursor of the famous golden Trumpy "T," were the 92-foot sister ships, *Thalia*, built for Thomas M. Howell of Chicago, and *Troubadour*, ordered by Webb Jay of Miami. The home bases of the two owners demonstrated that "all our boats are equally at home in Southern and Northern waters, on inland streams and along the coast."

The eye-catching centerfold gave "A partial list of men who have reordered recently:

"William M. Elkins, Philadelphia, Pennsylvania, who had the 87-foot *Pilgrim* in 1922, is taking delivery of the new-type 92-foot *Pilgrim II* in the summer. Judge Robert W. Bingham of Louisville, Kentucky, owner of the 77-foot Mathis *Dorinda*, will soon have ready the 93-foot *Eala*.

"F. D. Owsley of Greenwood, Virgina, whose 65-foot *Mariska* was built by Mathis in 1924 will take delivery in the fall of a 93-foot *Mariska*.

"A. J. Fay of Lowell, Massachusetts for whom Trumpy designed the 85-foot *Zenithia* in 1924 will take delivery of the 103-foot *Freedom* next year.

"H. B. Baruch of New York, New York, is replacing his 1919 *Riposo II* of 52 feet with the recently completed 92-foot

Riposo III.

"Dr. George Rosengarten whose 70-foot *Jane VI* Mathis built in 1916, replaced it with the 80-foot *Mariposa.*

"Richard M. Cadwalader, Jr. of Philadelphia, Pennsylvania had the Trumpy designed *Sequoia* built in 1924 and the 104-foot *Sequoia II* the following year."

Sequoia II is undoubtedly the best-known yacht of the hundreds Trumpy designed and built over a career spanning six decades. But Webb Jay's *Troubadour*, which he and the company dubbed the "Wonder Boat," was also featured in large advertisements. The April, 1926, issue of *Yachting* carried this bold type news: "Mr. Webb Jay takes little for granted; he wanted to see what the Mathis-designed and built houseboat *Troubadour* would do outside, with comfort to his guests. His party of six, and the whole crew, were astounded to realize that despite December seas it had made the whole distance from Morehead City down to Fernandina in 34 hours. For there had been no sacrifice of comfort.

"Just as surprising to the party of six in the guest quarters and the crew was the 24-hour record between St. Augustine and Miami—an outside run, because dredging blocked the inside route.

"If you want more detailed information regarding this new "wonder-boat" type of houseboat, rivaling yachts in speed and seaworthiness, yet possessing a degree of comfort to which no yacht of less than 115-foot length can aspire, we shall be glad to furnish it."

The *Sequoia II* was featured in *Yachting* the previous month with illustrations of the spacious salon (with a piano of course, a de rigeur furnishing on the larger yachts although some owners preferred fireplaces) and the ship in water flanking the text, "THE FLORIDA SEASON has been a MATHIS Triumph."

That boast was reinforced by this declaration: "Among all the boats in Florida waters this season, none have received so much interest and attention as the Mathis-built fleet of notable new houseboats. Broad beams, making for living comfort, have been concealed by yachty lines and the new type Mathis yacht stern. History has repeated itself. Once more Mathis has struck a new high keynote in general seaworthiness, luxurious comfort, yachty lines and efficient utility."

"Yachtiness" and "yachty lines" were as important to the buyer as they were to John Trumpy at the drawing board. "Comfort" was another buzz word for Trumpy and those who intended to live on the boats for extended periods of time, cruising or in harbor. Trumpy built in that comfort by designing higher head room, broad beams, wider passageways, more efficient galleys and engine rooms. Luxury was provided by the use of fine woods, long leaf yellow pine, Philippine mahogany and Burmese teak with high quality hand-brushed varnishes and paints. Durability was built into the woods and practicality in such conveniences as the patented Mathis metal shutters with ports which could be moved over windows from within.

The year *Sequoia II* was launched, 1926, the ad in *Yachting* emphasized that "Its large deckhouse is finished in teak inside and out. Its interior decoration is the last work in beauty and luxury."

Singled out for praise were both *Sequoia II* and Mrs. Coles' *Alscotia*, which had been "the center of interest in Florida this season," but then that was nothing new for the 98-

foot *Alscotia* for she had been "the center of interest when it first appeared at the New London Boat Races and everywhere since."

Sequoia II merited this description: "Never before has so much luxurious comfort been combined in a 104-ft. boat, with such yachtiness of line, such seaworthiness and such speed—15 miles an hour. The *Sequoia II* is of slender appearance despite its 19-ft. beam, its draft of 4 ft. 3 inches and its new-type Mathis yacht-stern, which give it speed and sea-going qualities seldom found in houseboats."

Sequoia II was purchased by the Department of Commerce in 1931 and she was used in the Mississippi River for a time as an inspection and decoy ship to trap rumrunners. In 1933 the Navy commissioned the boat an official presidential yacht. She served nine chief executives.

There have been presidential yachts since the 1880s when Rutherford Hayes used to entertain officials and friends aboard the 174-foot *USS Despatch*. In 1906, the *USS Mayflower* was made into an official presidential yacht. The 318-foot ship, designed and built in Scotland, had been purchased by the U.S. Navy during the Spanish-American War. She served admirably as the flagship of the U.S. fleet off Puerto Rico when rebels were conveniently creating the Panama Canal Zone. She also served as the secret site where President Roosevelt brought together the warring parties in the Russo-Japanese War and arranged a peace. Teddy must have had a "bully" time on board and he was rewarded for his efforts with the Nobel Peace Prize.

The *Mayflower* was decommissioned in 1928 as an economy move, but was put back in service as a patrol vessel during World War II, and then served as a Palestine refugee ship and finally as a training and patrol ship for the Israeli Navy.

The yacht of the presidents, known simply as *Sequoia*, was capable of carrying 38 passengers for cruising inland waters, and her five staterooms could accommodate eight. The mahogany-paneled dining salon seated 22.

It was just spacious enough for President Roosevelt who had an elevator installed for his moving between decks, and he greatly enjoyed entertaining political cronies, Supreme Court Justices, visiting dignitaries such as Winston Churchill who cruised the Chesapeake. FDR liked taking the *Sequoia* to New London for the annual Harvard-Yale crew competitions, attracting great attention. But then Mathis ads for years advertised the fact that their yachts "have been the social centers of the Harvard-Yale Regatta and along Northern coasts." *The Rudder* ad in October, 1930, reported that "the latest of our Diesel-powered cruiser-houseboats were the 'observed of all observers' while the *Enterprise* and *Shamrock V* competed" for the America's Cup.

FDR was an avid yachtsman and when he visited Miami as President-elect in 1933, he was aboard Vincent Astor's 264-foot *Nourmahal*. FDR left the yacht and was heading for a rally when an assassin fired at him but missed and killed Chicago's Mayor Cermak. But before he disembarked, he had the wit to inform his host that if the wealthy of the land could afford such luxurious yachts he probably should tax them more.

Far more than most presidents before or since, Roosevelt was a prisoner of the White House, unable to walk like Truman, jog like Bush, ride horses like Reagan or escape to the links in the manner of Eisenhower and Ford. The *Sequoia* was his primary getaway from the oppressive heat of Washington and he loved to cruise slowly along the Potomac. He had to walk or be carried aboard as the gangplank was too narrow for his wheelchair and he had a special elevator installed so he could move between decks.

FDR's "constant companion," Margaret "Daisy" Stuckley, was a frequent guest and she wrote in her diary that "The *Sequoia* is a delightful little boat . . . just a good size for a peaceful weekend."

President Nixon also liked cruising on the *Sequoia* but daughter Julie wrote that she didn't think anyone else in the family really enjoyed the rather public cruises, very public during the 1974 Watergate crisis when press and photographers jammed on board pursuit boats and lined the bridges in what she described as a "death watch."

Nixon entertained Soviet premier Leonid Brezhnev on board and planned with Secretary Kissinger the invasion of Cambodia, but for Julie the *Sequoia*, sailing about with no particular destination, was no better than a bottle bobbing along with all the deliberation and speed of a snail.

President Johnson, who had the shower stall floor lowered to accommodate his 6'3" frame, invited Queen Elizabeth and the Royals aboard in 1968 and drafted the Great Society program while cruising Washington waters.

The *Sequoia* was semi-retired during World War II, replaced by the larger and longer — 244 feet — *Williamsburg*, built as the private yacht *Aras* for Hugh Chisholm in 1930 and purchased by the Navy at the beginning of the war, despite the fact that it was not really suitable for rough seas, even after a couple hundred tons of iron were added to the bilges as ballast.

But President Truman, not the best of sailors, loved the boat, taking her north to New England and, more frequently, south to warmer waters, to Bermuda, Woodrow Wilson's favorite escape destination, or to Key West where a simple Little White House was established.

Navy Veteran Kennedy liked the luxury of yachting and frequently hosted receptions and dinners on board. He celebrated his last birthday on board, and was as fond of cruising as Navy veteran Nixon. But Navy veteran Ford and Annapolis graduate Carter had little interest and seldom took her out.

Carter, ever mindful of public image, decided it was too expensive to maintain. In 1977 he ordered it sold at public auction. It brought $286,000, less than a fifth of what it cost for the Presidential Yacht Trust, a private non-profit foundation in Washington, D. C., to buy it back a few years later after it had sunk into a pitiful state of disrepair.

$3.5 million was spent for *Sequoia's* restoration but a nationwide fundraising tour of the yacht failed to meet expenses and a Washington bank cried default on a sizable loan. The Trust's plans to make a gift of the boat to the President had to be canceled.

The distinctive stern that Mathis promotional material was so proud to point out was a rather brilliant adjustment by Trumpy to a problem caused by a collision of one of his boats with the Staten Island Ferry. Ferry officials and other critics blamed the accident on the fact that the yacht houseboat had only one rudder and therefore could not be controlled in open water. The fact that the ferry had only one rudder was pointed out but it was decided that the criticism could best be handled by installing two rudders on the new large yachts coming off the drawing boards. In order to accommodate a double rudder arrangement and change the chine, an elliptical stern was designed. It was quickly dubbed fantail.

For the next several years, the larger yachts were graced by fantails: the 92-foot *Trail* for William Wallace, Jr. of New York City, A. G. Fay's *Freedom*, the 104-foot *Truant* and 120-foot *Truant* built for Truman Newberry in 1927 and 1930, the 95-foot *Nicoya* ordered by Fred B. Lovejoy of Montclair, New Jersey, in 1927, with *Innisfail* and *Elsie Fenimore*, 85 feet and 87 feet, built for Chicago meatpacker millionaire Joseph M. Cudahy and E. R. F. Johnson of Camden in 1934 and 1935.

1926 was a banner year for Mathis Yacht with the launching of the fantails and the signing of new contracts for more long, lean yachty houseboats. Not all the news was good, however.

On September 17 and 18, 1926, the over-inflated South Florida bubbles of boom began to burst as the great winds of a hurricane roared on shore. Close to 150 boats that were at anchor in Miami's harbor and along the river were swept out of the water by 138 mph winds and cast aground.

James Deering's *Nepenthe* was blasted off her moorings and out of her shed into the Vizcaya gardens which were being ripped apart by the fury of the blast. Brother Charles Deering's boat was blown all the way from Cutler Ridge into a wall by the Vizcaya pool. During the clean-up process the *Nepenthe* was salvaged, her furnishings removed and burned. She was converted to a freighter working the Keys and islands.

The death of nearly 250 people, the destruction of close to 5000 homes and such landmarks as the Royal Palm Hotel sent shockwaves across the country, obliterating the paradise image of Miami and other parts of South Florida as well.

The hurricanes of 1928 and 1929 did not ameliorate the situation, and for a time there was a distinct lack of enthusiasm about cruising South Florida waters, in a Mathis yacht houseboat or any other vessel.

But there were other waters for Mathis yachts to cruise and in an August, 1930, issue of *The Rudder*, an enthusiastic houseboater, Edna F. Lane, described her

Nicoya's fantail stern (1927)

cruise from New York City to the Thousand Islands, "Houseboating Instead of Housekeeping:

"Before deciding to give up our summer home on land and transfer it to the water it was necessary to find a boat that could adequately take the place of a house in the country. Spaciousness, modern equipment, comfort, room for guests, room for servants, these and many other things had to be found. We did discover all this and more in our houseboat *Berto*, built by the Mathis Yacht Building Corporation.

"*Berto* is 70 feet 4 inches long, with a beam of 16 feet 6 inches. She has two 65 hp. Lathrop engines to make a speed of 10 knots—a comfortable cruising speed. The owner's quarters consist of a double stateroom the full width of the ship, containing a double bed and day bed, a full length clothes locker, dresser, and dressing table, a bathroom with a tub and shower, hot and cold running fresh and salt water, and pressure toilet. There is a guest cabin just like this and a second guest cabin with upper and lower berths.

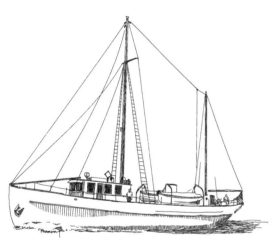

Elsie Fenimore, 1934

"Below is the dining saloon the full width of the boat, containing a divan, lockers, dressers and a table which can seat twelve people. This connects with the galley and engine room and crew's quarters.

"The deckhouse is a veritable living room with roomy, comfortable furniture, including a writing desk, radio and Victrola. There is vision on four sides giving delight at all times. The radio and speaker are built into the wall of this living room. A radio on board is better than on shore, due to the lack of interference from surrounding buildings and machinery. We believe a good radio to be one of the most important parts of the equipment of any cruiser, because it furnishes the news of the day and always brings a diversion in the form of music. Forward of the deck house is the pilot house, from which the boat is controlled and which

also contains couches and day beds to accommodate additional guests.

"The crew numbers five and includes the captain, who takes charge of the boat; the engineer who, under the captain, is in charge of all engines and machinery on board; the steward, in charge of all food supplies and who also cooks the meals; the waiter, who is responsible for the upkeep of the inside of the boat, and waits on the table; and the sailor, who cares for the decks and the outside of the boat.

"You can see the advantages of a houseboat. Principally, you are not tied down to any one particular spot, and with this equipment and staff you have every comfort to be found in your own home plus the freedom of the seas. You can move your marine home from place to place at your will; you have a variety of scenery instead of being confined to one place; if you find a place that particularly appeals to you, you can spend one or more summers at that place, and then move on to some other place without having to sell your house at a sacrifice and begin all over again. Waterfront property, to which a boat would correspond, is expensive and the amount of waterfront available is limited, but on a boat you have unlimited waterfront and at the same time, by belonging to a yacht club or other organization which has docking space, you have all the advantages of being on shore. In addition to that you have a degree of privacy on a boat, which you never have in a house. If your nautical neighbors annoy you, you move.

"The entertainment of guests on a boat is much simpler than in a house, due to the fact that boating has not as yet become as common as it undoubtedly will, and the very novelty of being entertained on a boat or yacht is in itself sufficient to amuse your guests without any effort on your part.

"As for a comparison of expenses the cost of running a boat is undoubtedly higher than running a house, especially when you take into consideration that, for the size of boat you get, a similar sized house would be much less expensive, except for the fact that a house is a constant expense, whether you use it or not, while a boat, if you choose not to use it, can either be of nominal expense by reason of being laid up, or else, if it is a desirable boat, it can be turned into a profit by being chartered. As far as entertainment is concerned, that is entirely a matter up to the individual owner and applies equally to a house and to a boat. The cost of food is exactly the same in one place as the other. The cost of servants as such is approximately the same, with the exception of the higher priced executives, such as the captain and the engineer."

*103' **Freedom**, contract number 181, built in 1926 for A. J. Fay who had the **Zenithia** (photo next page) built two years previously.*

*The Nov. 1926, **Yachting** editorial coverage of her states. "The designers have given her an elliptical yacht stern which has added a great deal to her appearance, and to her ability in a following sea, and which carries out the yacht appearance of the of the rest of the hull. The only things that bespeak the houseboat are the square windows amidships, and these add so much to the comfort below that they should never be omitted or changed.*

65' *Minken*, (above left) # 130, 1923, for Paul A. Schoelkopf. 70' *Ebenezer*, #131, 1923, for J. Aaron (above right) sunk in the C&D Canal during the winter of '95-'96. 70'4" *Ocoee*, #132, 1923, for W. S.Milne. 85' *Zenithia*, #141, 1924, for Albert J. Fay.

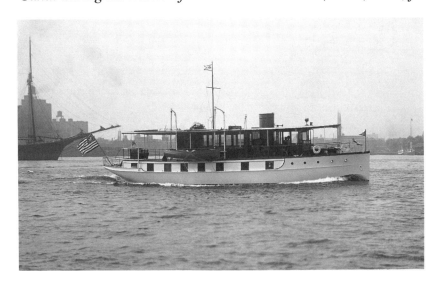

Chapter 8
BOOM TO BUST AND BEYOND

All the news from Florida wasn't bad. Progress was proceeding apace on the dredging and widening of the East Coast Canal, the 400-mile route from Jacksonville to the Keys, a four million dollar project to create the Intracoastal Waterway. By January, 1930, the job was finished and *The Rudder* could jubilantly proclaim in its issue the following month that "The age-old bugaboo of the Florida-bound yachtsman—the many troublesome toll chains across the Florida East Coast Canal—has at last been tossed overboard. The Federal Government has just ordered the last of the obstacles removed."

Mathis Yacht Building greeted the news with great enthusiasm. Their houseboats could now be assured a straight-shot channel at least 500 feet wide and a draft of eight feet at mean low water. Naturally, they had never really given up on the Sunshine State no matter how destructive the big winds. In the April, 1927, issue of *Yachting* their ad asked "Did you see them in Florida?" then pointed out that "To the Florida fleet during the past season was added the new class of 93-foot Houseboats Mathis Designed and Mathis Built distinguished by their new type of full deck stern."

Notable among these latest "Thoroughbreds of the Seas"

widely commented on for their comfort and general seaworthiness, are the **Trail**, Mr. Wm. W. Wallace, Jr., New York, New York, **Eala**, Judge R. W. Bingham, Louisville, Ky., **Summergirl**, Mr. R. G. Roberts of Philadelphia, Pa."

Orders flowed to Mathis offices at Front and Erie Streets. There was another 93-footer, **Mariska**, built for F. D. Owsley of Greenwood, Virginia and a 95-foot fantail houseboat, **Nicoya**, for Fred B. Lovejoy.

In 1930 Lovejoy ordered an even larger yacht, the 103-foot **Lanakila**, but the record length for that year went to the 120-foot **Truant** for Truman Newberry of Detroit, MI.

Newberry was another industrialist who made millions in the automobile industry—he was largely responsible for the formation of Packard Motor Car Company—and he served as Teddy Roosevelt's Secretary of the Navy and, after World War I, as Republican Senator from Michigan. The Newberrys had been prominent in midwestern shipping since early in the last century: Oliver Newberry was known as the Admiral of the Great Lakes and his steamship company was the first to establish regular service between Detroit and Chicago, which he opened to big ships by dredging the Chicago River.

Truman Newberry wanted a large, luxurious yacht, but his 1927 boat of 104 feet with a beam of 19 feet and draft of 3'9" and with Winton diesels, wasn't grand enough, so in 1930 he ordered a second *Truant*.

It was 121'3" with a 21' beam, 4'4" draft and the same set of 300 horsepower Wintons delivering a cruising speed over 13 knots. Displacement was 131.3 tons, 41 more than the first *Truant*.

W. H. Reynolds of New York, NY, and Walter H. Lippincott of Philadelphia, PA, also ordered super-size yacht houseboats, the 126-foot *Daydream* and 125-foot *Waleda II*.

Two of Mathis' wealthiest boosters, Arthur Curtiss James and George D. Rosengarten, upgraded their yachts with another *Lanai* and another *Mariposa*, the first of 85 feet, the second 98.

Two other 98-footers, *Luneta* and *Saunterer*, were delivered to Colonel S. L. H. Slocum of Washington, D.C., who replaced his smaller 1921 boat of the same name, and Jeremiah E. Milbank of Greenwich, CT. An active yachtsman and member of the New York Yacht Club, Milbank chose the name carefully, presumably to contrast with his other yacht, the 75-foot *JEM*, built in 1930 by Consolidated Shipbuilding Corporation of Morris Heights, NY, specialists in construction of those fast commuters that were so popular in New York in the years between the wars. Powered by Consolidated's Speedway in-line gasoline engines which gave a speed over 30 mph, that boat in a hurry was not intended to provide the kind of leisurely, carefree pace of a yacht sauntering along, a Trumpy houseboat yacht.

For General William W. Atterbury of Philadelphia, PA, Mathis built the 110-footer, *Arminia*, with a 21-foot beam, draft of eight feet and displacement of 153 tons. She was steel and not wood. The yard must have had the help of the John H. Mathis Company which was well-equipped with material and workmen skilled in steel construction. Atterbury was president of the Pennsylvania Railroad and had been in charge of U.S. military railways in France during World War I. His experience with iron rails and steel locomotives may have motivated him to think only of a steel boat. The only other such boat built by Mathis was the 148-foot *Alamo* designed by Tams, Inc., for William F. Ladd of New York, NY.

They were the largest yacht houseboats ever built by Mathis-Trumpy but they were dwarfed by the leviathans coming out of Pusey and James yards in nearby Wilmington the same year as *Daydream* and *Waleda II*. Their *Alder* built for Mrs. Boyce Thompson of the New York Yacht Club was 294 feet and their *Cambriona*, *Nakhoda* and *Rene* the following year, sister ships built off the same mold, were 236 feet and had twin screws.

A 106-foot houseboat, the *Mono*, was ordered at Mathis by George K. Morrow of Long Island, a director of Remington-Rand and McLellan Stores; and one of 108 feet, *Minoco*, for the Mills Novelty Company of Chicago. Mills manufactured slot machines and its president, Herbert S. Mills, was a member of the Chicago Sportsmen's Club, collection agency for graft and payoffs for operation of those "slots."

A less controversial customer was Francis V. duPont, who ordered the 85-foot *Tech, Jr.* in 1930. He was a member of the greatest boat-owning family in the country. His father had *Tech I, Tech II* and *Tech III*, and his uncles had mini fleets. Largest were Alfred's 125-foot *Nenemoosha* and 101-foot *Gadfly*. Up to 1936 the only duPont with a Trumpy other than Francis was A. Felix duPont who had the *Bolo* for a time, the 90-foot houseboat originally built as **Enada III** for George Thomas.

1931 was as bad a year as 1930 had been good. Three boats were ordered compared to eight. One was that giant steel houseboat **Alamo**; another was **Virago**, a 98-footer for Thomas N. McCarter of Rumsen, New Jersey and the third was the 111-foot **Captiva** for Mrs. Helen Hay Whitney of Manhasset.

That threesome was not alone in taking possession of monster yachts at the worst time in history for such manifestations of conspicuous consumption. That year Eldridge R. Johnson from Camden, member of the New York Yacht Club, took the wheel of his 278'11" **Caroline** built by Bath Iron Works; and Emily Roebling Cadwalader took delivery of her German-built 408-foot **Savarona III** which weighed in at 4,656 tons and required a crew of 83. Her 20-foot draft prevented her from entering small harbors and mooring at most private docks. The greatest nonroyal yacht ever built, she was a four million dollar white elephant and eventually, in the mid-1930s, wound up as a training ship for the Turkish Navy.

1931 was a crisis year for the entire country and for the private boat-building industry, it was the beginning of a disaster that continued into the Great Depression. Six years of drought and hard times followed twelve of plenty and prosperity.

The contrast can be seen in the annual meetings of the company and the compensation paid the directors and key personnel. At a monthly meeting of the directors on January 27, 1921, the salaries were set for president Robinson and vice president Trumpy at $12,000. W. F. Eddleman received half as much, but a year later those salaries were adjusted to $5400, $8400 and $3000.

John Mathis had not been on the payroll or been a director since before the beginning of World War I, but he remained a major shareholder in the company.

At the time of the increase of the capital stock from $50,000 to $150,000 in 1918 he held 153 of the outstanding shares. President Robinson, by that time president of the Mathis Company as well as Mathis Yacht Building, had 352 and L. M. Robinson, 90. Yard foreman Alfred May had 87 and secretary-treasurer E. F. Eddleman, 78. Trumpy had 240. Within four years, Trumpy was the largest single stockholder with 403 shares; W. W. Robinson had 397 and Eddleman, 163. That year a 6% cash dividend was declared on all shares outstanding.

Robinson represented the parent Mathis company when re-negotiating the three-year lease for ground rights of the building the offspring had purchased—175 feet on Erie Street and 400 feet on Front plus the sole use of a wharf, a track for hauling yachts out for repair, and the office building. Metered water bills and a portion of the overall insurance were extra expenses and the total cost was $3000, payable in monthly installments.

By 1925, Trumpy was receiving $8400 a year, Robinson $5400 and Eddleman $3000; and foreman Alfred May had his compensation increased from $3600 to $4200 per annum. A $25 per share dividend was declared.

At a July meeting that year the board, reacting to the solid success of sales and new contracts, voted an immediate 100% cash dividend. That generous bonus was supported by the semi-annual audit made the end of June, 1925 which showed a surplus of $223,721.28.

In 1928 a cash dividend of $37.50 per share was declared and the salaries were set at $8400 for both Robinson and Trumpy and $3000 for Eddleman. Those salaries were readjusted two years later when Trumpy received $12,000, Robinson $10,000, Eddleman $3500 and foreman George May $6000. A cash dividend of $30 per share was declared, $15 to be paid immediately and $15 sometime between April 1 and May 1 "as finances permit."

The same salaries were paid the following year but the cash dividend was reduced to $12.50. In the 1932 annual meeting, after a year in which only one new boat contract was drawn up, Trumpy proposed and the board passed a 30% reduction in salaries. Payments were reduced to $7000 for president

87' Elsie Fenimore, #219, built in 1934 for E. R. F. Johnson

Robinson, $8400 for vice president Trumpy and $2450 for Eddleman, but four days later the board voted an adjustment so that Eddleman's compensation was increased to $3000 and Robinson's to $8400, the same amount as Trumpy's. In 1933 those figures were reduced 15% to $2550 and $7140 but that year a 6% dividend was declared, $3 per share. Foreman May was put on a weekly basis, $60 per week or $3120 a year.

There were three contracts signed that year, one for the 48-foot *Seagoin'* for William K. Barclay, a 59-foot schooner, *Minel*, for R. K. Walling and a 30-foot cutter, *Lodsen*, for F. M. Doan.

The following year only one buyer signed up and that was for the first grand scale yacht the yard had built in three years. She was the 87-foot *Elsie Fenimore* ordered by E. R. F. Johnson of Camden. Salaries were again reduced, to $2500 each for Robinson and Trumpy, $1500 for Eddleman and $1800 a year for May. Robinson, ever the businessman with an eye on his pocket, moved that those salaries be changed "any time during the year as business warrants."

The annual rent payment to the John H. Mathis Company was approved at $3600 and a cash dividend of $5 was approved. At the end of the year, an additional $10 per share dividend was declared.

In 1935 that amount was increased to $25 while the salaries of the three officers remained the same. Another $25 was declared the following year but Trumpy's salary was increased to $5000 and Eddleman's to $2000.

The years 1935–1938 witnessed considerable improvement over the lowest-of-the-low market of 1932–1934. Twenty boats were built, including a few echoes from the good old days. R. L. Heverling ordered the 72-foot *Edrus*; William J. McCahan, III, the 80-foot *Florence V*; Chicago meatpacker Joseph Cudahy the 85-foot *Innisfail*; T. Munroe Dobbins of Atlantic City and Philadelphia, the 90-foot *Consort IV*; and Eugene E. duPont the 85-foot *Morning Star*, replacing his 50-foot non-Mathis built *High Tide*. Francis duPont added a 36'6" Trumpy, *Suitsus*, to his boat shed.

During that time span Mathis Yacht also turned out a quartet of 30-foot cutters and one of 36-feet, plus a half dozen 61-foot and 61'6" houseboats, and a 55-footer, designed by Frederick C. Geiger, the *Nameni*, for L. Rodman Paige. Geiger later became the staff naval architect when Trumpy moved to Annapolis.

The yard cost for constructing the four 61-foot houseboats and the two that were 61'6" ranged from $27,817 to $33,884, including labor costs between $11,871 and $15,028.

Six years earlier, when the 111-foot *Captiva* was built for Helen Hay Whitney, the total cost had been $127,990 including a $10,000 commission and a pair of launches, a 19'6" boat for the owner with sedan top and one of 18 feet for crew. Labor's total cost had been $41,576. Cudahy's *Innisfail* in 1935 cost $56,819 to produce, of which $23,244 was labor.

The yard wasn't really generating much money with such a limited number of contracts and such boats as small as the 46-footer, *Egret*, for the coal company magnate Porter Schutt and the 47'4" *Far Cry* for Colonel Edwin M. Chance, president of a large construction and engineering company in Philadelphia and member of both the New York Yacht and Mantoloking Yacht Clubs.

A far cry indeed from the Roaring Twenties when the trio of 98-footers *Luneta, Mariposa* and *Saunterer* with their half dozen launches meant close to $300,000 was added to the Mathis Yacht cash flow.

Cudahy's 90-foot *Innisfail* was built in 1939 but she would be the last over 80 feet for 25 years. A 69-foot yacht houseboat was built for A. M. Stoner, the 71-foot *Martha* for William M. Davey and 76-foot *Drifter* for Frank O. Sherrill. But more typical of the era, one in which down-sizing was the trend of the time, was the order of Francis duPont for a new *Tech, Jr.* to replace the 85-foot boat of that name he had bought eight years earlier. His new boat was only 45 feet.

In the 1930 register of the New York Yacht Club there had been 81 yachts of 200 tons or more. But by 1939 with war clouds darkening the skies and dampening desires and opportunities for pleasure yachting of any kind, there were half as many.

1939 was a pivotal year for Trumpy and his Mathis Yacht Building Company. The 30-year-old firm became in fact his company. John Mathis died that year; William Robinson was removed as president and died the following year. Trumpy was elected president and his 32-year-old son, John Trumpy, Jr., was elected vice-president. The younger Trumpy, a graduate of the Penn Charter School and the Drexel Institute of Technology across the river in Philadelphia, had been working in the company since 1928, learning all aspects of the boat-building business just as his father, grandfather and great-grandfather had done. His salary for the first half of 1930 was set at $1200 and raised $500 for the last six months. His father's six-month salary payments were $2500 and $3750. Eddleman, who continued as secretary-treasurer, received $900.

John Trumpy had 604 of the 1755 outstanding shares in the company. John Jr. had 25 and Eddleman, 105. The Robinsons, four of them, had 1021 shares but after the death of patriarch William, they remained pretty much in the background and posed no objections to the negotiations the company was carrying on with the Navy about possible contracts, or the increases in the payments to the three key figures. The senior Trumpy had his annual salary boosted to $18,000, John Jr. to $12,000 and Eddleman to $7,200. Those salaries remained the same through 1945, a year in which bonuses of $4000 were paid to John Trumpy Sr. and Jr., and half as much to Donald Trumpy and Eddleman. But by that time the country had gone through the greatest war in history, the company had been reorganized and the Trumpys had control of 1124 of the outstanding 2000 shares. The Robinsons' 771 shares were purchased by Trumpy for the company at $60 per share in 1946.

110' Maemere, #199, built in 1929 for DeWitt Page. Forward end of main deckhouse (above) and main stateroom (below).

Chapter 9
SUBCHASER REDUX

The initial months of U.S. involvement in World War II were a repeat of the experience a quarter century earlier. German U-boats raided sitting duck tankers and freighters like a free Friday in a shooting gallery. In the seven months after Pearl Harbor German submarines torpedoed nearly 400 ships along the east coast, in the Gulf of Mexico and Caribbean.

German commanders, sinking at will whatever appeared in their sights, called the Eastern shoreline their "happy hunting ground." Critics condemned the inadequate U.S. Navy response, as the "worst-ever defeat at sea," and accused Navy top brass of failing abysmally to respond to the ample warnings from the British about the impending German attacks on shipping. British cryptanalysts had broken the codes and were reading the traffic when Hitler ordered the German High Command on December 12, 1941 to launch all-out submarine warfare in American coastal waters.

For the first time since Columbus' historic voyages there was a break in contact between Old World and New, as the Navy tried to make do with its pitiful arsenal. They were forced to defend some 1500 miles of coastline with only twenty ships including a quartet of 110-foot wooden hull subchasers from

World War I and a like number of 170- to 245-foot private yachts converted in 1941, plus half a dozen 125-foot Coast Guard patrol cutters. None of them had speeds capable of catching German U-boats on the surface and none was inadequately armed.

However, subchasers, even if outgunned by the Germans,

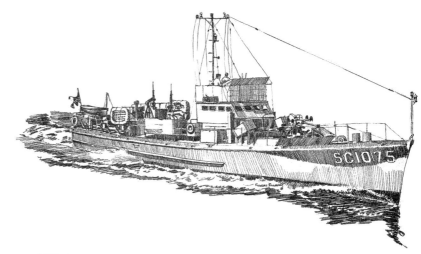

USN 110' Subchaser, 1942; Sparkman & Stephens Design

could ram a conning tower and periscope and clear the decks by spraying with .50-caliber machine gun fire.

President Roosevelt, a real Navy man—Assistant Secretary of Navy in World War I—was a lover of small boats especially his Trumpy-built presidential yacht, *Sequoia*. He pushed the Navy and prodded Admiral Stark, who staunchly believed that little boats, no matter how stout the hearts of their crews, were no match for the German submarines, so very much improved since World War I. Roosevelt persisted and admitted to Churchill, whom he had entertained on board the *Sequoia*, that "my Navy has been definitely slack in preparing for this submarine war off our coast."

FDR wanted an immediate crash construction program of the World War I type 110-foot subchasers, even though Chief Naval Operations Admiral William D. Leahy fought the president's repeated pressure declaring that the 110-foot boats "weren't worth a damn."

Later analysts sided with FDR and the official naval historian, Admiral Samuel Eliot Morison, who concluded that if the president's advice had been heeded and more naval small craft constructed, the Navy and the country would have been far better prepared to meet the threat of submarine warfare.

Something had to be done without a hint of delay, procrastination or excuse making. In the United Kingdom the Fairmile design subchaser was being built with great speed in 45 shipyards, some of them very small. The U.S. Navy decided that the same could be done in this country, just as in World War I, so contracts were let as the Germans continued to pound the east coast, concentrating on the Newfoundland–New York corridor where convoys for the UK were being assembled.

In February, 1942, alone, 71 ships, 384,000 tons, were torpedoed and sunk in the Atlantic. The Germans, doing all this damage with only twelve to fifteen submarines, blew oil tankers out of the water all along the Carolina and Florida coasts. By the end of our first year in the war, nearly 200,000 tons had been sunk off the coasts of the U.S. and Canada.

The Navy did not think much of the British Fairmile, dismissing the design as basically an adaptation of the type of subchasers built in the U.S. during World War I and supplied to Britain.

But the Navy's design also had to be based on the earlier vessels, decided upon after a naval design competition and elimination of the ELCO PC449 and the American Car and Foundry's PC450. Neither could meet the challenges posed by the vastly improved modern German submarine fleet.

The entire program might have been terminated had not the old Westergard Boat Works in New York—certainly a familiar name to John Trumpy—come up with an improved hull design and General Motors developed a new pancake diesel which doubled the horsepower to 2400 shp, increasing the speed to 22 knots.

Westergard's SC 497 design won the day and was therefore forever on the number of the class of ship, the SC 497. But it was Trumpy and his Mathis Yacht Building Company which won honors as class leader. Their SC 507 was completed in record time, on January 19, 1942, three months before Westergard's SC 497. Designation of the class was changed from PC to SC in September, 1942.

These updated, upgraded subchasers were more graceful, more yacht-like, than their World War I forebears. They were also built of wood, with yellow pine or Douglas fir planking over 109 frames covered with quarter inch white oak sheeting on the entire hull. Some New England yards also used juniper.

There were seven watertight bulkheads with fore and aft crew's quarters, galley, magazine, engine room, freshwater and fuel (capacity 4,400 gallons) tanks, officers' quarters with radio, and an engine room with a pair of GM pancake diesels, each 1200 horsepower, or two GM 8-268A diesels, each of 500 horsepower.

The pilothouse was replaced by a flying bridge and abaft the bow was a single mast mounting the radar, standard SF or SG surface search radar, along with WEA-1 sonar.

The main armament was initially a short barrel 3-inch/23, but it was not a very accurate weapon and had to be replaced by a better and more reliable Bofors 40 mm. Two and then three 20 mm guns were located amidships and at the stern were twin racks each containing six depth charges. They were replaced by more modern Type-C racks, six individual holders port and starboard. In addition there was a double set of what were called mousetraps, each containing eight fast-plunging projectiles fired a couple hundred feet in front of the bow. Some ships also mounted .50-caliber machine guns on the bridge.

There were 27 crew members crammed into tight quarters fore and aft and three officers, "60-day wonders" trained at the national subchaser headquarters at Pier Two off Biscayne Boulevard in Miami. The Submarine Chaser Training Center (SCTC) conducted the crash courses that enabled the Navy to man the hundreds of subchasers suddenly flowing out of the yards.

Pier Two always had nests of subchasers, some of them being equipped for their first operational assignments, others being repaired, modernized and fitted out with the latest gear. The Merrill-Stevens shipyard in Miami did the work, including installation of the new radial diesels with variable-pitch propellers, allowing for greater maneuverability and speeds up to 20 knots.

The subchasers, all too often denigrated by the men on the "real ships" as toys and stepchildren, were seldom manned by old salts, wise in the ways of the Navy but those "60-day wonders" and inexperienced reservists at least found them easy to handle as they went to sea and did their duties of screening and shepherding convoys across the ocean, leading LSI and LST landing craft to invasion shores, shielding them from enemy fire, laying down smoke, rescuing seamen and soldiers whose ships had been shot out from under them, and aiding the larger minesweepers search for another kind of unseen deadly threat.

The second Mathis subchaser, SC 508, was completed March 27, 1942, a couple weeks before Westergard's SC 497. After service on submarine patrol, both boats were transferred to France two years later. They were renumbered CH 85 and CH 95.

SC 524–529 were completed at the Mathis yard from April through June, 1942. Four of them were transferred to France immediately, and were renumbered as CH 84, 101, 102 and 114. The other two, SC 527 and SC 528, served in the U.S. Navy until they were sold two years after the war.

A half dozen more subchasers, SC 630–635, were completed in the time frame of August–October, 1942, and after the war, one was transferred to the Coast Guard and two to the Maritime Commission. SC 634 was shipped to the Soviet Union. Two were destroyed.

Three of the next group of six, SC 1023–1028, were completed November–December, 1942, and another six in the first two months of 1943.

The need for subchasers was still severe. The underwater enemy was still snipping and slicing into the vital trans-Atlantic supply line, charging out of wolf packs to attack the merchantmen stocking the larders and stoking the engines of war, keeping alive the hopes of the beleaguered British. In November alone, 106 ships were lost to torpedoes and for the next four months, an average of 50 were sunk each month.

One of the Mathis series of six was also lost at sea—it collided with another vessel. After the war, three of the surviving subchasers were transferred to the Coast Guard and two were turned over to the Maritime Commission.

SC 1067–1076, the final ten members of Mathis' mini-fleet of forty subchasers, were completed between March and August, 1943. Three of these were immediately transferred to the Soviet Navy and after the war, three were picked up by the Coast Guard. Two were converted to PGMs in October of that year.

Eight of the 438 wooden and steel SC class subchasers built by Mathis and other yards during the war were converted to motor gunboats, PGM. The Mathis SC 1071 and SC 1072 were converted in December, 1943, by replacement of the pilot house with an open bridge and removal of all ASW air safety gear and the addition of 40 mm guns within semi-circular shields. Two pairs of Mark 17 twin ½-inch turrets were installed port and starboard and an SG radar was mounted atop a bipod mast aft of the bridge—an arrangement similar to that on the PT boats. Later refinements, after the war, called for 40 mm guns both fore and aft. After the initial conversion of the 110-footers, larger craft were used and armed with six 20 mm guns and twin power-driven 40 mm.

The PGM conversions were part of the restructuring program of anti-submarine warfare. The battle of the Atlantic was being won. FDR and the Navy canceled 1944 orders for additional 110-foot vessels, but increased armament and firepower on those built for use in clearing beaches and supporting invasion landing craft.

At the same time Trumpy and his crews were working around the clock on the conversions, they were producing another thirty subchasers, 63-footers instead of their standard 110-ers. Actually, they were intended to be crash boats, small fast craft put in service to rescue downed pilots at sea. There were numerous smaller boats put to this purpose, mainly 36- and 45-footers, but there was also a need for boats able to handle longer range, rougher water situations, rescuing downed crews of bombers far from shore.

The 63-foot boat was developed by Miami Shipbuilding not far from the Submarine Chaser Training Center. They had built a couple of PT boats the year before Pearl Harbor, and between April and August, 1943, they produced fifty of their 63-footers. Almost half—24—were transferred immediately to the USSR.

Watching over the production was John Trumpy's son, Donald, by then a Lt. Commander in the Navy. His was a valuable presence and he served as link between Miami and Mathis Yacht.

Twenty-five of Mathis' thirty 63-foot PTCs, finished between October, 1943, and August, 1944, were transferred to the Soviets under the terms of lend-lease. The Soviets were not interested in sea rescue boats but wanted subchasers, so 25 were adapted for that purpose and PTC 37–66 were redesignated RPC 51–80. Five of the series, PTC 49–53, remained as crash boats; one of them, PT 51, was transferred to the Army, and two of them were put to use as torpedo retrievers for the Navy Air Force.

The Mathis Yacht yard was chockablock with frames and forms, scaffolding and steam pressers with fitters, joiners, shipwrights and carpenters rushing to complete the Navy order for subchasers. But Mathis Yacht Building Company was running out of room and big brother in the yard next door, the John H. Mathis Company, was also pushing the limits, urgently needing more yard capacity to complete its own government contracts for minesweepers, the *Sway*, *Swerve* and *Swift* (AM 120–122), the *Teaberry*, *Teak*, *Pepperwood* and *Yew* (AN 34–37).

At a special board meeting of Mathis Yacht on April 28, 1942, John Trumpy explained the situation, pointing out the fact that their lease on the Mathis property was due to expire in two months, on July 1.

Trumpy briefed the board on his meetings with Mathis and also with various Navy officials in Camden and Washington, concluding with the rather unpleasant facts of the company's present plight. Without a yard, they could not complete the current contracts or accept any new ones. But, if they could find a suitable space, acquire it without delay and put it into operation immediately, the contracts would be saved. The Navy promised a contract for an additional ten more subchasers, in addition to the six boat contracts presently pending and the partially built dozen other vessels.

Trumpy saved the good news for last. He had found a suitable property down river in Gloucester City, at the foot of Water Street, across Newton Creek from giant New York Shipbuilding Corporation where he had started his Delaware Valley career forty years earlier.

For $237,000 they could buy a gigantic waterfront building, 550 feet long and 127 feet wide, formerly occupied by the American Radiator and Standard Sanitary Corporation. The board approved the following resolutions:

"RESOLVED, that the Mathis Yacht Building Company purchase from the American Radiator and Standard Sanitary Corporation its premises located in Gloucester City, New Jersey, as more particularly shown by survey made by Remington and Vosbury, Civil Engineers, Camden, New Jersey, dated September, 1925, for the sum of $237,500, of which $50,000 shall be paid in cash and the balance secured by a purchase money mortgage, upon such terms and conditions as may be acceptable to the President and Secretary of this Company.

"AND BE IT FURTHER RESOLVED, that the President and Secretary of this Company be and they hereby are authorized and directed to execute and deliver on behalf of this Company an agreement of sale in such form as they may determine to be satisfactory for the purchase of the aforesaid property, and upon settlement for such property to execute and deliver on behalf of this company to the American Radiator and Standard Sanitary Corporation a bond in the amount of $187,500, secured by a purchase money mortgage in the same amount, which said bond and mortgage are to carry interest at the rate of four per cent per annum payable semi-annually, and are to be payable as follows: $37,500 one year from the date thereof and $18,750 each six months thereafter until paid in full, said bond and mortgage to be substantially in the form used and approved by New Jersey title companies.

"AND BE IT FURTHER RESOLVED, that the President and Secretary be and they hereby are authorized and directed to execute and deliver any and all instruments and to carry out and complete any and all transactions necessary or proper to complete the purchase of said property.

"AND BE IT FURTHER RESOLVED, that the President and Secretary of this Company be and they hereby are authorized and directed to make arrangement to borrow from such bank or banks as they may determine such sum or sums of money as may be necessary or needed to complete the purchase of said property, to move the equipment, inventory, and partially completed boats from the present yard of the company to the new property, to make such improvements to and constructions on the new property as may be necessary."

The Trumpy team moved swiftly to convert the property to its needs. They cut six large doors along one side of the building, erecting six building ways opposite them inside the building, each of them with a track connecting with a main line leading to a newly constructed 350 ton marine railway.

A fitting-out wet basin and over 700 feet of frontage at the northern end of the building handled boats too big to be built inside. A 300 ton wharf for fitting-out and a 25 ton derrick completed the facilities which were converted in good time to satisfy the Navy. They issued a contract for four YT-class tugs, a new type, diesel-electric driven with a double armature propulsion motor of 1000 shp direct-connected to the shaft, developed especially for the boats by the Crocker-Wheeler

Company. The main generators in the tugs were driven by two Enterprise 625 hp diesels.

The move was made so quickly and the greatly expanded yard capacity operated so efficiently that another star, the third, was placed on their Army-Navy E. But it wasn't awarded to the Mathis Yacht Building Company. It was awarded to John Trumpy & Sons, Inc. At the January 28, 1943, meeting of the company a resolution was passed "that for the best interest and benefit of all parties involved, the Charter name of Mathis Yacht Building Co. be changed to John Trumpy & Sons, Inc." Seventy-four years after Hans Jacob Trumpy of Bergen partnered his son into the family's shipbuilding business, another J. Trumpy & Sons opened for business.

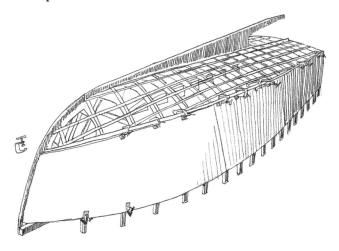

24 Ft. Personnel Boats
Contract #322 1942

US Navy 24' plane personnel boat,
96 built under contract 322, 1942

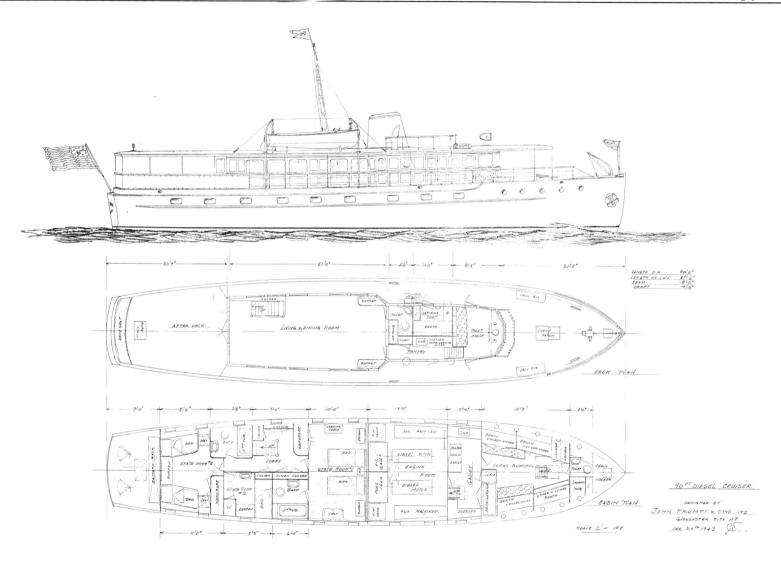

Proposed 90' Diesel Cruiser, design dated December 20, 1943.

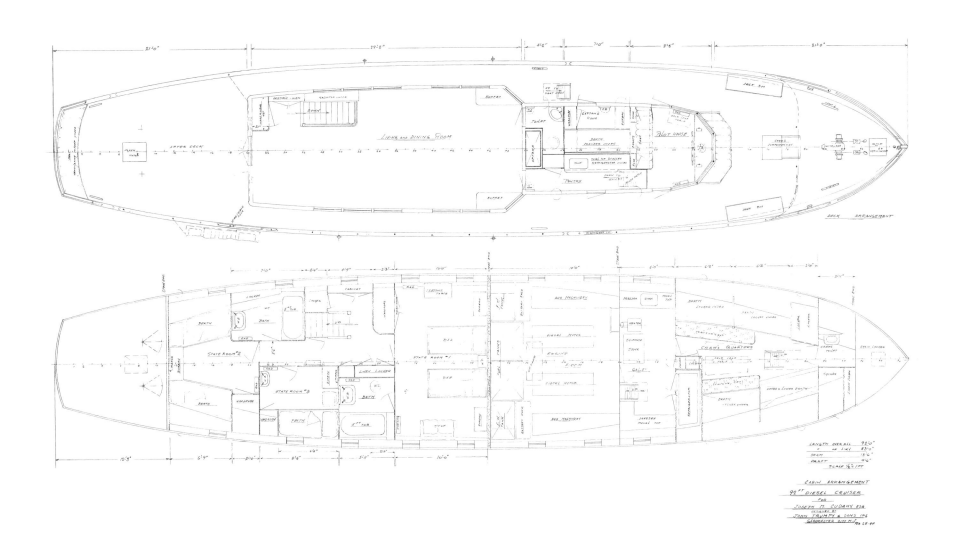

92' Diesel Cruiser for Joseph M. Cudahy, drawings dated February 28, 1944

Chapter 10
ANCHORS AWEIGH FOR ANNAPOLIS

There had been such hectic activity in the many shipyards along the Delaware River during the war, and such an outpouring of wartime-impelled production by all the neighboring chemical companies that the river water was like syrup. Leaded paints poisoned the fish and the fumes of sulphur mixed with other chemicals assaulted the nostrils and created a black haze in the sky. The freshly painted white hulls of the Trumpy yachts turned a sickly shade of yellow and ghostly gray.

Trumpy had to move out of the area, but to where? He and his directors examined sites and boatyards along the eastern shore and of course in Florida, which they and their clients knew so well. As they were considering the several possibilities, a ready answer was supplied by the owners of a highly respected yard in Eastport, strategically situated across Spa Creek from the Annapolis Yacht Club, the yacht basin and the Naval Academy.

Annapolis Yacht Yard was a ten-year-old company which had built a series of 46-foot cruisers before the war, but the origins went way back, all the way to 1903 when Chance Marine Construction Company was founded. It concentrated on building and servicing Chesapeake Bay work boats, but it did manage to build a single subchaser, SC 409, during World War I. Its second one, SC 410, was canceled when only 40% completed at the time of the armistice.

Other cancellations came during the Great Depression as Chance, which had built the Annapolis Yacht Basin, did not generate enough business to stay afloat—despite the fact that it enjoyed an enviable location on the main waterway for pleasure yachts moving to and from northern ports, the Carolinas and the subtropics. There just wasn't enough traffic and need for repair and maintenance work. By the mid-1930s, the yard went into bankruptcy and Eastport went into mourning.

The Reconstruction Finance Corporation took it over and a group of wealthy Annapolitans bailed out the Yacht Basin. In July, 1937, a man on a white yacht appeared—New York ship designer and builder Chris B. Nelson. Armed with an MIT degree in naval architecture, he had started as a draftsman for Tams, LeMoyne and King, moved over to the Dawn Boat Company and then started his own firm, Nelson-Reid, Inc.

His partner, Frederick I. Reid, previously manager of the Hutchins Yacht Company, joined Nelson in the new venture, as did another New Yorker, Erik Almon, who had earlier worked for the Frank Browne Jones Company, Thomas Hanson and finally, Dawn.

The new team revitalized the company, renaming it Annapolis Yacht Yard and pumping into it some much-needed money and modern ideas. They also demonstrated at the very beginning that they had a fine feel for public relations.

Their very first customer was no less a personage than the son of the President, James Roosevelt. He docked his *Sewauna* and placed an order for a general overhaul and copper sheathing of the boat bottom.

As the local press headlined the news, Nelson took advantage of the attention by announcing that he already had in hand orders for three new boats, a 65-footer, one of 54 feet and a 50-foot ketch.

But the doldrums of the Great Depression still had a deleterious—for some a disastrous—effect on the yacht-building business, as Trumpy well knew. Nelson had to come to the harsh realization that Annapolis Yacht's days were limited and its future bleak, despite the success and general acceptance of their fine 46-footers, primarily used for fishing. They built nearly twenty of them, but that was not enough to keep the work force fully employed and the accountants happy.

Managing director Nelson was a man of action and considerable determination and he realized that unless he could negotiate additional contracts, hopefully official government contracts, he'd be forced to shut down his operation. In April, 1941, the month after Congress passed the $7 billion Lend-Lease Bill, he managed to make his way to England where he negotiated a license agreement with Vosper in Portsmouth to build their Navy patrol boats in Annapolis.

Two months later, the British Navy sent over an officer to expand the agreement to include other U.S. shipyards. Nelson was appointed chief coordinator by BuShips acting as liaison between the British and the Robert Jacobs Company of nearby Bay City, Herreshoff of Bristol and the Harbor Boat Building Company of Terminal Island, California.

The first Vospers were all built by Annapolis Yacht which laid keels for eight of them in September and October, 1941, BPT 21–28, redesignated by the Royal Navy as MTB 275–282, and transferred to the Indian Navy. Four of the next series of twenty went to the Indians, eight to the Soviet Navy and the remainder to the Royal Navy—five of the British boats were transferred to the Italian Navy in 1947 and 1948.

Keels were laid for another thirty boats, PT 400–429, between September, 1943, and February, 1944, all destined for the Soviet Union. The keel for PT 661 and those for PT 677–692 were laid between August, 1944, and January, 1945, and another 15, PT 662–676, were sent to the Soviets in kit form.

Another 38 Vosper boats, PT 693–730, were completed between March and October, 1945, for the Soviets but were not delivered. Two were converted to small boat duty and the remainder were sold, many to Chesapeake Bay fishermen. Two of them, PT 715 and 716, went to Cuba where they were redesignated R 41 and R 42.

The Annapolis Vosper had a low silhouette in the water, was equipped with SO radar and weighed in at 33 tons. 71'1/2" long with a beam of 19'2" and drafts between 4'1/2" and 7'1/2", the vessel had a power plant of three shaft Packard gasoline engines, developing 4055 hp and a speed of 40 knots. She carried a crew of twelve and armament of a 20 mm. Oerlikon automatic gun and twin .50-cal. Browning machine guns, four depth charges and two 21-inch torpedoes.

Annapolis Yacht also built ten of the kind of 110-foot subchasers Mathis Yacht had been sliding down its slips with such regularity, and their payroll mushroomed mightily from a low of 18 before the naval contracts, to nearly 500 during the war years.

The pace was non-stop, especially when assembling the torpedo boats which yard workers dubbed "Devils With Hornet Stings." The wives of the workers were called upon to serve as sponsors, crashing the compulsory champagne bottle christening the ship. On one auspicious occasion, when the 30th of the hundred torpedo boats destined for the USSR was launched on May 19, 1944, Russian and British admirals were in admiring attendance, joined by the commandant of the Naval Academy, gathered under the Army-Navy E proudly waving overhead.

Those were the glory days of Annapolis Yacht. The end of the war brought a return to reality rather quickly. By 1946 there were only four new PT boats on the Navy list and these were sold to South Korea in 1952. Their place was taken by fast patrol boats.

With the sudden cessation of naval orders, and only a trickle of orders from the private sector for the 46-footers and a few other craft, the work force had to be drastically reduced. The same thing was happening elsewhere as the country ground back to a peacetime economy. Cramps of Kensington, once the primary naval contractor of big ships, shut down in 1946 and the mighty ELCO company in Bayonne closed the last day of December, 1949. It was a repeat of the post World War I situation when such giants as Bath Iron Works were put on the auction block.

Annapolis Yacht Yard did not suffer a similar indignity, but when Chris Nelson died in 1947, partner Fred Reid decided he did not want to run the company alone. When John Trumpy got that news, he immediately contacted Reid to start negotiations. They were quickly brought to a successful and satisfactory conclusion. Trumpy was eager to place his yard in such a strategically advantageous location, one that was as much in the center of all the action as his father's and grandfather's shipyards had been in Bergen.

At a special July 9, 1947, meeting of the Board of Directors—held in the new offices of John Trumpy & Sons, Inc., at 204–214 Severn Avenue in Eastport with the secretary recorded that:

"All of the directors having taken part in negotiations with Annapolis Yacht Yard, Inc., for purchase of its plant and equipment and for agreement to complete construction of seven yachts now under construction by Annapolis Yacht Yard, Inc., and each director being thoroughly familiar with the elements of the transaction with Annapolis Yacht Yard, Inc., and satisfied that such transaction should be consummated, it was.

"Resolved that the vice-president and secretary of this company be and they hereby are authorized and directed to execute in the name and on behalf of this company two certain contracts with Annapolis Yacht Yard, Inc., one for completion by this company of seven yachts now under construction by said Annapolis Yacht Yard, Inc., and the other for purchase, for the sum of $200,000 of the land, buildings and yacht building equipment of Annapolis Yacht Yard, Inc., at 204–214 Severn Avenue, Eastport, Maryland, which contracts shall be in the form attached hereto.

"It was further Resolved that the president and secretary of this company be and they hereby are authorized and directed to take all necessary action to procure proper authority under the laws of the State of Maryland for this company to do business in said state.

"It was further Resolved that the president and secretary of this company be and they hereby are authorized and directed to borrow in the name and on behalf of this company from First Camden National Bank and Trust Company the sum of $50,000 upon such terms and with or without security as they deem advisable."

One of the contracts inherited from Annapolis was a new PT boat for the Navy. The Bureau of Ships had issued the general specifications and a list of requirements to four companies in June, 1946—Bath Iron Works and the naval

US Navy PT 811, 1947

architectural firm of Sparkman and Stephens, ELCO, the Philadelphia Navy Yard and Annapolis Yacht. PT 811 was built by Annapolis, ultimately by Trumpy which took over the yard and the contract in mid-1947; PT 810 by Bath, PT 809 by ELCO and PT 812 by the Philadelphia Navy Yard, which designed a round-bottom boat.

PT 811 was built of aluminum with a long V-bottom and four rudders, one abaft each propeller, plus a special fin, added to improve turning maneuverability at high speeds. During the trials she reached speeds of 47 knots.

Overall length was 95 feet with a beam of 24'11" and drafts of 3'4" forward and 6'4" aft. With 173,000 pounds displacement, she was the lightest of the four boats in the competition and carried the same kind of armament—two 40 mm guns, twin 20 mm cannons and 81 mm mortar. The power pack was the same in all boats—four Packard W-100 gasoline engines and a pair of Hobart 25 kW, 120 volt generators.

BuShips found that the Trumpy boat, with her heavy-shelled, welded hull, ran into too many troubles in rough seas, taking on a great deal of water topside, and planing when riding the crest of swells but slowing considerably when settling into the troughs. After the trials, it was determined that the boat needed additional structural members and internal bracing. Equally important, the main engines were not judged to be reliable, lacking in power and durability to perform the required cruising range of 1,500 nautical miles.

Navy evaluations were of interest to Trumpy, but not if they meant his yards had to build aluminum boats. John Trumpy & Sons did not want to work in aluminum or any other kind of metal, despite all the research and experimentation they had done learning and perfecting the processes of what was then a rather novel approach to boatbuilding.

The Trumpy team, led by the founder, president and chief designer, wanted to work in wood, and only wood. They rejected any additional tests and informed the Navy they were not metal boat builders.

After the trials and assessments, PT 811 served for a time as a presidential "escape yacht," meaning she was on standby call to whisk the president to safe harbor in the event of an enemy attack. She was withdrawn from service in 1957, but reinstated as PTF 2 in December, 1962, as the Navy launched a new series of fast patrol boats.

PTF 2 (PT 811) ended her days in Vietnam.

Model of USS Nasty (PTF)

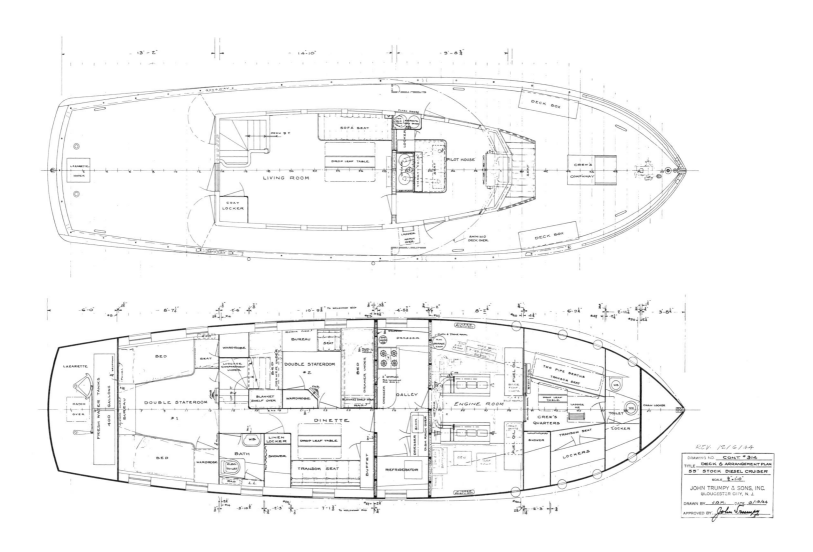

*55' **Aurora**, #314, built in 1947 as pilot model for new houseboat series.*

Chapter 11
SWORDS TO PLOWSHARES & PLOWSHARES TO SWORDS

In the early stages of adjusting to the post-war market, Trumpy launched a program of down-sizing to meet the demand for smaller boats just as he had done after World War I with his 61-footers. He started in the last months of the war, as soon as the last subchaser was off the boards and out of the Gloucester City yards. He designed a new 55-foot diesel cruiser with a beam of 15' and draft of 4', which he claimed "rivals pre-war 60- to 70-foot models," and demonstrates "how well our thirty-five years experience in designing and building yachts of all types has enabled us to include in this new 55-footer many features which have proven so satisfactory in our 60- to 70-foot designs."

Proud of the clipper bow and graceful rounded stern, Trumpy assured potential customers that "in no other design will you find such comfortable living conditions in a yacht of this size, combined with seaworthiness, strong construction, economical maintenance and a cruising speed of 12 miles."

The two engines were 75 horsepower, 6 cylinder, 4 cycle diesels with fresh water cooling, bronze propellers and shafting with rubber bearing struts. The 32 volt, 1500 watt generator was attached to the motor, eliminating the need for a separate gasoline engine. 350 gallon welded steel fuel tanks were in the engine room and fresh water tanks of 400 gallons capacity were in the lazarette. Forward of the engine room were "exceptionally good accommodations" for a crew of two.

All the furniture was built-in including the sofa, easy chairs, and drop-leaf table which were in the 15'6" x 10' deck house living room that was finished in light walnut with a paneled insulated ceiling. The staterooms were 11'6" x 8'9" and 10'9" x 6'6".

The main deck extended without break from stem to stern with full headroom and the dinette, with a sofa seat providing additional accommodation for two people, was located next to the galley which had built-in gas stove, electric fridge, dish racks, cabinet, linen locker and buffet.

As was usual with Trumpy, the first boat of a new series or a special kind of yacht that could serve as sales model was called *Aurora*. That was the name of the first 55-footer but before she was finished, three others were ordered, the *Marion II*, by R. F. Bain, *Sylvia IV*, by Samuel S. Bell, Jr., and A. R.

Gross's *One Forty Four II*.

It was a short-lived series as customers wanted yachts a little or a lot longer. The first year after the war, R. W. Johnson ordered a 65-foot motor yacht, *Makaira*, which was later lengthened to 70 feet by Charles F. Johnson.

The motor yacht was similar to the 65-footer built for Samuel S. Sanford in 1940, the *Chanticleer*, which was commandeered by the government to serve as a coastal patrol boat for the Navy during the war.

Mrs. Whitney's 111-foot *Captiva* was also requisitioned by the Navy during the war but did not take on the hazards of patrol duty; she was anchored in the Cape Cod Canal and served as officers' billets. Cudahy's 91-foot *Innisfail* was taken over in 1942 by the Navy and designated YP 354.

In 1946 the Gloucester City yard built the 60-foot *Carol Anne* for R. Foster Reynolds, the 71-foot *Silver Swan* for Arthur W. Conley and the 61'3" *Malova V* for J. Rodman McCoy, who renamed her *The McCoy* a few years later. With a beam of 16 feet and draft of five, she cruised at ten knots powered by a pair of four cylinder GM diesels with 3:1 reduction gear. Designed by Frederick C. Geiger of Philadelphia Yacht Sales and Service, she had an unusually heavy displacement, including her one ton iron keel. The Port Orford cedar planking in 40-foot lengths was on 2" x 2 1/2" oak frames. Bulkheads, engine room floors and beds were galvanized steel and the tanks held 1,413 gallons of fuel and 400 of water. Unique for any boat built by Mathis was her solid mast crowned by a crow's nest. Accommodations were for two forward and the owner aft in quarters that provided more space than usual.

The following year there were a pair of 45-foot cruisers, *Curlew* for R. Snowden Andrews and Edward H. Ellis' *Jinofor*. But the Zinns, Roland and Gertrude, ordered a 60-footer, *Gretchen III*, as did Thomas T. Keane with his *Tomadge*. George Codrington's Diesel Towing Company and Connecticut Colonel Frederick Pope wanted 80-footers, *Seaplay* and *Marylin*.

Those post-war boats were all finished in Gloucester which is where another prototype was started, the last of the 15 yachts built there, the 61-foot *Aurora II*. She was shipped to the new yards at Annapolis and completed.

Also completed in the new home of John Trumpy & Sons were the seven yachts they were obliged to complete in accordance with the contract for purchase of Annapolis Yacht Yard. Largest was the 60-foot *Do-Ho III*. Smallest were the 46'7" *Jennie Belle IV* for Jules Gorliz and *Tamarack* for the University of Rhode Island. The others ranged from 47 to 54 feet.

After Annapolis Yacht's customers were satisfied and the finishing touches were put on *Aurora II*, the Trumpys and their new work force proceeded to work on nine other boats of their own design.

They weren't exactly flooded with orders, as happened in the booming twenties following the first World War. Only three a year in 1948, '49 and '50. The duPonts ordered two in 1948 including Francis' new 60-foot *Tech, Jr.* She was the first keel laid by the company on the banks of Spa Creek. Another duPont ordered a 61-footer, *Seaholm*. *Tech, Jr.* was later taken over by Coleman duPont who donated the boat to the Maryland Militia.

The most impressive vessel the new yard could show their new neighbors in Eastport was the 72-foot *Mikaro* built in 1948 for G. M. Stull. *Co-ed II* was a 50-footer built for A. R. Gross to replace his 55-footer, and *Florence VI* was a 56-footer that William J. McCahan III ordered to take the place of his much larger 80-foot *Florence V*.

William McKelvey and E. E. Dickenson, the witch hazel king, ordered 60-footers, *Rumak II* and *Alva*, designed by Sparkman & Stephens. And John Trumpy built for his own use a 40-foot sloop, *Sea Call*.

John Trumpy was a sailor at heart. And he had been ever since he sailed those magnificent models built for him in his father's yard at Jekteviken. Under other circumstances he might have been able to concentrate on building sailboats exclusively, but he could not fathom how that would have had the same kind of market potential or given him the kind of financial future he was hoping for in the New World.

He contented himself with watching an occasional sailboat come to life on his drawing board and in his shipyard. In 1950 he designed and built *Sea Call IV*, a 40-foot auxiliary sloop with a pair of headsails, fore staysail and jib. She replaced the 36'3" auxiliary cutter, *Sea Call III*, Trumpy had designed and built for himself in 1940 which in turn had replaced the 1928 *Sea Call II*, his 44-foot auxiliary schooner.

The senior Trumpy seldom if ever missed a day at the yards except when the family was, in the best Norwegian fashion, spending summer holidays at their seaside cottage on Barnegat Bay. There he could relax and recharge, sailing on the bay and instructing family members on the fine art of catching the winds with the skills and experience passed down and perfected since Viking times.

It was most appropriate, and not at all surprising, that the grand trophy Trumpy contributed to the Annapolis Yacht Club—to be awarded to the overall winner of the fall series of races—was a beautifully crafted silver Viking ship, one of those "surf dragons."

In the midst of the Great Depression, Mathis Yacht built ten sailboats, auxiliary cutters, schooners, sloops and yawls ranging from 30 feet all the way to 59 feet. But after the war, other than the boats for the boss's personal use, only three were built, the 42-foot ketch *Sanbar* in 1959 and four years later, the 48-foot cutter *Oceanus*. The first was for George F. Johnson and the second for Charles Owen. C. Porter Schutt, head of Diamond Ice and Coal Company, ordered the 62-foot *Egret* in 1972.

Sanbar and *Oceanus* were designed by Fred Geiger, the Philadelphian who had caused a stir in Gloucester City with his design of *Malova V*. He was as sure-handed a draftsman and as artistic a designer as his mentor John Trumpy, who brought him aboard officially in the early 1950s.

Schutt's *Egret* was the second to last boat built by John Trumpy & Sons. But before the company reached that end of the line, they had to survive another naval attack from the Bureau of Ships—after the North Koreans swept across the 38th parallel and the United States, leader of the Free World and the United Nations, was back at war. The Navy again called on John Trumpy for help.

Sid Peters did the calling. He was the powerful head of the Small Boats Division of the Navy's Bureau of Ships and a good friend of the yacht builder whose design skills and nautical knowledge he greatly respected. Peters was charged with the responsibility of responding to an immediate need for minesweepers.

After the dramatic turnaround of the ground war with the brilliant amphibious assault on Inchon, General MacArthur and his staff wanted to follow up that stunning success with a similar landing at Wonsan. But the Wonsan harbor had been heavily mined, thanks to the Soviets using their extensive arsenal of mines, some of them vintage 1904 from the Russo-Japanese War.

The Russians had been great believers in the efficacy of defensive mine warfare ever since the Crimean War when Immanuel Nobel, founder of the Swedish-Russian Nobel dynasty, supplied the underwater "torpedoes" which blew up British ships attacking the fortress of Kronstadt.

The Soviets supplied the North Koreans and advised the North Koreans who were able to humiliate the U.S. Navy by laying some 3000 mines, magnetic and pressure types, in Wonsan harbor in just three weeks. The UN forces were stymied and the most powerful Navy in the world found to its embarrassment that it could not go where and when it wanted to. As Admiral Allan Smith succinctly summarized the situation, "We have lost control of the seas to a nation without a Navy, using pre-World War I weapons, laid by vessels that were utilized at the time of the birth of Christ."

The need for minesweepers was urgent. UN forces were planning other amphibious landings and wanted to be able to bring their warships closer to shore for more accurate bombardment of entrenched enemy positions.

Five years earlier, the Navy had close to 550 minesweepers (300 were off Normandy on D-Day and 100 off Okinawa when that island was invaded), but when the North Koreans invaded the South, that number had dwindled to four 180-foot steel-hulled Admirable class AMs and a half dozen 136-foot auxiliary AMSs, redesignated YMSs. The others had been scrapped or were mothballed.

Sid Peters selected John Trumpy as chief designer and project coordinator for all yards involved in building a new type of minesweeper. They were basically a conversion of the LCVPs, the Landing Craft, Vehicle and Personal, 57-footers intended for close-to-shore harbor clearance and capable of sweeping ahead of the bigger steel-hulled boats. Trumpy built a dozen, MSB 3–9 and MSB 25–29, nicknamed "Mighty Mites" and "Splinter Fleet" by the sailors. Trumpy, the biggest business in Annapolis with a payroll of 150, also built two skiffs designed by Sparkman and Stephens and a half dozen 50-foot utility boats for the Navy in 1952.

The shallow-draft, wooden hull MSBs could sweep both moored and magnetic mines, operating in shallow waters closer to shore than the larger minesweepers. In deeper water, they were able to open lanes for the others to follow with more sophisticated gear.

They operated like brood chicks running out from a mother hen, housed in large square-sterned vessels that could be flooded to take on and disgorge the splinter fleet. The timing of aircraft carrier deck operations was required for launching the Mighty Mite MSBs to do their detective work, sweeping in prearranged patterns.

Initially, LSTs were used, Landing Ship Tank, housing four MSBs on the tank deck—a novel technique but not successful in rough seas. The LST bow yawed too much and it was difficult, if not dangerous, to re-embark the MSBs. LSDs, Landing Ship Dock, were substituted and used until the end of the war, although the need for extensive sweeping operations, the kind required at Wonsan, was no longer on an emergency basis.

It took eight days and more than 200 casualties to clear channels at Wonsan and by the fall of 1951, minesweepers were suffering more damage and casualties from shore fire than by mines. During the entire course of the Korean War, the Navy lost only four minesweepers but they suffered more than 20% of the casualties in the war even though their ships and boats constituted barely 2% of the total naval craft committed. The Navy had hopefully learned the lesson well articulated by Admiral C. Turner Joy, Commander Naval Forces, Far East, that "no so-called subsidiary branch of the naval service, such as mine warfare should ever be neglected or relegated to a minor role in the future."

With a sudden, post-Wonsan freeing of funds the Bureau of Ships restructured its minesweeper fleet, building, converting and reactivating vessels and authorizing a new, larger and more powerful MSB, an 82-footer.

Peters and Trumpy analyzed the evaluations of MSB combat performance and learned that they were not easy to handle, and were difficult to turn when both drag hooks were out. Trumpy designed the wooden, non-magnetic MSB 29 to solve the problem. She was a compromise size between the large and small boats of its type, and when launched on October 5, 1956, with the wife of a retired Navy captain doing the champagne-crashing honors, there were some 250 guests present, including a local Congressman who praised the Trumpy shipbuilders for their excellent construction record, producing craft which "contributed immensely to the effectiveness of our naval effort and the victory we ultimately achieved."

He reminded the audience that the building of boats with wooden hulls is a most demanding task and requires skills that certainly cannot be learned overnight. The Rear Admiral in charge of Fleet Operations' Undersea Warfare Division echoed those sentiments and indicated that the new Trumpy minesweeper was the first of several to be built for the Navy.

But in 1958 the program was canceled as Mine Countermeasures, MCM, reverted to its usual back of the budget status. The not-so-glamorous mission of minesweeping was not the route to an admiral's rank. No other MSB 29s were built.

John Trumpy & Sons could again concentrate on its own primary mission, the building of pleasure yachts. The prototype *Aurora IV* came off the boards and into the mold lofts in 1954. She was a 67'6" stock cruiser powered by a pair of GM diesels capable of delivering 478 shaft horsepower at 2300 rpm which gave a top speed of 21.6 knots and cruising speed of 19.4.

Constructed of double planked mahogany over a frame of white oak, the trim and deckhouses were teak. Teak is a smooth fine grain tropical hardwood used extensively by Trumpy and worked into precise mortice and tenon joinery. Tectona grandis is impervious to weather, wind and water, resistant to rot, mildew, boring bugs and warp-splinter proof.

Forward quarters accommodated a crew of three and the pair of double staterooms aft each had a head. The 19'6" long lounge deck was partially enclosed with sliding glass panels and

67'6" Aurora IV, #366, built in 1954

newest Trumpy prototype. L. M. Miller ordered one before she was even finished, calling her *Sereno*, and Herbert W. Stone took possession of his *Silver Mist* in 1955. Richard E. Riegel waited a few years before ordering his *Blue Hen* and so too did Howell van Gerbig and Roger Firestone, who christened his boat *Tireless*. She turned heads whenever she arrived at a new dock, especially when traveling in tandem with brother Russel Firestone's *Flameless*, a 50-foot cruiser originally built as *Aries* for Henry Gibson. *Tireless* and *Flameless*, what a pair!

In the decade from 1954 through 1963 John Trumpy & Sons launched 41 boats and a special series of ten 40-foot patrol boats under a contract with Radio Corporation of America. The designer was Sparkman and Stephens and the designee was the coastal patrol service of Fulgencio Batista. It was a giveaway to the Cuban government which, under Castro, no doubt used them during the Bay of Pigs invasion. With the durability of Trumpy-built boats, there are probably some still in service.

Trumpy experimented with 50-foot and 55-foot fisherman cruisers, the *Jinofor II* for Edward H. Ellis, *Shelly Kay V* and *Willit* for John B. Rich and Lammot duPont.

Jinofor II had a beam of 14'3" and draft of three and a half

there was total temperature control, heat and air conditioning. Frigidaire units, including a freezer, were built into the galley, installed by a small army of workmen from various trades who swarmed and nested once the basic boat had been completed—cabinetmakers, welders, sheet metal workers, mechanics, plumbers, electricians and painters.

The finished product was an artistic achievement, but also a major engineering, mechanical and electrical production, one that provided precisely what John Trumpy had been promising since his earliest days designing and building yacht houseboats—comfort.

It wasn't long before orders started coming in for the

feet and was one of the few yacht fisherman Trumpy ever designed or built. Sleeping six in a trio of staterooms with three heads and two showers, the boat boasted a swimming platform and ladder, teak deck, a roomy flybridge with lounge seats on both sides, and a large open deck area aft with steps to the fishing cockpit. The engines were twin Cummins diesels 8V-370M, capable of 18 knots cruising and 20 top speed.

For the standard 55-foot cruisers, the foremen returned to the mold shed to build the last three in that particular series, *Bunky* for Stephen Paine, *Vael* for Allison F. Fleitas and *April Showers* for George Senn.

53-foot cruisers were built as sister ships for Dwight P. Allen, *Fin V*, and for John B. Rich, who replaced his three year old *Shelly Kay V* with *Shelly Kay VI*. Another pair was built in 1962, the *Martha P V* for William N. S. Pugh and the *Aries* for Gibson.

Fifty-seven-foot cruisers were ordered by Frank Michaux and Howell van Gerbig who christened them *Valor* and *Tonda*; but when company representatives went to upper New York state to pick out the wood they bought so much there was enough left over for another sizable yacht. Gerbig promptly

67'6" Tonda, #394, built in 1960 for Howell VanGerbig

ordered one of the 67'6" series of six and also named that *Tonda*. Other 57-foot flush deck cruisers were bought by Harald Pitcairn who named his *Clara*, Lester Finkelstein, *Irene C.*, Ralph Atlas, *Wind IV*, R. W. Bartram, Jr., *Exchange II*, and J. W. West, whose *Westerly* was the last of the series.

With a beam of 14 feet and draft of 4'6", the 57-foot flush deck cruisers built of double-planked Honduras mahogany, bronze fastened with teak handrails and decks, were powered by twin GM 6-71M engines, each generating 270 horsepower producing a speed of 12–14 knots. Owner's and guest staterooms were aft, each with head and stall shower, the first with queen-size double berth and walnut cabinetry, the second with two lower berths plus an upper Pullman berth.

The salon was walnut paneled and in the bow there were upper and lower berths, with a separate head and stall shower. The 22-foot long pilot house aft deck with a teak wet bar and six-foot raised helm seat provided 360 degree visibility. The furniture was hand made teak designed and made by the same master craftsmen responsible for the wood finishing and cabinetry of the boat. Trumpy teak furniture have always been prized possessions among Trumpy owners.

While the 57-footers were taking their place in the Trumpy Hall of Fame, the company underwent a basic reorganization, transferring the corporate identity from New Jersey jurisdiction to that of Maryland, merging John Trumpy & Sons of New Jersey into the Maryland corporation. Directors were John Trumpy Sr. and Jr., William J. McWilliams, Frank W. Wrightson and James H. Kimberly, three new names in the company records. McWilliams of 212 Duke of Gloucester Street, Annapolis, MD, was the resident agent of the corporation which was voted the authority to issue 3,000 shares of stock at par value of $50 per share.

Officers (and annual salaries) of the new corporation were John Trumpy, chairman of the board ($12,000); John Trumpy, Jr., president and treasurer ($23,000); C. E. Hires, vice-president and secretary ($10,350); Lyle W. Gaither, vice-president and superintendent ($12,000); and William F. Hastie, assistant treasurer ($8,000).

The new position of chairman of the board had been created on April 29, 1952, on the occasion of the 50th anniversary of the arrival of John Trumpy in the U.S. The directors realized the company "needed the counsel and naval architectural advice" of the founder and they weren't about to let him retire from the scene.

In 1952 the senior Trumpy had a salary of $14,400, his number one son $16,080 and son number two, Donald, World War II Navy veteran, and by then vice-president and secretary, $14,880. (Donald died in 1958.) The then assistant secretary C. E. Hires earned $9350, assistant treasurer Hastie $6000 and yard superintendent Gaither, a key figure in the success of the company, $9,900.

The chairman of the board had no intention of retiring. While he retreated from the daily grind he still put in time at the drawing board and oversaw the fulfillment of new orders, whether the client was a newcomer or repeater, whether the model built was from one of the prototypes or constructed from scratch. He treasured the time-honored procedures of drawing the plans, calculating weight and trim, and working in the mold loft where patterns were made for each individual part of the boat. Trumpy watched the white oak timbers being cut for the keel, wood being steam-bent for ribs and frames, mahogany planking being measured and teak sized for deck, railings and furniture.

Whether the yacht was stock or custom-designed, each step of the process, of working the woods, was meticulously executed with the constant supervision of the foreman, the shipwright, the "old man" himself.

A man of few words—in the best Norwegian manner—John Trumpy's presence and his perfectionism were always felt in the yards. At one point during the construction of ships for the Navy, he was making the rounds and noticed a workman carefully sanding a joint. "Don't bother with that," advised

Trumpy, "this boat's going to get shot at and might sink; just paint over it." The workman replied, "Mr. Trumpy, I only know one way to do this and that's the way you taught me."

One of the largest boats built from 1954 to 1963 was almost as long as the prototype minesweeper, 79 feet, but certainly more commodious for passengers and crew having a good many more luxurious features. She was built for William M. McKelvey of Pittsburgh, a winter resident of Florida who was replacing his 1949 60-foot **Rumak II**. As soon as his captain took possession, he revved up his pair of GM 6-110 diesels and **Rumak III** was off to the Sunshine State, gliding gracefully along at 16 knots, cutting the characteristic Trumpy slice at the sleek prow, leaving a flat wake.

Other long, lean yachts built during those ten years were the 71'5" stock cruiser **Aurora**, another prototype, the 75-foot cruiser **Beatrice** for Jack Meyerhoff, an 80-foot cruiser, **Claybeth**, for Clayton Gengras and a pair of 84-foot cruisers, **Pintail** for Colonel David Flagstaff, and **Eskimo** for John R. Kimberly, whose 67-foot houseboat built in 1958 had been named **Eskimo III**. The head of the giant Kimberly-Clark Paper Company was a winter resident of Palm Beach, a good friend of John Trumpy, Jr., and an important, charged-up promoter of Trumpy yachts. In 1965 he ordered a 46-

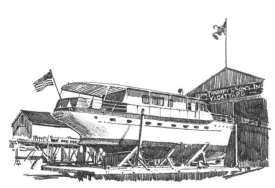

*Fantail stern on **Aurora***

foot cruiser for running about, giving her the name of **Wavey II**.

The **Eskimo** and **Pintail** had three double staterooms with baths, dining salon, living room and a fishing cockpit aft. Quarters for the four-man crew were forward, with a separate head, shower and dinette. Cruising speed was 17 knots with a top speed of 19.

But John Trumpy never had the chance to go out on Spa Creek and the Severn with the last of his yard's great 80-footers. He died, in his 84th year, on September 4, 1963.

John Trumpy 1879-1963

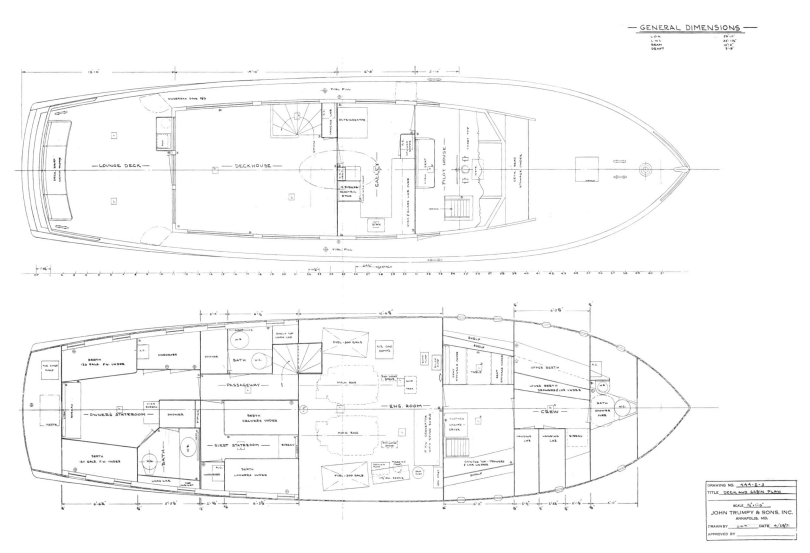

*58' x 53'1½" x 15'3" x 3'9" Houseboat **Aurora V**, Contract number 444, built in 1971 for John Trumpy & Sons*

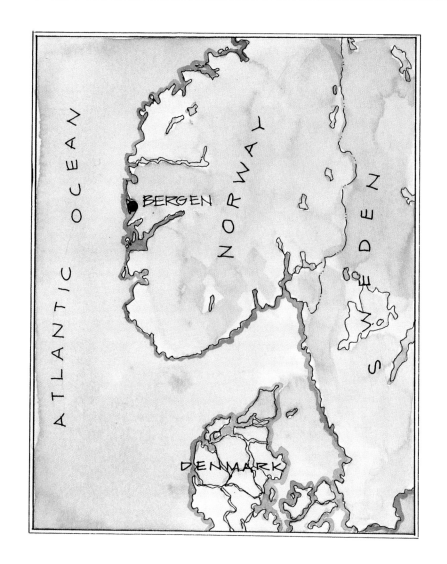

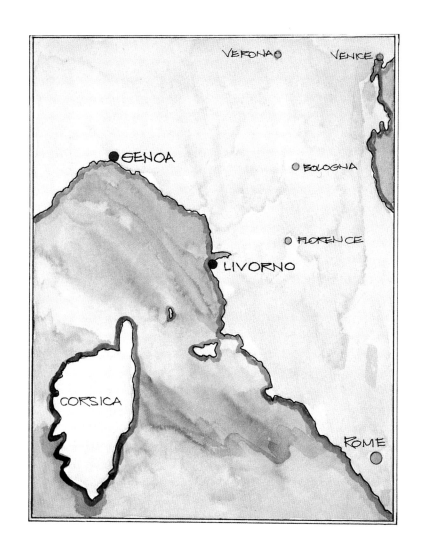

Trumpy Yard in Bergen, Norway & Trumpy Yard in Livorno & Genoa

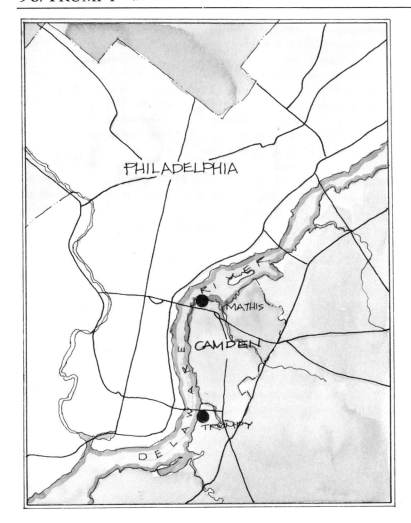

Mathis Yard in Camden, NJ

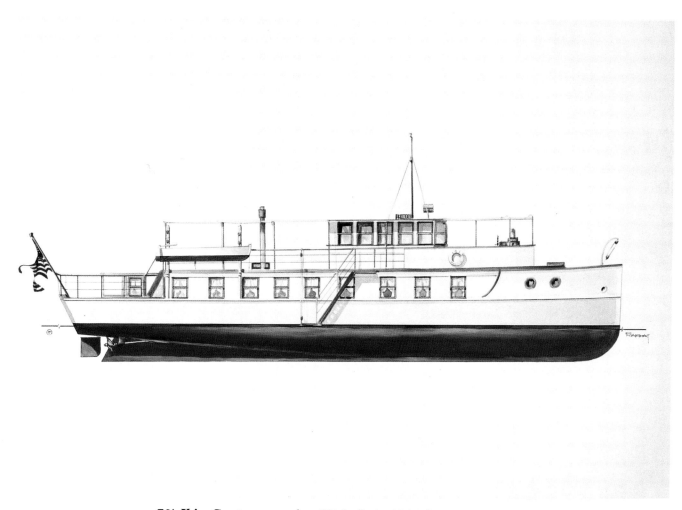

70' *Ibis*, Contract number 27, built in 1912 for F. F. Christie

68' **Nahmeoka**, Contract number 38, built in 1913 for H. N. Baruch

90' *Nepenthe*, Contract number 67, built in 1916 for James Deering

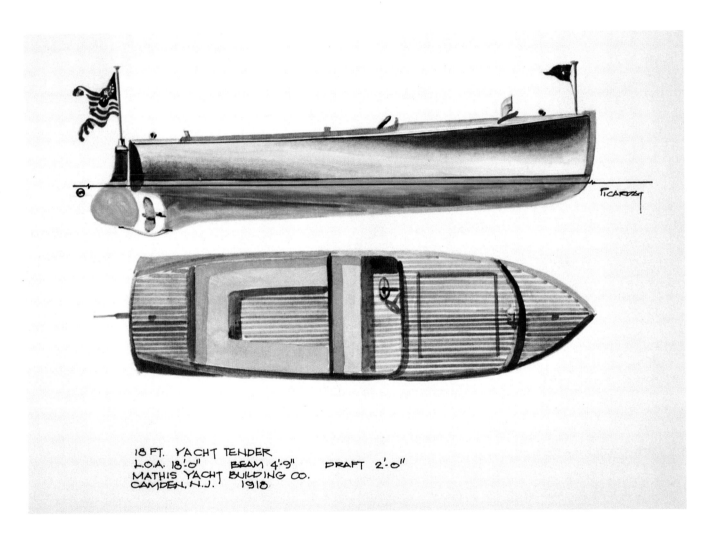

18 FT. YACHT TENDER
L.O.A. 18'-0"   BEAM 4'-9"   DRAFT 2'-0"
MATHIS YACHT BUILDING CO.
CAMDEN, N.J.   1918

18' Yacht Tender, typical of Mathis work, built in 1918

75' Patrol Boat Contract number 142, built in 1924 for the USCG

104' *Sequoia II*, Contract number 174, built in 1925 for Richard Cadwalader, Jr.

104' *Sequoia II*, Contract number 174, built in 1925 for Richard Cadwalader, Jr.

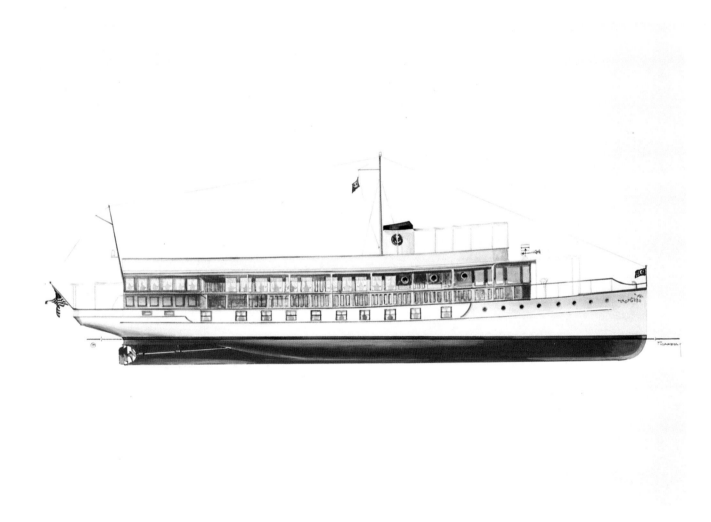

104' *Sequoia II*, Contract number 174, built in 1925 for Richard Cadwalader, Jr.

94' *Nicoya*, Contract number 189, built in 1927 for Fred B. Lovejoy

The 44' knockabout, centerboard schooner *Sea Call II*,
(1928, no contract number), built for John Trumpy.
44' x 30' x 11'6" x 3'6", 8.93 tons, 725 sq. ft. of sail.

110' *Maemere*, Contract number 199, built in 1929 for Dewitt Page

120' **Truant**, Contract number 207, built in 1930 for Truman Newberry

85' *Innisfail*, Contract number 228, built in 1935 for Joseph M. Cudahy

90' *Consort IV*, Contract number 230, built in 1936 for T. Monroe Dobbins

90' *Innisfail*, Contract number 242, built in 1939 for J. M. Cudahy

70ft Trumpy

MARY ANN

Commissioned 1941

76' *Drifter*, Contract number 244, built in 1939 for Frank O. Sherrill

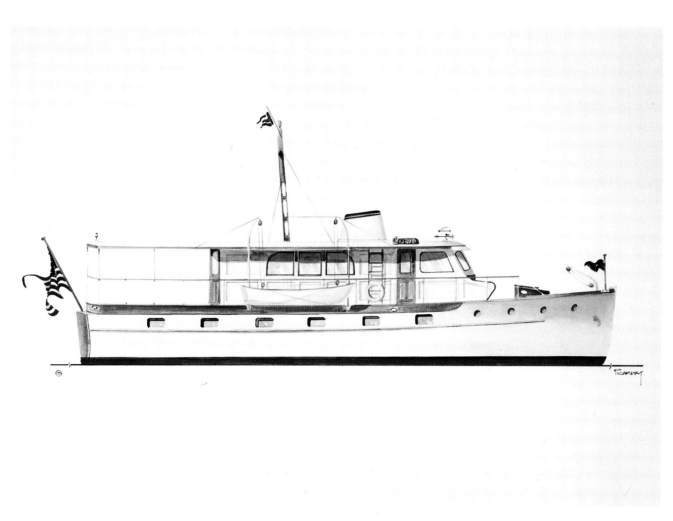

55' *Aurora*, Contract number 314, built in 1945 (Pilot model), built for John Trumpy

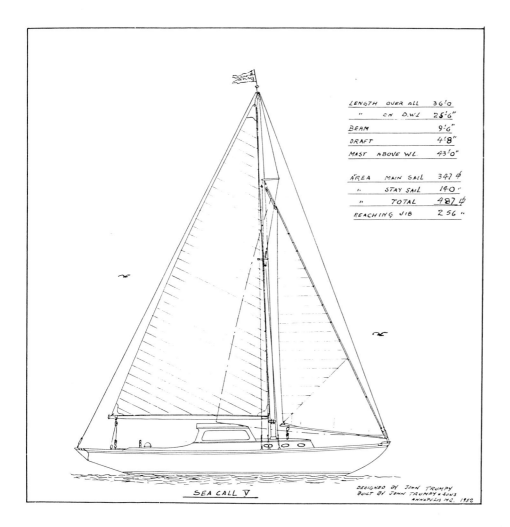

LENGTH	OVER ALL	36'0
"	ON D.W.L.	25'6"
BEAM		9'6"
DRAFT		4'8"
MAST	ABOVE W.L.	43'0"
AREA	MAIN SAIL	347 ⌀
"	STAY SAIL	140 "
"	TOTAL	487 ⌀
REACHING JIB		256 "

SEA CALL V

DESIGNED BY JOHN TRUMPY
BUILT BY JOHN TRUMPY & SONS
ANNAPOLIS MD. 1952

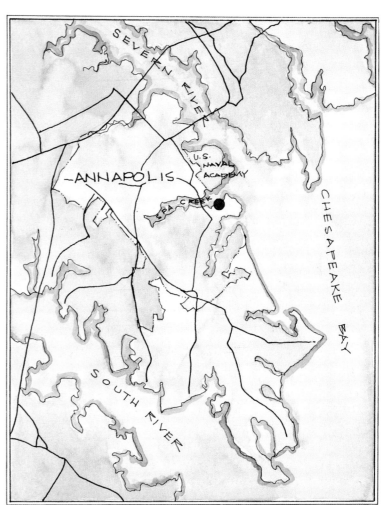

Trumpy Yard in Annapolis, MD

80' *Sea Play*, Contract number 328, built in 1947 for Diesel Towing Co.

57' *MSB-5* Minesweeper Contract number 345, built in 1951 for the U. S. Navy

53' *Jinofor II*, Contract number 367, built in 1954 for Edward H. Ellis

79' *Rumax III*, Contract number 372, built in 1955 for Wm. McKelvy

71'5" *Aurora*, Contract number 380, built in 1958 for John Trumpy

67'6" *Tonda*, Contract number 394, built in 1960 for Howell van Gerbig

83' *Eskimo*, Contract number 400, built in 1961 for John Kimberly

75' *Polaris*, Contract number 415, built in 1964 for Ben Tobin

75' *Jimiana*, Contract number 420, built in 1965 for James L. Knight

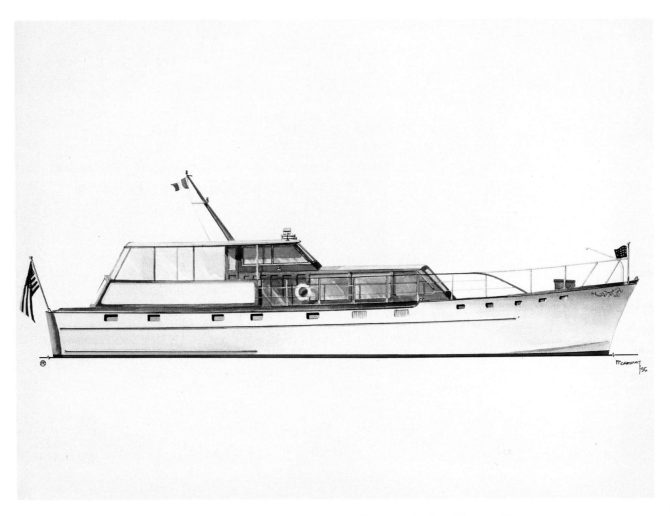

67' *Georgejan*, Contract number 421, built in 1965 for George Wasserman

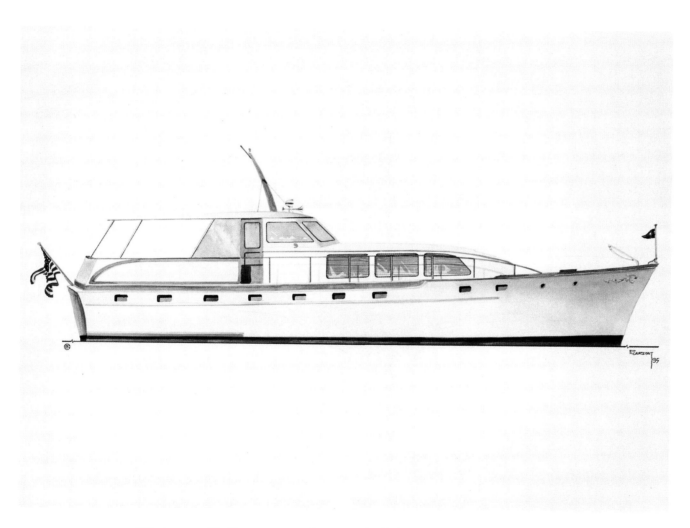

58' *Aurora V*, Contract number 444, built in 1971 for John Trumpy

60' *Sirius*, Contract number 448, built in 1972 for Henry C. Gibson

Chapter 12
LAST HURRAHS

When the founder of John Trumpy & Sons died, he held 759 shares of company stock. Son John Jr. had 771 for a Trumpy total of 1530 of the outstanding 1663 shares. Next most important shareholders were Lyle W. Gaither with 60 and C. E. Hires with 40.

Annual compensation of the officers in 1963 was $14,000 and $24,000 for chairman of the board John Trumpy, Sr., and president-treasurer John Trumpy, Jr.; vice president in charge of production Gaither $14,000; vice president-secretary Hires, $11,950; and assistant treasurer William F. S. Hastie, $9,000.

The same salaries were paid in 1964 with end of the year bonuses of $2,500 to John Trumpy, Jr., $2,000 to Gaither, $1,300 to Hires and $1,000 each to Hastie, designer Fred Geiger, and shop superintendent Edward Roberts. Another nine shop foremen received $750 each, two received $500 and one $250. Similar bonuses were paid in subsequent years.

A special meeting of stockholders was called in September, 1965, to elect John R. Kimberly as a director. His brother, James, had been a director since 1959 and John had bought three Trumpys over the years. He had also bought 500 shares of the company from the estate of John Trumpy, Sr.

The presence of such corporate heavyweights as the heirs to the giant Kimberly-Clark fortune was an important plus and John was named business and sales administrative assistant to the president at an annual salary of $5,000.

President Trumpy reported to the shareholders that "the business prospects for 1965 were very good," and he outlined plans to paint the main building and shed at a cost of four to five thousand dollars, and to put up a new $15,000 paint shop, large enough to accommodate boats from the Syncrolift. A final extraordinary expense was the conversion of the heating system from coal to oil for $4,500, a sum that would easily be saved by eliminating the stokers who during winter months had to work around the clock.

Trumpy also briefed the board on a prototype yacht under consideration. She was a 54-footer that could be built for an estimated $88,157, including carpeting, basic furniture and a power pack of Cummins or General Motors diesels. He speculated that the selling price could be in the neighborhood of $125,000, but gave no figures on the amount of money received from the U.S. Navy for repair work done on the fleet of three presidential yachts, including *Sequoia*.

Company representatives made no effort to publicize that kind of work, to confirm or deny that the boats were pulled into the wet shed. Similar discretion was shown each time the Trumpy-built *Sequoia* was in the yard or the *Williamsburg*, but it was not too difficult for the press to catch a glimpse of these boats, especially the *Williamsburg* with her length of 244 feet and beam of 36.

President Eisenhower spurned that biggest of all Presidential yachts as "too rich for my blood," but in the fall of 1954, the Navy did commission Trumpy to perform extensive renovation and restoration on a more modest cruiser, a 92-footer built in 1931 as the *Lenore*, requisitioned during World War II to serve as Navy patrol ship off Long Island, and put in the presidential fleet in 1945. Truman named her *Lenore II* but he preferred the *Williamsburg*.

Eisenhower changed the name to *Barbara Anne* in honor of his granddaughter. She was intended to be a day cruiser only, the White House quickly assured the press, but it would not confirm the cost of Trumpy's conversion. The press reported that "estimates by outside sources placed it in the neighborhood of $300,000." That was probably a considerable exaggeration, because when the Kennedy Administration put her in for maintenance and repair seven years later—after changing the name to *Honey Fitz*—the bill was between $20,000 and $25,000. (Nixon renamed her *Patricia* but, preferring the *Sequoia*, put the vessel up for auction in 1970.)

That was about ten percent of what it cost the company in 1965 to produce one of the trio of 75-foot houseboats, modeled on the mold of Jack Meyerhoff's *Beatrice* from 1959.

The first was the *Polaris* for Ben Tobin, a prominent Miami developer and philanthropist whose many projects included the landmark Hollywood Beach Hotel. The yard cost of construction of his yacht was $187,376 of which $105,510 was for labor.

The second, *Jimiana*, was for James L. Knight with a yard cost of $206,216 of which $112,930 was labor, and the third, *Rebel II*, for Mary Perry Alexander who took delivery two years later than the others, at a time when the company costs were $229,711 with labor's share $121,284.

Knight was part of the Ohio newspaper family which bought control of the *Miami Herald* in 1937 and founded the Knight-Ridder organization, a mass market media company. It and its predecessor companies also owned *Florida Shipper* and *Gulf Shipper* as well as the New York-based *Journal of Commerce*, a trade publication covering shipping and world trade developments.

Jimiana and the other 75-foot cruisers were 18'3" in the beam and drew 4'6" The power pack consisted of two GM 12V-71N diesels driving Colombian propellers through Monel shafts. At 2100 rpm the cruising speed was 17 knots with a top speed of 19.7 knots.

The 75-footers were as solidly and gracefully built as all the other Trumpys, with double planked mahogany over white oak keel and frames, fastened throughout with Everdur. Deckhouse trim and the main deck were teak. The boat deck was fiberglass covered adding additional strength and easing maintenance.

Accommodations were generously laid out with three double staterooms, each with head and shower and quarters for a crew of three—a separate stateroom for the captain and a forecastle for the crew. The deckhouse was 19'4" long and the lounge deck abaft 15 feet. Knight's *Jimiana* was fully equipped, to say the least. In addition to the Cruisair reverse cycle unit which provided complete temperature control, she had, in the words of the Trumpy technicians, a good deal more modern gear:

"*Jimiana* is an all-electric ship with a main power supply of two 14-kilowatt alternating current Mercedes diesel generators. Her galley range, refrigerator and deep freeze units are standard units built by Frigidaire. She is fully found, and among her other equipment are an Ideal windlass, a Sendure hot water heater, Burke water pressure system, an automatic Kidde fire extinguisher system, a Penguin bar refrigerator, Danforth anchors, Buell air horns, Panish engine controls, Exide batteries, Konel radio-telephone, Sperry automatic pilot, Decca radar, Digit depth sounder, Loran navigator, Bogen intercom system, and a Constavolt rectifier."

All state-of-the-art stuff installed masterfully and compactly so as not to interfere with the smooth functioning of the boat and providing maximum comfort in a yacht houseboat with elegant, classic lines, a grand achievement by designer Fred Geiger and the craftsmen of Trumpy & Sons. As president Trumpy stated in a Christmas 1965 company newsletter to friends, fans, actual and would-be Trumpy owners, "Every plank laid, every fastening driven, every joint made, is fashioned not only to last, but to last in the face of some of the most powerful forces in nature."

John Trumpy, Jr., was presenting his reaction to "an element that seems to have become part and parcel of modern living . . . the thing generally known as 'built-in obsolescence,' which, in the last few decades, has become recognizable to even the most untutored among us."

"To us," declared Trumpy, "the whole idea is utter nonsense and it is the one skill that we have absolutely no interest in. There certainly is no place for it at sea under any circumstances, and it will be a cold day, indeed, when it crops up there. At any rate, you can be

assured that it will not crop up in our Yard . . . we are as proud of those old Trumpys still afloat on the waterways as we are of the *Jimiana*, one of the most recent off our ways."

Jimiana was launched in August and three months later the traditional bottle of champagne was broken on the prow of a 48-foot cruiser *Megaera*, built for a former commodore of the New York Yacht Club, Henry Sears.

A pair of 67-foot cruisers, *Georgejan* and *Odyssey*, slid down the ways shortly after, built for George Wasserman and Wallace Whittaker. Then there was the sleek and speedy 70-foot *Minnow* for Phillip Miller who spent close to a quarter million for the privilege and pleasure of having one of the most beautifully designed boats ever to glide off the drawing boards of Fred Geiger. No matter that she was so narrow in the beam that staterooms and deckhouses were far too restrictive in size. Other Trumpy captains said "it ran like a scared rabbit," and the company control sheet showed she had required no fewer than 875 hours of drafting time—at a cost of $3,448. The total company cost was $198,231, of which labor accounted for well over half, $109,452.

Trumpy's February, 1966, progress report to the directors was on board the 53-foot Trumpy cruiser *Dee Dee*, docked at the Palm Club in Miami. The boat had been built in 1959 for Dwight P. Allen as *Fin V*, then sold to William B. Griscom, Jr., when Allen ordered a 60-foot *Fin V* in 1966.

But Allen was a mite slow in paying for his new boat and at a meeting of the directors in November, 1966, the board was informed of the delinquent account. It was particularly distressing at a time of tight money when the corporation had to borrow funds at a high rate of interest. The directors voted that "aggressive action" be initiated immediately and that "strong action be taken to collect from other regular customers who have failed to make payment of repair bills on a current basis."

Another important item on the agenda concerned negotiations with the U.S. Navy. Trumpy was empowered by the board to enter into a new contract, one which he expected would be signed within the next few weeks. But first, Trumpy informed the board, a "concentrated effort" would have to be made to finish the three new yachts currently under construction as early as possible in 1967.

One of them was the 54-foot *Sea Dream VII* for John M. Rutherfurd replacing his 60-foot houseboat *Sea Dream VI* built two years earlier. Another was the 64-foot cruiser for John P. Blair, named *Admiral Blake*, and the third was Mary Perry

Alexander's 75-foot houseboat *Rebel II*.

As soon as the naval contract was signed and the slips cleared, John Trumpy & Sons took on its final government assignments, its last challenges from the Bureau of Ships.

The first was the design and construction of some kind of mini-sub. Overseeing production, which was confined to a hidden corner of the Trumpy yards in an effort at concealment, were a pair of trench-coated, hush-hush types whose dress and demeanor called a good deal of attention to their presence and caused questions to be raised about their special project. The boat was semi-submersible, apparently intended to transport frogmen who had to keep a very low profile in the water while moving from a mother ship to a point off an enemy coast—Korea, Vietnam, Russia, wherever—and then back again upon completion of the mission.

The second challenge was a response to the Navy's needs in Vietnam where riverine warfare demanded fast patrol boats. Trumpy was called upon to supply them and to coordinate the efforts in other yards producing similar vessels.

It was the company's last contract with the government and it was a remarkable one, demonstrating in its own way what goes around, comes around. John Trumpy & Sons found itself working with Norwegian boatbuilders on a new class of speedy motor patrol boat.

In 1957 the Norwegians had developed a desirable prototype, an 80-foot, wide beam, V-bottom, fast wooden torpedo boat with a rounded bottom forward and a hard chine aft to increase speed in rough water. The boat was powered by British Napier Deltic 18-cylinder engines producing a smooth-water sustained speed of 41 knots.

The Norwegian Navy ordered twenty and the manufacturer also produced two for the Turkish Navy and six for Greece, plus fourteen for the U.S. Navy. BuShips determined, after extensive study and tests, that the boat, named *Nasty* by the Norwegians, was better than any other being built in European yards. But the Buy American Act posed barriers to the purchase of foreign-made vessels, so the Navy again began to consider the experimental PT 811 Trumpy had constructed along with PT 810 and PT 812 from other yards as model for the new class of fast patrol boats.

The Defense Department did arrange for a partial subsidy for Norwegian production of *Nasty*s and had rights under the contract for construction in the U.S., but the conversion from metric was seen as too great a delaying factor and it was finally decided that the boats would be bought directly from Norway. There was no ready alternative and attack boats were urgently needed in Vietnam.

The Secretary of Defense also wanted eight *Nasty*s for duty off Cuba but Congress balked at increasing the number of foreign purchases. A successful side-step was arranged by having the Norwegian yards ship keels and frames directly to Trumpy for *Nasty*s to be assembled and finished at the Annapolis yard.

Trumpy could not have built the ships from scratch in any event; its laminating gear could not handle anything as big as the 25-foot beam of the *Nasty*. Yards that had larger laminators did not want to take on the project. So the Norwegians sent over six keels and six sets of frames on a freighter which unloaded at Baltimore. From there they were taken, two at a time, by barge directly to Annapolis where they

werc immediately off-loaded by crane and set on the rigs where Trumpy workmen swarmed all over them assembling and constructing.

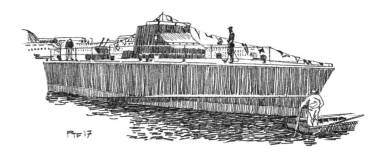

PTF 17, 1967

The company was concerned about the law that specified no foreign material could be used in Navy vessels, so they wanted to finish the boats as quickly as possible. The first, PTF 17, was launched November 17, 1967. Construction was on schedule, Trumpy was pleased to report to the board a month later, adding that the launching cradle had been repaired and reinforced to accommodate the new boats and that he was considering replacement of the "big railway" with a 150 ton Syncrolift.

By July, 1968, the first two patrol boats were completed and were berthed across the water at the Navy dock at North Severn awaiting a tow to Baltimore where they would be hoisted aboard a ship, placed in specially constructed cradles and transported to Vietnam. The trial run on the third boat was held in mid-July.

Progress on the patrol boats was discussed in detail at the

July 9, 1968, board meeting, one in which a new director was named to replace Frank W. Wrightson who died the previous year. He was J. Pierre Barnard, chairman of the board of Annapolis Banking & Trust Company. Three years later, the fifth generation of Trumpys were brought onto the board: Johan, who was then a special assistant to his father, the president; and Donald, in charge of the maintenance and repair facilities just as his father had been. Designer Fred Geiger was also put on the board.

In 1968 the board approved annual salaries of $35,000 for president Trumpy; $17,000 for vice-president Gaither; and $13,000 each for vice-president, Hires in charge of purchasing, and secretary-assistant treasurer Hastie. Bonuses totalling $29,450 were approved for eight of the administrative staff, including officers, and ten shop foremen.

Also in 1968 the board approved the plans for production of a 58-foot diesel cruiser as a stock boat with a basic price and a list of suggested extras to be determined by the purchaser. Construction was to start as soon as the patrol boats were completed. In a November board meeting that year, it was reported that trial runs on the fifth boat would take place by the end of the month. Both the fifth and sixth boats were to be delivered to the Navy in February, 1969.

In keeping with company precedent, the new 58-foot cruiser was christened *Aurora V*. From 1969 to 1971 the yard built a half dozen of them just as they had planned. Fifty-eight feet long with a beam of 15'3" and draft of 3'9", a standard stock hull and layout, with appointments, equipment and power all custom designed for the individual yachtsmen. Leonard Butscher called his *Peaches*, Gilbert Verney named his *Katuna*

V, C. W. Schooley renamed *Aurora V* the *Vega*, F. Eugene Dixon took over *Target* after the original client, Ferdinand Eberstadt, died; and Gerrish H. Milliken, Jr., who did the same when Monroe Dreher died before his cruiser, *Spindle*, could be built. A second *Aurora V*, was launched two years after the first had been bought by Schooley.

Powered by a pair of Cummins VT8N 370M diesels, the new boats could reach a speed of 21.3 knots at 3000 rpm and cruised at 19.2 knots with a throttle setting of 2700 rpm. Tankage provided for 550 gallons of fuel and 250 of water. In the words of the attractive flyer circulated by the company:

"*Aurora V* is fitted with the latest in marine equipment, including Bendix Auto-Pilot, Danforth-White compass, Onan diesel generator, Konel Radio Telephone, Ideal electric windlass, and Raritan marine heads. In addition a U-Line ice maker and Cruise-Air air conditioning have been installed to add a touch of cool luxury to below-decks living."

Writing in the *Aurora V* flyer, Trumpy reminded potential buyers that "We are not mass producers nor interested in production lines. We supply the kind of quality a discriminating yachtsman wants and will be proud to own without having to consider the cost." He did not hesitate—and he was seldom contradicted—to point out that Trumpy & Sons was building "custom yachts admired the world over for their elegance and seakindliness.

"From the distinctive scroll on the bow, to the luxurious interior appointments, every detail of construction is carefully supervised to deliver a truly custom yacht. In the cluster of sheds that form Trumpy, every component is built by hand including the furniture that is individually made for each yacht."

Trumpy believed that the boats sold themselves, provided the buyer had the wherewithal to finance such a purchase, and he used the reputation of the company and his father when making his own rounds to sell boats, and in circulating among the Trumpy captains and crews he invited to an annual party at the yard. It was a time when they could swap sea stories and talk shop, while being reminded of the superb repair facilities and shown the newest boats being built.

Trumpy was apparently a natural born salesman and he used his skills to full advantage when calling on customers, be they in Wilmington, Washington, Miami-Palm Beach or Rochester, New York.

Rochester is where Fred H. Gordon lived and he and his wife were very interested in buying a Trumpy—a new Trumpy—to replace their 23-year-old *Sinbad* which they had purchased in 1964. She was one of John Trumpy's postwar 55-footers, built originally as *One Forty Four II*. They discussed new boats, and old John Trumpy, Jr., when he personally visited them and signed the contract, listening no doubt to Fred Gordon's stories of his experiences as a young boy aboard the first Trumpy he had known, the 1912 *Ibis*. More than half a century earlier, before World War II, he had sailed with her all the way to Florida, taken there by his father and his father's friend, who owned the boat.

The Gordons signed up for a 63-foot cruiser they called *Sinbad*. She was on the slips the same time as a 62-foot houseboat ordered by Bayard Sharp. Trumpy didn't have to go far to sell that multi-interest businessman.

Sharp's office was in Wilmington but he had thoroughbred farms in the surrounding countryside and lived the life of a country baron. That is, when he was not running things at his rambling Florida fishing escape, Gasparilla Inn in Boca Grande — tarpon fishing capital of the country and a place for laid back wealth to relax and for the socially prominent to stop being so prominent.

Built, typically, of double planked mahogany on oak frames, Sharp's Trumpy was named *Galpo*, a 62-foot houseboat with a 16-foot beam, draft of 4'2", and double diesels producing a top speed of 23 knots. She could accommodate four of the owner's party and a two-man crew, with master and guest staterooms and a winding staircase leading up from the centerline hall to a spacious salon on the main deck. Double doors led to the large afterdeck area where there was a wet bar, and a swinging door from the salon led to the fully equipped galley. There were full walk around decks on both sides of the salon leading to the foredeck.

Galpo looked so much at home, so proper docked at Sharp's superb Gasparilla Inn, a memory bank built in 1912. When a Florida broker was offering her for sale in the 1980s, he was quick to point out that "She is a delightful combination of traditional elegance and modern technology . . . a one owner yacht, maintained by a most knowledgeable captain and the most knowledgeable 'open pocket book' owner."

Trumpy also continued his sales promotion calls to Florida marinas and yacht clubs. In late 1969, he authorized Wade Levering to set up an office in Palm Beach, at 271 South County Road, to act as the corporation's representative for contacting customers ordering new boats, selling used boats and arranging charters—on a commission basis.

Trumpy's 1970 trip to Florida was a disappointment. As he told the board, "Several prospects for the building of new boats had diminished due to the uncertainty of the stock market." As Trumpy had learned through the years the slightest swells in the economy hit the boat market like a tidal wave. To counter such a downturn, he was actively pursuing the alternative of another contract with the Navy to build four more patrol boats. His efforts were intensified when he was informed that Braith Davis's contract to build a new yacht had to be delayed. The reason? The decline and the uncertainty of the stock market. At the annual meeting in April, 1970, the salaries were reduced, the president by $5,000, and each of the others by comparable amounts relative to their pay levels.

Lyle Gaither and C. E. Hires retired that year, and they were not replaced. Fred Geiger took over as the single company vice-president and William F. S. Hastie combined the offices of secretary and treasurer.

1971 was the year of disaster and decision for the company. The independent union, the only one in any area yard, which had been formed by the 73 workers the end of 1969, struck the company at the busiest time of the year, walking out and picketing from March 19 until the signing of a new contract on May 17. But, Trumpy complained to the board at its December meeting, "The bulk of the men, however, did not return to work until Monday, May 24."

The strike, he complained, probably with a fair portion of bitterness, had adversely affected the repair and shop sales; but equally important, many qualified personnel never returned to work. In addition, shop plant superintendent Edward Roberts and Charles Atwell, foreman in charge of new construction, resigned.

Also delayed were two houseboats under construction, the 68-foot *Little Sissie* for automobile dealer John W. Koons, Sr., and the 72-foot *Gerifay* for Earle Cantor.

The positive news in 1971 was the promotion of Donald Trumpy to be plant superintendent and Johan Trumpy to be assistant to his father. Both were made directors along with Fred Geiger.

The other promising developments concerned the approaches by Trojan Boat Company and Hargrave Boat Company, the first with a proposal that Trumpy & Sons complete construction of 68-foot hulls it would provide, the second involving completion of fiberglass hulls shipped to the yard. Both proposals were set aside as the directors agreed that neither alternative could be implemented if sufficient orders for Trumpy boats were received.

The company was at a crossroads with labor costs causing as much of a dilemma as the shortage of skilled workers capable of building custom-made wooden boats. As early as 1965, president Trumpy was concerned about "our craftsmen—a dying breed, to be sure," and later commented to the press that there simply were not enough old-fashioned, dedicated craftsmen left to do the job right. When building the last boats, "there were so many mistakes made, so much that had to be done over." "We just had a devil of a time maintaining quality," he confessed to the *New York Times* which characterized Trumpys as "the Rolls-Royce of American motor yachts."

It was certainly no secret in Annapolis that there were few apprentices coming along who were eager to spend the four years necessary to become a shipwright. They could forego all that and short-cut their way to twice or three times as much money by becoming a "wood-butcher," a carpenter, on one of the many construction projects underway in town. Plumbers, fitters, welders, electricians could also find higher wages outside. Not in another shipyard—Trumpy was paying the best and considered to be the best—but in outside industries.

As labor costs mounted at the yard, the availability of skilled labor—native-born and immigrant—declined. In the glory days, labor accounted for less than a third of the total yard cost of construction; after World War II and into the 1960s and 1970s it was well over half and steadily rising.

But there were other important factors at work, which had driven wooden boatbuilders earlier into the disappearing mists—Lawley and Luders, Consolidated, New York Launch and Engine, Jacobs, Nevins and Herreshoff.

Fiberglass, speeded-up serial production and lower labor costs answered the new boating public's demand as America's waterways began to swarm with flotillas of vessels that were vastly different from the laboriously assembled yachts of the rich and well-born.

Synthetics and thermoplastics were not for Trumpy, however. Nor was aluminum, despite the fact that they had mastered the art far better than most when building the PT 811 patrol boat

The Trumpys had started as wooden boatbuilders and they would finish as wooden boatbuilders. And they would finish in style, even if it took constant supervision during construction. As Trumpy explained to the *New York Times* when discussing work standards since the 1960s, "you have to watch, watch, watch or the boat would sink when you let it off the railway."

Earle Cantor's 72-foot houseboat, *Gerifay*, was one of the last built and she was followed by C. Porter Schutt's sea-going sailboat, the 62-foot *Egret*.

The last hurrah, the testament that ended a century and a half of Trumpy tradition, was a 60-foot cruiser built for Henry C. Gibson who took possession in March, 1973. She was his third Trumpy, following those ordered in 1962 and 1964. The first was named *Aries*, the second and third *Sirius*.

It was a felicitous, an historic name, inspired by heaven above: *Sirius* is one of the closest stars to earth, a brilliantly twinkling gem of blue-white brilliance. That was the name of the 1788 flagship of a fleet of eleven ships that sailed into Sydney harbor carrying some 700 convicts to start the settlement of Australia; and it was the name of the ship which 50 years later set a trans-Atlantic crossing record of 18 days, 10 hours, beating the record of the *Great Western* by a full day. *Sirius* was also the name of one of the last boats built at the Trumpy Bradbenken yard in Bergen.

Gibson's last Trumpy set no records and established no precedents, cruising against the tidal waves of fiberglass promoters trumpeting the terrors of *Teredo navalis*, the *mollusk terredo, Limnoria lignorum*, and the crustacean gribble, the infamous worldwide wooden boat borers which thrived in warm waters.

Worms and wood-borers were nothing new to Trumpy whose predecessors had been careening ships for Bergen bottom repairs since the early nineteenth century. What was new to the company were the economic sea changes, with new money replacing the old and recreational boaters bobbing up and down racing plastic clones that resembled the cars they used to tow them to the ramps. Houseboats once again began to resemble boxcars on scows, or rather RVs on rafts, as yachtsmen were replaced by boaters.

The death knell was sounded at the October 18, 1972, meeting of the board of directors. John Trumpy, Jr., reported that "it was increasingly difficult to produce quality yachts for the following reasons:

"(a) Lack of skilled workers. This condition, to a certain extent, can be traced back to the strike of eight weeks duration in the Spring of 1971. Many of our good workers left then and have not returned.

"(b) Our commodity is in demand. A $380,000 contract was turned down for Mr. Aborn last week because we do not have the skilled craftsmen to produce the quality product for which the Trumpy name is renowned.

"(c) If new work is eliminated the yard is too big for repair work alone."

After "considerable discussion," in the words of the minutes, "The Board appoints John Trumpy, Jr., and John R. Kimberly, the major stockholders, as a committee of two, to investigate the possibility of sale and liquidation of the corporation and to report back to the Board at the earliest date possible."

The pair then proceeded to meet with accountants, tax consultants, lawyers and eventually a real estate developer interested in constructing a $10.5 million, 156 unit condominium, similar to the high-rise condos flanking the yard and the six-story Hilton 200 yards across Spa Creek. Ironically, the developer was a subsidiary of American Cyanamide, a New Jersey-based conglomerate producing plastics and synthetic fibers.

The Annapolis City Council balked, turning down the request five to four and refusing to change the zoning. Opponents protested the over-development and strains on utilities; proponents took the man's home is his castle approach, eliciting considerable press support.

The last meeting of the board, the only meeting in 1973, was on December 20 when it was decided to close down the yard the following day. President Trumpy was allowed to buy the corporate title of John Trumpy & Sons, Inc., for the sum of one dollar.

The final paragraph of the final report of the final board meeting was cryptically recorded by secretary Hastie:

"It was mentioned by one of the directors that this was a sad meeting for a renowned concern with such a good reputation, come to an end. The main reason for closing was the lack of skilled personnel not for the lack of orders. Young people were not coming into the organization to learn the skill and art of boatbuilding."

An auctioneer was brought in and tags were put on everything from anvils and cranes to clamps and grinders, dies, routers, filing cabinets and office furnishings, forges, chains, 50,000 brass and bronze bolts. As the *New York Times* reported, "all that was not sold here was the smell of sawdust, varnish and tidewater, and the cries of gulls."

The *Annapolis Evening Capital* called the bidders and buyers "harpies," dramatically citing the famous poem of Oliver Wendell Holmes' protesting the proposed scrapping and pleading for the cause of the Constitution, declaring it would be better she be cast adrift to the "God of storms" than be abandoned so the "harpies of the shore shall pluck the eagle of the sea."

The paper's reporter described the plucking:

"So the harpies had their day. Big sweaty men hauling boxes and machines to waiting vehicles of as many kinds as there were items (10 typewritten pages) for sale as fast as they could get them into handcarts, and little sweaty men in straw hats waving pads: 'How much've yer got? D'yer have a bill? I got ter ask for bills.'"

The paper also cited a July 3 letter from the Navy Department expressing to John Trumpy & Sons "a profound sense of loss and regret . . . Your reputation and performance in the industry will not easily be surpassed, if ever . . .

"It had been a well-earned reputation, gleaned from the famous old wooden subchasers of the Great War, 110-foot armed corks that rolled

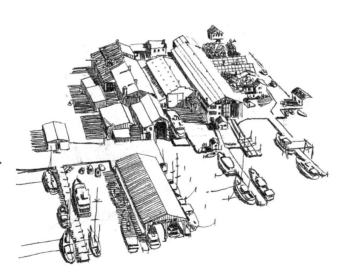

like scalded cats and were crewed by jackass officers and riffraff—S.C. 1-x-4 had a cook whose only qualification was peddling lemonade in a circus, and a skipper who was a professor of Arabic—but Trumpy's 'matchstick Navy' made it en masse under its own power across the North Atlantic with a foot of ice on deck in the worst winter in 75 years, and stopped the Kaiser's U-boat stranglehold dead. Statistic: from the moment of arrival until the Armistice not one Allied merchantman was lost where they patrolled. Trumpy had produced eagles."

Other newspapers marked and mourned the sliding of John Trumpy & Sons into history but none said it better than the *Baltimore Sun* in its lead editorial on Sunday, October 14, 1973:

Master Builders

Along Spa Creek in Annapolis, the John H. Trumpy & Sons Boatyard became an international symbol of quality craftsmanship. Trumpy's yawls, ketches and sloops sail the harshest waters, and their majestic goldleaf scroll is easily identified in the far-flung harbors of the globe. The firm's hallmark was pride, rubbed into the smallest fitting, built into the sleekest bow. Serious yachtsmen, as well as wealthy weekend sailors, reflect that pride when under full sail or power of one of Trumpy's custom-builts.

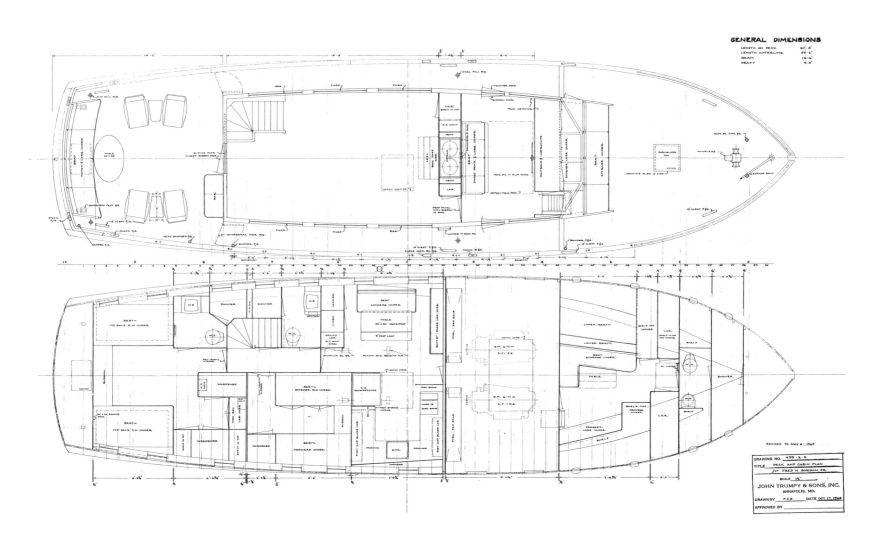

Deck and Cabin Plan drawing for the 63'5" x 59'2" x 16'6" x 4'0"
Houseboat **Sinbad***, Contract number 439, built in 1970 for Fred H. Gordon, Jr.*

EPILOGUE

The last words of the Baltimore Sun editorial obituary proved to be prophetic. "Though the craft may end, the product is certain to last a long time to come."

John Trumpy knew that and he always declared that a wooden boat, properly built and properly maintained, would outlast all others. The first yacht that came off his boards and out of the Mathis yard proved his point. He was proud to explain to the press on the occasion of his 75th birthday that he had seen his 1909 *Caliph* in Miami in 1951, "still in commission — the first of 366 boats we've built." *Caliph* was still around in the 1970s.

As long as yachtsmen and patrons of the arts continue to define the word "classic" to fulfill their dreams on the water; as long as there are those who want to own historic memories and possess pedigree standards of excellence, enduring year after year, there will be Trumpys around.

Ninety-one standards of Trumpy excellence survive today. The veteran is the 1912 *Ibis*, one of the show-stoppers at the Classic Boat Rendezvous during the 1995 Fort Lauderdale Spring Boat Show. It's at the Chapman School of Seamanship in Stuart, Florida, looking for a new owner, someone who can come up with $150,000.

Alongside the *Ibis* at the show was another Trumpy triumph, a 1963 cruiser named *Principia*. The 68 footer was originally built for Roger Firestone as *Tireless* and has a current price tag of $449,000.

Other Trumpys are for sale in other marinas and by other brokers, some of whom have probably turned them over several times---to owners who have the time, treasure and talent to lavish massive doses of TLC. As the full-time crew member of June Watkins McNelis' *Patience II*, built for James Knight as the 1965 *Jimiana*, put it: "working on great Trumpys is real job security." McNelis bought her Trumpy in 1988, inspired and encouraged by her uncle who had his own Trumpy, the *Hummingbird*, built in 1971 as *Little Sissie*.

There are always going to be rescues and restorations, such as that currently being worked on the third to last boat built by the company, the *Gerifay*, launched in 1972 for a successful New Jersey developer, Earle Cantor. Fort Lauderdale classicist Carolyn Weaver saved that lovely 72 foot houseboat from further abuse in May, 1995, and immediately launched an extensive one-year program mid-wiving the lady to rebirth.

"I now have 132 feet of Trumpy," she proudly announced when she added the houseboat to her 60 foot cruiser, *Sirius*, built in 1964 and maintained in absolutely impeccable condition by its devoted owner.

She had bought *Sirius* from South Florida automobile super-salesman Roger Dean, who called it *Petite Ruth*, the same name he had given to his other Trumpy, the 1966 *Minnow* and 1967 *Rebel II*, purchased in '77 and '81.

John Kimberly's 85 foot *Eskimo* from 1961 sailed to several docks before Edward Bronstien got hold of it and worked the miracle of full scale renovation. An expensive process of course, but Bronstien has his own shipyard, Spencer Boat Company in West Palm Beach. Recognizing that "The days of elegant wood-built boats are gone" and that "Those skilled craftsmen are extremely rare," he used to great advantage the few qualified woodworkers on his payroll, producing in the process the beautifully reborn *Dreamboat*. Since the end of 1991, George Horne has been at the tiller and he renamed it *Olde Guarde*.

The 1954 *Aurora IV* was beautifully restored to its original mint condition in 1990 after going through several owners, including Colonel and Lizz Whitney Tippett of Llangollen Farms, with a plantation home reportedly used as Tara in "Gone With The Wind." They called it *Adventurer* and it was the ultimate party boat, cruising to the races in Saratoga and to Newport for the season, entertaining the Rockefellers, Jack Lemmon, Charleton Heston, Elizabeth Taylor and Fred Astaire, who gifted them with a small piano for their salon decorated in fuschia and purple, the racing colors of their thoroughbreds.

Another Trumpy, the 1947 80 foot *Marylinn*, became a California party boat, renamed the *Mauretania* and chartered for weddings, receptions, business meetings and floating set for movie crews. The owners let it be known their pride and joy was a "close cousin" of the *Sequoia*.

That claim was considerably more modest than the one made by the new owners of the 60 foot *Nahmeoka* built for Harty Baruch in 1921. The William Claypools of New Orleans purchased the yacht, then known as *Vizcaya* and docked in the Bahamas' Paradise Island, in 1989 and immediately took her up the Tennessee-Tombigbee Waterway to Stillwater, Minnesota---informing the press en route that Baruch's old boat was a "sister ship to the former presidential yacht *Sequoia*."

No such extravagant claims of kinship were made for another sturdy survivor, the 61'6" *Abadab* built in 1938 and rescued from oblivion in Haiti by an Atlanta real estate developer, R. Hugh Daniel, Jr. In writing about her complete renovation at Fort Lauderdale's Pearson-Potter Yacht Basin in the 1970s, *Yachting* in its October 1974 issue described the makeover of the old *Abadab* into the new *Mariah* in detail---the transformation of the plumb stem into a clipper bow and the plumb stern into a canoe stern, adding some ten feet to the length. "The old hull was in astonishingly good condition . . . keel, longitudinal stringers, bilge clamps---all were sound . . . even the deckhouse framing, and the overhead carlins, were good as new."

Joseph Cudahy's 1939 *Innisfail*, taken over by the Navy to perform patrol duty (YP 354) in World War II, and known as *El Presidente* since 1973, had its configuration altered when, in order to pass Coast Guard inspection, it put in double bulk heads, adding a couple feet to the prow.

Minor changes were made to the Trumpys bought by Atwater Kent, Henry Mancini and Winthrop Aldrich who took over the 1960 *Claybeth*, re-naming it *Wayfarer*. When Jacksonville's mega-developer Peter Boss took it over, he named it for one of his most ambitious projects, *Sandestin*, on Florida's Panhandle.

When Trumpys are sold, the specification sheets from the broker usually give the reason why someone could possibly bear to part with a Trumpy. In the August, 1989 offering of the

Janal, a 67'6" cruiser built in 1963 as the **Blue Hen**, the remarks section states the following:

"*Janal* is an extraordinarily beautiful Trumpy Cruiser. Her graceful lines typify Fred Geiger's genius in design. Her present owner has maintained his boat beautifully during his 19 years of ownership. The captain of 18 years passed away recently and this is the primary reason for the boat being put on the market."

The comments for the **Lazy Tiger** that same year described the 1964 **Sea Dream IV** as "one of the most immaculately kept yachts available; literally 'like new.' No expense has been spared by the owner to put and keep her in top condition. She is a comfortable cruising house afloat."

When the 1958 **Aurora** was put on the market the following year as **Litchfield Lady**, the commentary was as enthusiastic as it was informative:

"**Litchfield Lady** is the only fantail Trumpy of her size ever built with a fantail stern and modern bow. She is one of the few fantail Trumpys of any size still afloat. Originally designed and constructed for John Trumpy's personal use, she has been authentically updated and lovingly cared for by her former and present owners. She represents the finest in craftsmanship of a bygone era and is an exceptional offering that must be seen to be appreciated!"

As Fort Lauderdale yachtsman Walter McCrory put it when turning over the 57 foot cruiser, Fairlee, originally the 1960 Wind IV, 'I will have another boat but I will never have a more beautiful boat or a better boat."

Truman Newberry and the subsequent owners of his 120 foot **Truant** of 1930, including Leon Mandel and Walter Chrysler who whet his appetite for another Trumpy a few years later,

might have expressed the same sentiments when they were at the wheel in their pilot house.

That pilot house was rescued from the remains of the **Truant**, then named **Manatee**, when it was broken up a few years ago at Jones Boat Yard in Miami. It was carefully restored by Nautical Furnishings, Inc. of Fort Lauderdale and no doubt will eventually find its way into one or another theme restaurant.

Just how appealing a Trumpy can be was demonstrated dramatically by none other than Howard Hughes. He saw a picture in a boating magazine of the 1939 **Martha**, a 71 foot houseboat, and ordered his staff to buy it immediately. 'To ship to California?" one boldly asked. 'No! Keep it in Florida but hire a captain and crew and make sure it's ready whenever I want to use it down there." Five years later, the **Vita** as he renamed her, was sold. He never saw the boat. It survives today — in perfect condition — as the **Barchrisda**.

One of Trumpy's many naval vessels faced a far different fate, in the Buffalo and Erie County Naval and Servicemen's Park along the river in Buffalo. Among the several land-locked vessels on permanent open-air display is patrol boat PTF 17.

A patrol boat or one of Trumpy's subchasers or minesweepers would be a grand addition to the site where the shipyard once stood---sitting proudly and providing a great sense of place across the water from the Naval Academy.

It could be anchored close to the old Trumpy wet shed, now housing the Chart House, a sensational case book study of adaptive restoration. The old marine rail lines are gone, but a portion of the cog wheel protrudes from the pavement and close by are the former Trumpy offices.

Flanking the old yards are condominium-marina

developments and boat dealers who have filled other sheds---Back Yard Boats and a fuel dock boasting it's the only one in town with 93 octane gasoline.

Across the street is Marmaduke's which took over a popular bar about the same time Trumpy & Sons went out of business. It used to be a refuge for the workers slugging a shot and beer over lunch and a hideaway for the designers and foremen taking a break from every-day demands. Today it's a great place for Sunday brunches with non-stop mimosas and Bloody Marys. On Wednesday nights the crowds come for videos of the weekend races. I like it for the etched glass portrait of Norwegian great Roald Amundsen, contemporary of John Trumpy, who in his way was every bit as extraordinary as the great explorer.

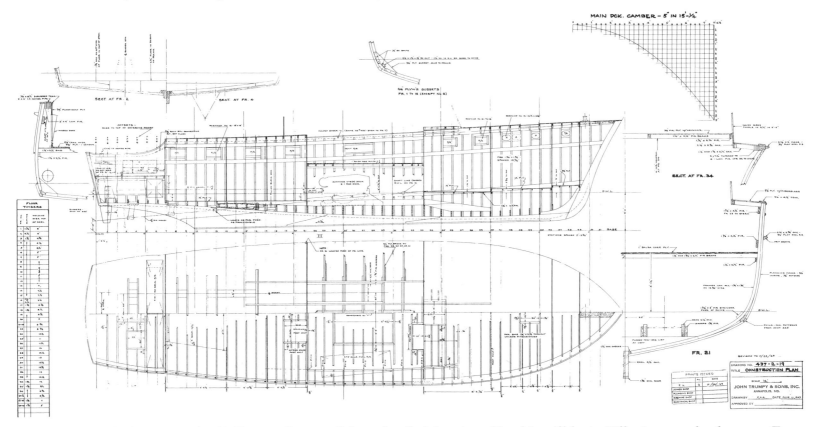

*58' **Target**, #437, built in 1970 for F. Eugene Dixon. (More detailed drawings like this will be in Tiller's second volume on Trumpy.)*

APPENDIX A
SHIPS BUILT AT BRADBENKEN 1837-1879

Date	Name	Type	Net Registered Tonnage	Date	Name	Type	Net Registered Tonnage
1837	*Preciosa*	Brig	156	1855	*Christopher Hansteen*	Brig	159
1838	*Eidsvold*	Schooner	123	1856	*ProfessorSchweigaard*	Bark	340
1838	*Den 11te April*	Schooner	110	1857	*Breidablik*	Schooner-brig	145
1839	*Johan Gerhard Ameln*	Bark	206	1858	*Rivalen*	Sloop	51
1840	*Peder Schr der*	Bark	220	1859	*Czar*	Schooner	127
1841	*Augusta*	Bark	231	1860	*Concurrent*	Sloop	62
1842	*Concurrent*	Schooner-brig	126	1859/61	*President Harbitz*	Bark	358
1842	*Newcastle Pacquet*	Schooner-brig	102	1861	*Herman Engen*	Schooner-brig	132
1846	*Avanse*	Schooner	90	1861/62	*Herman*	Sloop	71
1847	*Lofoten*	Brig	236	1862	*Activ*	Sloop	72
1848	*Sleipner*	Brig	181	1863	*Kong Carl*	Bark	434
1849	*Henrik Wergeland*	Brig	209	1864	*Eliezer*	Bark	292
1850	*Hans Holmbo*	Brig	157	1864	*Harald Haarfager*	Bark	499
1851	*Immanuel*	Bark	292	1866	*Ceres*	Bark	526
1853	*Olav Kyrre*	Brig	212	1867	*Dynaborg*	Schooner-brig	191
	Laura	Bark	327	1867	*Ludvig Holberg*	Bark	413
1854	*Amalia*	Schooner-brig	127	1868	*Valkyrien*	Bark	565
1855	*Dronning Victoria*	Bark	372	1869	*Prinsesse Louise*	Bark	422

Date	Name	Type	Net Registered Tonnage
1870	*Professor Schweigaard*	Bark	502
1871	*Kong Sverre*	Bark	541
1872	*Alpha*	Steam	272
1872	*Idr't*	Steam	172
1873	*Johan Irgens*	Bark	783

Date	Name	Type	Net Registered Tonnage
1873	*Zaritza*	Steam	314
1874	*Italia*	Schooner-brig	265
1874/75	*Professor Mohn*	Frigate	973
1876	*Sirius*	Schooner	371
1875	*Jacob Trumpy*	Frigate	921
1877/79	*Carl Konow*	Bark	491

*92' Houseboat **Riposo**, contract number 177, built in 1926 for Dr. H. B. Baruch.*

APPENDIX B
MATHIS/TRUMPY LIST OF BOATS
BUILT 1909–1972 WITH NAME AND OWNER CHANGES AS OF JUNE 1, 1995

Compiled by Captain Jerry Foster on the basis of company contract lists, Lloyd's Register of American Yachts, the records of Fort Lauderdale yacht broker John Dulany, Donald Trumpy of Annapolis and Carolyn Weaver of Fort Lauderdale; edited by Robert Tolf. Additions and corrections would be greatly appreciated and should be sent to Jerry Foster; Apartment 404, 100 Paradise Harbor Boulevard, North Palm Beach, FL 33408 and to Tiller Publishing, P. O. Box 447, St. Michaels, MD 21663. Phone (410) 745-3750, Fax (410) 745-9743.

Underlining of original boat names indicates that boat survives.

Contract Number	Year Built/ Documentation Number	In Lloyd's Register	Original & Subsequent Boat Names	Length	Original & Subsequent Owner(s)	Lloyd's Register Reference
1			*Caliph*	60'	Martin B. Brigham	(to19p63)
		(1923)	*Caliph*		Robert J. Luedemann	(41p90)
2	1910/207587		*Dielta*	94'4"	J. J. Riker	
		(1919)	*Kemah*		E. W. Scripps	(23p141)
			Kemah		Hiram W. Johnson, Jr.	(28p164to41)
3	1909/207413		*Ocoloqua*	65'	Andrew L. Riker	(to28p217)
			Ocoloqua		T. B. Davis, Jr.	(35p260)
		(1939)	*Ocoloqua*		William C. Bedell	(41p336)
			Ocoloqua		Edward L. Hatch	(47p322)
4	1910/208011		*Cocopomelo*	69'8"	William Disston	
			Cocopomelo		Benedict Crowell	(15p74)
			Cocopomelo		Arthur H. Marks	(19p73)
		(1923)	*Golden Days*		James Elverson, Jr.	(28p132)

Contract Number	Year Built/ Documentation Number	1st in Lloyd's	Original & Subsequent Boat Names	Length	Original & Subsequent Owner(s)	Lloyd's Register Reference
5	1910		*Gleam*	36'	Archer G. Riege	
6	1910		*Mascot*	36' (stock)	E. J. Mickley	
7	1910/208469		*Sybilla II*	82'6"	John F. Betz III	(to19p230)
			Sybilla II		Irving R. Raymond	(23p240)
		(1928)	*Typee*		Herman A. DeVry	(39p441)
8	1910		*Viola*	17'	Robert F. Welch	
9	1911		*Chelwood*	39'10"	Rufus King Lennig	(to41p102)
			Chelwood		M&M H. G. Henry	(47p97)
10	1911				William Cramp & Co.	
11	1911/209046		*Lodona*	77'	E. J. Greacen	
			Lodona		E. A. Richard	(19p147)
			Lodona		Frederick Wolstenholme	(23p151)
			Miss Gray Seas		W. E. Davis	(29p199)
12	1911		*Ednada III*	90'	George C. Thomas, Jr.	
			Zianetta	(89'7")	Charles Van Bergen	(15p270)
			Palmetto			
			Bolo		A. Felix duPont	(19p59)
	(1923/208897)		*Penguin*		Henry D. Whiton	(23p195)
			Ilah		Arthur F. Elliott	(28p148)
			Ilah		Clyde A. Coulter	(35p168)
		(1939)	*Charmer*		Charles Blount, Jr.	(79p89)
13	not used					
14	1911/209363		*Pauline*	57'6"	William Disston	
			Millie K	(50'0")		
			Esther D.		George F. Adams	(19p97)
			Osprey		Millard E. Swift	(23p189)
			Osprey		Clarence Hay	(28p221)
15	1911		*Lunaria*	70'	A. J. Quackenbush	
16	1911/209514		*Lanai*	70'	Arthur Curtiss James	
		(1919)	*Lanai*	(Len 7'6" 1918)	Mrs. A. C. James	(23p146)

Contract Number	Year Built/ Documentation Number	1st in Lloyd's	Original & Subsequent Boat Names	Length	Original & Subsequent Owner(s)	Lloyd's Register Reference
			Lanai	(75'6")	William M. Kingsley	(28p169)
			Argo		Powel Crosley, Jr.	(35p46)
			Argo		Eugene Jones & Richard C. Hill	(39p51)
			Argo		Eugene Jones	(41p53)
			Argo	(76')	Earnest L. Willis	(56p58)
	(Rebuilt 1936)	(1947)	*Argo*		William V. Cox	(60p61)
			Argo		Cdr. Gail H. Gilliam, U.S.N.	(73p38)
		(1962)	*Argo*		Jack W. Ross	(79p26)
		(1975)	*Argo*		At 79th St. Boat Basin, NYC, in 1996	
17	1911/210142		*Nahmeoka*	95'	H. N. Baruch	
			Hildebrat			
			Awa		A. De Witt Cochrane	(15p53)
			Kama			
			Kismet		Louis Kann	(19p139)
			Lady Grace		Frederick S. Fish	(23p145)
		(1928)	*Colleen*		James H. Cullen	(35p92)
			Colleen		Sylvester Sparling	(39p106)
		(1941)	*Colleen*		Bruce & Virginia Wallace	(62p146)
		(1964)	*Colleen*		Mary Saye	(71p161)
18	1911		Tender		G. W. C. Drexel	
19	1911		Tender		J. F. Betz	
20	1912		*Mary C.*		John C. McHugh	
21	1912/231628		*Black Duck*	50'	Alexander Sellers	
		(1919)	*Black Duck*	(Len 5' 1913)	Michael G. Prices	(28p71)
			Black Duck		Acme Boat Works, Inc., George T. Gravenstine, Pres.	(35p65)
		(1939)	*Black Duck*		John E. Leach	(47p69)
		(1954)	*Pirate*		D. C. Wilson	(60p450)
22	1912		*Vipi*	51'0"	Glass Bottom Co.	

Contract Number	Year Built/ Documentation Number	1st in Lloyd's	Original & Subsequent Boat Names	Length	Original & Subsequent Owner(s)	Lloyd's Register Reference
23	1912		*Inspector*		State Board of Health	
24	1912/210659		*Calabash*	70'	William J. Matheson	(to23p66)
		(1928)	*Mary Ann*		J. B. Thompson	(35p223)
			Mary Ann		Robert W. A. Wood	(39p273)
25	1912				G. W. C. Drexel	
26	1912				G. W. C. Drexel	
27	1912/210832		*Ibis*	70'	F. F. Christie	
		(1919)	*Ibis*		F. F. & W. F. Christie	(23p124)
		(1928)	*Ibis*		W. F. Christie	(39p201)
			Ibis		H. Van Benschoten	(41p207)
		(1947)	*Ibis*		Howard Bond	(50p224)
		(1954)	*Ibis*		Tatem Wofford	(55p247)
		(1956)	*Ibis*		Robin I. Bryant	(75p238)
			Ibis		Jeff Siben	1983-1995
28	1912		*Georgena*		F. F. Proctor	
29	1912/211169		*Content*	60'	M. Byron Megargee	(to23p79)
			Content	(58'6")	Dr. Lewis Yerger	(28p93)
		(1935)	*Content*		Robert J. McCormick	(41p113)
			Content		T. Larsen Snik (et al)	(47p107)
30	1912/211104		*Ruffled Grouse*	63'	J. H. Carstairs	
		(1919)	*Ruffled Grouse*		Edward E. Gold	(28p247)
			Marybeth		Alfred J. Hoffmann	(35p223)
		(1939)	*Marybeth*		Lawrence J. Johnson	(41p286)
??	1912		*Clare III*	40'	John H. Drexler	(15p72)
			Ma			
			Mardys			
			Champ		William E. Bond	(19p67)
			Champ			(23p71)
31	1913/211220		*Alela*		A. H. Disston	(to15p39)
			Alela		George T. Lippincott	(19p38)

Contract Number	Year Built/ Documentation Number	1st in Lloyd's	Original & Subsequent Boat Names	Length	Original & Subsequent Owner(s)	Lloyd's Register Reference
			Alela		Henry Gilsey	(23p42)
32	1913		*Gondola*		Price & McLanahan	
??	1913/211427		*Margo*	64'0"	George H. McNeely	(19p156)
		(1923)	*Pandora III*		Arthur T. Vance	(32p280)
33	1913/213623		*Margo II*	45'0" Cruiser	G. H. McNeely	
			Lorowa	(40')	R. D. Heaton	(19p148)
			Lorowa		Henry Harrison Lewis	(23p152)
			Lorowa			(28p176)
			Lorowa		Edward R. Ammon	(32p220)
		(1935)	*Lorowa*		George A. Smith, Jr.	(50p278)
		(1954)	*Lorowa*		Mac Summer Mullin	(56p310)
34	1913		*Trinitaria*	40'	S. H. Clarke	
			Trinitaria		Louis S. Clarke	(19p239)
		(1923)	*Trinitaria*		Wm. M. Francis	(28p292)
		(1935)	*Milani*		Ralph P. Minnick	(41p298)
35	1913		City Tug *Passyunk*	(Pilot, Dk Hse.)	T. Smith & Sons	
36	1913		Dredge Hull		T. Smith & Sons for Dept. of WD&R, Phila, PA	
37	1913		Houses For Patent Pump			
38	1913/211847		*Nahmeoka*	68'	H. N. Baruch	
			Nahmeoka II		H. M. Slater	(19p172)
			Alona		C. B. & E. L. Maloney	(23p45)
			Flamingo		David Rumsey	(28p123)
			Flamingo		Aubert J. Fay	(35p135)
39	1913		*Bethel*	Tugboat house		
40	1913		*Fred Nathan*	Tugboat house		
41	1914		Tug *Perry*		U.S.E.D. Norfolk	
42	1914		Tug *Skycoak*		U.S.E.D. Jacksonville	
43	1914		*Alice*	43'0" (Stock)	J. J. Smith & Mary Scofield	
			Alice		Mrs. J. J. Smith	(15p41)

Contract Number	Year Built/ Documentation Number	1st in Lloyd's	Original & Subsequent Boat Names	Length	Original & Subsequent Owner(s)	Lloyd's Register Reference
44	1914		*Okisko*		U.S.E.D.	
45	1914		*Young America*	46'0"	Boy Scout Houseboat, Charles Longstreth	
			Maggie Jane		R. N. Whaley	(19p152)
			Jan Jan		J. R. Philips	(23p133)
46	1914		*Abeona*	(Stock)	E. J. Mickey	
47	1914/213710		*Miakka*	42' (Stock)	T. C. Allison	
			Miakka	(43')	T. Ellwood Allison	(19p164)
			Miakka		Walter C. Grey	(23p167)
			Miakka		Louis Calder	(28p196)
			Miakka		Sound Properties, Inc. E. Calder, President	(35p230)
		(1939)	*Miakka*		John B. Absmeier	(41p296)
48	1914		*Vira*	37'7" Exp. Cruiser	George N. Degerberg	(19p248)
49	1915/213334		*Akbar*	72'6"	George W. C. Drexel	(to23p40)
			Akbar		U.S. Navy	(19p36)
			Akbar		William M. Butler	(28p46)
			Akbar		Samuel I. Davis	(35p27)
50	1915/213306		*Enchantress II*	74'2"	Louis Burk	(to19p96)
51	1915/213550		*Lady Baltimore*	77'	Hall-Seeley Motor Co.	
			Lady Baltimore		E. F. Hutton	(19p142)
		(1923)	*Lady Baltimore*		Arthur C. Hardy	(39p232)
		(1941)	*Lady Baltimore*		L. G. Proctor	(50p258)
		(1954)	*Lady Baltimore*		Gerald W. Ford	(62p327)
		(1964)	*Lady Baltimore*		Nils Lommerin	(67p360)
52	1914		*Ace*	48'8"	George W. C. Drexel	(to41p25)
		(1915)	*Ace*		Ellery Tuck	47p25
53	1914		8 Small Boats		Carman & Bowes	
54	1915		*Mifflin*		U.S.E.D	
55	1915/213723		*Dorinda*	77'	Henry W. Savage	(to23p89)

Contract Number	Year Built/ Documentation Number	1st in Lloyd's	Original & Subsequent Boat Names	Length	Original & Subsequent Owner(s)	Lloyd's Register Reference
		(1928)			Mrs. Frank T. Lloyd	(35p112)
		(1939)	*Maybick*		Bickford's, Inc.	(41p291)
		(1954)	*Wilamar*		William A. & Marie C. McCutcheon	(56p583)
			Wilamar		Int. Salvage & Charter Co.	(60p642)
		(1962)	*Wilamar*		International Marine Inc.	(69p788)
56	1915/213013		*Palisades*	120'	Bessey (Perkins)	
			Palisades		Van Lear Black	(19p188)
	Rebuilt 1919		*Pioneer* (see contract 107)		Interstate Park Commission	
57	1915		*Adios*		L. L. Biddle	
??	1915		*Vira* (see contract 48)	37'7"	George N Degerberg	
58	1915		Stock			
59	1915		Stock			
60	1915/214285		*Marpessa*	50'	William J. Matheson	(to19p158)
			Marpessa		David G. Joyce	(23p161)
			Marpessa		Kathryn K. Rice	(28p189)
			Marpessa		William J. Hermann	(35p221)
			SP-787		U.S. Government	1941-45
61	1915/214019		*Vigilant*	65'	Alvah H. Martin	(to19p247)
		(1923)	*Vigilant*		Samuel L. Kent	(35p367)
			Vigilant		Ogden W. Headington	(39p454)
		(1947)	*Vigilant*		Frank S. Jacobus	(41p479)
			Vigilant		Harold T. Ray	(50p506)
			Vigilant		John B. Wathen	(54p551
62	1915/215230.		*Inquirer*	62'0"	Col. James Elverson, Jr.	(to23p127)
63	1915/214866		*Ameera*	71'5"	Alexander Sellers	
			Ameera		U.S. Navy	(19p42)
64	1916/214293		*Agnes B.*	57'	Charles F. Well	
			A. R. M.		John M. Mauser	(19p33)
		(1923)	*Pastime*		John W. Hubbard	(28p224)

Contract Number	Year Built/ Documentation Number	1st in Lloyd's	Original & Subsequent Boat Names	Length	Original & Subsequent Owner(s)	Lloyd's Register Reference
		(1935)	*Muriel*		Margaret Brooks	(41p312)
			Muriel		John F. Hoppe	(47p300)
			Muriel		S. Owen Leider	(50p328)
			Muriel		Henry G. William	(54p355)
			Muriel		M&M Pio Zuclich	(55p357)
65	1916/214868		*Zenith*	73'3"	Charles Longstreth	(to19p263
			SP-61		U.S. Government	1941-45
66	1916/214601		*Jane VI*	72'	A. P. Ordway	
			Jane VI			(19p128)
			Jane VI		George D. Rosengarten	(23p132)
			Jane VI		A. W. Brown	(28p155)
			Jane VI		S. I. Wilkinson	(35p175)
			Vasagus			
		(1937)	*Jane*		Alberto & Jane Santos	(39p211)
			Loraymo		Raymond Loewy	(41p259)
		(1947)	*Loraymo*		Paul C. Case	(50p277)
		(1954)	*Loraymo*		Warren W. Collamer	(55p303)
			Sno-Foolin'		William A. Snow	(56p492)
		(1960)	*Virginia J.*		Virginia Farrell, Inc.	(62p647)
		(1964)	*Virginia J.*		D. E. Rivers	(69p763)
67	1916/214676		*Nepenthe*	90'	James Deering	(to23p180)
			SP-112	(80'0" in 1923 Lloyds)	U.S. Government	1941-45
68	1916/214678		*Chieftain*	106'3"	A. W. Armour	
		(1919)	*Chieftain*		Charles W. Armour	(23p73)
		(1928)	*Chieftain*		Albert B. Dick	(35p87)
			Chieftain		Albert Pack	(39p100)
			Chieftain		Howard Bond	(41p104)
			Chieftain		J. W. Metzler, Jr.	(46p13)
		(1947)	*Chieftain*		Barbara Campbell	(56p123)
69	1916/215231		*Leonie*	106'	Murry Guggenheim	(to39p241)

Contract Number	Year Built/ Documentation Number	1st in Lloyd's	Original & Subsequent Boat Names	Length	Original & Subsequent Owner(s)	Lloyd's Register Reference
			YHB-19		U.S. Government	1941-45
		(1947)	*Leonie*		Leonie Guggenheim	(to1955)
			Leonie		Putman Publishing Co.	(56p300)
		(1960)	*Leonie*		Dorothy Martin	(62p340)
??	1917/215036		*Alba*	43'		
			Bud Jr		Frank B. Harris	(19p62)
			Elaine		Benjamin J. Rosenthal	(23p94)
			Elaine		Gifford B. Crary	(28p113)
			Alba		Alex Littlefield	(35p28)
			Alba		Samuel M. Leidy	(39p30)
			Snoopy II		Thomas Jones	(41p424)
			Snoopy II		C. R. Hubbell	(47p405)
			Floris		J. Stephen Thomas	(50p175)
		(1954)	*Tortoise*		Wm. S. & Clara F. Stephens	(62p621)
??	1917/215364		*Riposo*	44' (40')	Herman B. Maruch, M.D.	(19p202)
			Riposo		Col. C. W. Fowler	(23p207)
70–84	1917		SC 65–74 & 209–213 (total 14 boats)		U.S. Government	
85	1918		75 airplane hulls		Standard Aircraft Corp.	
86–90	1918		SC 381–385 (total 5 boats)		U.S. Government	
91	1918		10 airplanes		U.S. Navy	
92–93	1918		Tugboat No. 75–76		U.S. Navy	
94	1918		airplane hulls		U.S. Navy	
95–99	1918		SC 426–430		U.S. Government	
100	1919/218989		*Bilma II*	52'	W. G. Selby	
			Bilma II		Dr. F. T. Rogers	(23p61)
			Tramp		Mrs. Wm. K. Townsend	(28p291)
			Dorymar		Ralph H. Hubbard	(30p122)
		(1933)	*Tramp*		Ralph H. Hubbard	(39p436)
			Tramp		Charles F. DuBois	(41p460)

Contract Number	Year Built/ Documentation Number	1st in Lloyd's	Original & Subsequent Boat Names	Length	Original & Subsequent Owner(s)	Lloyd's Register Reference
			Tramp		Sommer B. Jaquith	(54p530)
		(1978)	*Tramp*		John M. Gould	(79p532)
101	1919/219193		*Loaf Along*	52'	John C. King	
			Loafalong		Harry A. Lawton	(23p151)
		(1928)	*Loafalong*		Clarence B. Kugler, Jr.	(39p247)
			Loafalong		George S. Ruhland	(41p257)
			Loafalong		Harvey Lore	(47p249)
		(1950)	*Loafalong*		M&M George W. Cummings	(55p301)
			Loafalong		Peter Ball	(56p307)
		(1960)	*Loafalong*		N. F. Ryder	(62p349)
		(1964)	*Loaf Along*		John N. Kabler, Jr.	(71p392)
102	1919/219190		*Riette II*	52'	George G. Shelton	(to23p207)
			Alexandrea			
			Edith III		Franklin M. Doan	(28p112)
			Connie I		L. B. Reeb	(35p94)
			Ariadne		C. A. Hansen	(39p51)
			Entre Nous			
			Hapala III		Christian Henry Hecker, Jr.	(41p192)
			Marjella II		W. E. Perry	(47p272)
		(1950)	*Marjella II*		W. Braith Davis	(54p324)
		(1955)	*Marjella II*		J. V. Leddy	(56p333)
			Grand Lady		W. Phillip Fuller	(79p196)
103	1919/219191		*Scarus*	54'6"	John H. Eastwood	
			Azile			
			Elsara		Col. William T. Starr	(23p98)
			Elsara	(52')	Joseph E. Black	(28p116)
			Elsara		Dr. Walter H. Snyder	(35p124)
			So What			(39p406)
			Entre Nous		C. A. Hansen	(41p152)
			Entre Nous		C. N. Drennen	(47p145)

Contract Number	Year Built/ Documentation Number	1st in Lloyd's	Original & Subsequent Boat Names	Length	Original & Subsequent Owner(s)	Lloyd's Register Reference
		(1954)	*Entre Nous*		Benjamin F. Bunn	(56p179)
			Homeport Too		George Bradley	(60p269)
		(1962)	*Homeport Too*		C. J. Elliott	(71p311)
104	1919/219296		*Zigan*	52'	Edward S. Moore	
			Zigan		Charles K. Kotcher	(23p273)
			Zigan		C. C. Coddington	(28p321)
		(1935)	*Zigan*		Charles B. Prettyman, Jr.	(39p483)
			Zigan		George Lauder	(41p511)
		(1947)	*Zigan*		E. C. Fogg, Jr.	(50p537)
		(1954)	*Zigan*		George A. Naumann	(56p598)
		(1960)	*Zigan*		William G. Hawkins	(62p684)
		(1964)	*Zigan*		Charles Clapp	(73p705)
105	1919/219475		*Helen Louise*	52'	V. B. Hubbel	(to23p120)
			Helen Louise		William H. Reddy	(28p142)
			Helen Louise		M. E. Kinnan	(35p160)
			Helen Louise		Janet F. Kelso	(39p192)
		(1941)	*Merrillan*		James C. Merrill	(54p339)
		(1955)	*Bobalong*		Ms. Corinne P. Long	(56p92)
		(1960)	*Bobalong*		Francis James Duff	(62p102)
			Bobalong		Paul Zimmer	(64p99)
		(1967)	*Bobalong*		Jeffrey Arnold	(75p72)
		(1977)	*Darian*		Quin L. Gilchrist	(79p116)
106	1919		*Buzzer*	38' Cruiser	A. D. J. Paul	
		(1935)	*Bon Doon III*		Barron Collier Est.	(41p82)
107	1919/213913		*Palisades* Rebuild	120'	Van Lear Black	(19p188)
			Pioneer		E. H. Kluge	(23p197)
			Pioneer		Sumner Ballard	(28p230)
			Pioneer		Frank W. Ballard	
			Pioneer	(120')	Edward Coppage	(35p275)
			Pioneer		Interstate Park Comm.	

Contract Number	Year Built/ Documentation Number	1st in Lloyd's	Original & Subsequent Boat Names	Length	Original & Subsequent Owner(s)	Lloyd's Register Reference
108	1919/219424		*Nadesah*	80'	J. H. & J. D. Carstairs	
		(1923)	*Sangamo*		Robert Oglesby	(28p251)
			Sangamo		Sherburn M. Becker	(35p301)
		(1939)	*Sangamo*		Phillip R. Mallory	(41p391)
			Sangamo		John B. Kutchey	(47p375)
		(1950)	*Sangamo*		Herman Langleben	(56p451)
		(1960)	*Sangamo*		Carleton L. Witham	(69p606)
		(1971)	*Sangamo*		E. R. Pipping, Jr.	(77p397)
			Friendship			
109	1919/219427		*Osana*	80'	Clayton G. Dixon	(to23p189)
			Lena H		Tillinghast L. Huston	(28p172)
110	1919/219426		*Kingfisher*	80'	E. L. King	(to35p188)
			Kingfisher		Sherburn M. Becker	(39p228)
		(1941)	*Mimosa*		Horace C. Stebbins	(47p289)
			Mimosa		Hubert Scott-Paine	(50p316)
		(1954)	*Mimosa*		H. Braith Davis	(60p387)
		(1962)	*Mimosa*		C. P. Coady, III	(64p407
		(1967)	*Mimosa*		Eugene E. Mori	(77p295)
		(1978)	*Spring Lake*		Eugene E. Mori	(84p693
111	1919/220262		*Tosca*	52'	Albert C. Middleton	
			Dorothy		Hugh L. Willoughby, Jr.	(23p90)
			Aileen II		John L. Cannon	(28p45)
			Barbette		Jefferson L. Ford, Jr.	(35p57)
		(1939)	*Barbette*		George Ortsiefen	(47p61)
			Barbette		George C. Williams	(50p64)
			Joya			
		(1954)	*Oluolu*		Bertha D. Bloomfield-Brown	(56p388)
			Oluolu		Charles J. Phillips	(60p427)
		(1962)	*Islander*		Charles J. Phillips	(75p247)
112	1919/215364		*Riposo II*	44'	Herman B. Baruch, M.D.	(19p202)

Contract Number	Year Built/ Documentation Number	1st in Lloyd's	Original & Subsequent Boat Names	Length	Original & Subsequent Owner(s)	Lloyd's Register Reference
			Riposo	(40'0")	Col. C. W. Fowler	(23p207)
			Riposo	(44')	O. R. Saint	(28p242)
113	1920/220253		*Donaldo*	52'	Sailing W. Baruch	
			Marylin		S. K. Demick	Mar. 1922
			Clare		Fredrick Pope	3/1/22
			Clare		Dr. Charles Van Bergen	(23p75)
			Comford		William Scheer	9/26/24
						(28p92)
		(1935)	*Abadab*		Mac Thurnauer	5/28/31
					Mathis Yacht Co.	8/18/38
		(1939)	*Albatross*		A. Atwater Kent	11/30/38
						(41p31)
			Albatross		A. Atwater Kent, Jr.	8/12/46
						(47p32)
			Albatross		Theatle E. Rodenhaver	12/9/48
						(50p32)
			Albatross		Anthony Waterer	6/7/49
		(1954)	*Albatross*		J. Raymon & Mary F. Greenhill	7/5/51
						(56p35)
		(1960)	*Albatross*		Asa H. & Margaret G. Coale	4/27/55
						(67p37)
		(1969)	*Albatross*		James S. & F. Gooch Fitzgerald	4/27/69
						(77p8)
					David H. & Maureen D. Bayer	10/8/80
					Scott L. Betten	12/29/81
			Kings Glory		Urban Crisis Center	7/17/82
			Helva		Robert Barton & Sandra Burke	Aug. 1990
			Helva	(47'6")	Robert F. Barton	Dec. 1990
114	1920/220395		*Reverie*	60'	Arthur K. Bourne	

Contract Number	Year Built/ Documentation Number	1st in Lloyd's	Original & Subsequent Boat Names	Length	Original & Subsequent Owner(s)	Lloyd's Register Reference
			Riposando			
			Maroya	(61'0")	Roy F. York	(23p161)
		(1928)	*Edora II*		Paul Lindenberg	(30p127)
			Maroya		Albert Pack Corp.	(33p233)
			Tropic		Albert Pack Corp.	(35p353)
		(1939)	*Tropic*		Mrs. Webb Jay	(41p463)
			Tropic	(61'0")	Nolan-Brown Motors Inc.	(47p445)
		(1950)	*Tropic*		Connor Brown	(54p534)
		(1955)	*Tropic*		Charleston Marine Co.	(60p602)
			Tropic		Southeastern Properties Inc.	(62p627)
		(1964)	*Dunvegan*		Colin MacLeod, Dunvegan Farms	(79p137)
115	1921/220393		*Nahmeoka*	60'8"	H. N. Baruch	
			Arline			
			Anado		J. Adolph Mollenhauer	(23p47)
			Domino II		Montgomery Maze	(28p106)
		(1935)	*Domino II*		R. W. Trimpi	(56p157)
			Domino II		Century Am. Corp.	(60p170)
			Domino II			(62p177)
		(1967)	*Vizcaya*		Bruce W. Whitcombe	(79p554)
			Vizcaya		Will Claypool	at least 2 yrs.
??	1921/220886		*Nahmeoka*	85'6"	Arthur J. Grymes	(23p175)
		(1935)	*Tred Avon*		William H. Pierce	(41p461)
		(1947)	*Tred Avon*		Samuel W. Johnson, III	(67p701)
		(1964)	*Tred Avon*		Mrs. Samuel W. Johnson, Jr.	(79p533)
116	1921/220394		*Cyrene*	60'8"	Robert M. Bond	
			Amril			
			Surina II		S. S. DeLano	(23p239)
		(1928)	*Bee Cee*		David G. Joyce	(35p60)
		(1939)	*Rosalind*		Mrs. Rosalind H. Croft	(41p382)

Contract Number	Year Built/ Documentation Number	1st in Lloyd's	Original & Subsequent Boat Names	Length	Original & Subsequent Owner(s)	Lloyd's Register Reference
			Rosalind		Harvey & Betty Gardner	(47p366)
		(1950)	*Kyanis*		G. T. Shirres	(56p287)
117	1921		*Equitorial*		Carib Syndicate	
118	1921/220882		*Luneta*	85'	Col. S. L. H. Slocum	(to23p154)
			Jane			
			Luneta		S. A. Lynch	(28p178)
			Lucerne		George Leary, Jr.	(35p205)
119	1921/219191		*Scarus*	85'	John H. Eastwood	
120	1921/220887		*Miramar*	72'10"	Edward H. Garcin	
			Bolo		Charles M. Swift	(23p63)
			Venetia		E. S. Griffiths	(28p301)
		(1933)	*Venetia*		Louis Calder	(35p364)
121	1921/221338		*Enchantress III*	85'	Louis Burk	(to35p126)
			Enchantress III		Louis J. Kolb	(39p148)
		(1941)	*Enchantress III*		Edwin N. Belcher	(47p144)
			Jedge II	(83'0")	Lamson Co.	(50p236)
		(1954)	*Mabel Claire*			(55p310)
122	1921/222299		*Pilgrim*	86'11"	William Elkins	(to23p197)
			Pilgrim		Alfred P. Parker	(28p229)
			Marlen III		William T. Grant	(35p220)
			Marlen III		Frank M. & Joseph Dunbaugh	(39p270)
			Deltra II		D. R. Traver	(41p125)
123	1921		*Seaway*	30'	Louis W. Wheelock	
124	1921/222117		*Amitie*	75'	Charles B. Prettyman	(to23p46)
			Amitie		Joseph H. Adams	(28p54)
			Friendship II		H. C. Yeiser, Jr.	(35p142)
			Friendship II		William M. Davey	(39p168)
			Loller		F. Worthington Hine	(41p258)
			Loller		Random Trips, Inc.	(47p250)
			Loller		Clara May Downey	(50p276)

Contract Number	Year Built/ Documentation Number	1st in Lloyd's	Original & Subsequent Boat Names	Length	Original & Subsequent Owner(s)	Lloyd's Register Reference
		(1954)	*Marana*		Henry Frazer Harris	(55p319)
		(1956)	*Marana*		E. W. Coppage	(60p359)
			Marana		Gustave G. Coplan	(62p371)
		(1964)	*Marana*		Richard B. Lurie	(75p317)
125	1922/222260		*Nedmac*	56' Aux Sloop	Albert C. Middleton	(to41p322)
		(1947)	*Nedmac*		Samuel L. Clark	(50p337)
		(1954)	*Trade Winds*		E. H. Holzworth	(56p540)
		(1960)	*Sea Castle*		Capt. Herman E. & Annie G. Offhouse	(79p446)
126	1922/222261		*Snug*	63'	Arthur Block	(to23p231)
			Rene			
			Margaret		Charles W. Kotcher	(28p185)
			Marjoclaire		Joseph E. Block	(35p219)
			Marjoclaire		S. J. Daly	(39p269)
			Marjoclaire		W. B. Campbell	(41p281)
			Lazy-Me	(63'6")	W. V. B. Campbell	(47p240)
			Lazy-Me		Charles H. Weber	(50p266)
			Tunky Too			
		(1954)	*Stray Winds II*		J. V. Lindsley	(56p508)
127	1922/222335		*Lazy Lady*	68'	Robert Wolstenholme	(to23p148)
		(1935)	*Lazy Lady*		Wm. D. Stanger	(50p266)
128	1922/222463		*Elise*	74' Aux Cutter	Frank B. Bower	(to41p146)
			Elise		James R. Hensler	(47p139)
			Elise		D. C. Rimmer	(54p168)
		(1955)	*Elise*		Paul Roberts	(56p173)
129	1923/222952		*Emeska*	65'	John L. Kemmerera	
			Marilyn IV		Dr. C. Wadsworth Schwartz	(28p191)
			Priscilla		R. M. Barwise	(35p279)
		(1939)	*Charming Alice*		Richard H. Trimpi	(54p116)
		(1955)	*Capricorn*		Albert J. Schwarzter	(60p116)

Contract Number	Year Built/ Documentation Number	1st in Lloyd's	Original & Subsequent Boat Names	Length	Original & Subsequent Owner(s)	Lloyd's Register Reference
			Capricorn		John Townshend Benjamin	(56p109)
130	1923/222954		*Minken*	65'	Paul A. Schoellkopf	(to24p175)
			True Blue			
			Moonlight		Fred W. Weller	(28p202)
		(1935)	*Moonlight*		Charles E. Penny	(41p310)
		(1947)	*See Rest*		Oscar C. Seebass	(69p638)
			Sandy Mae			
??	1923		*Marian III*	65'		
		(1963)	*Ce-Bo IV*		Robert B. Hollander	(69p145)
		(1971)	*Ce-Bo IV*		Dr. Gordon Dunn	(79p84)
131	1923/223047		*Ebenezer*	70'4"	J. Aaron	
			Marlen		William T. Grant	(28p188)
			Mendota II		Herbert W. Warden	(35p228)
			Shy-Ann II		Mrs. Sylvia Louise Leland	(39p394)
			Agase		Margaret M. Fraser	(47p29)
			El-Ja		James J. & Eliz. T. Archbold	(41p147)
			Corsair		Daytona Beach Boat Works	(50p120)
			Corsair		Williams G. Oaks	(54p132)
		(1955)	*Corsair*		Irene P. Brett	(56p137)
		(1960)	*Corsair*		Guy Tripp Hemphill	(67p167)
		(1969)	*Corsair*		Emery J. Buckner	(71p171)
132	1923/223049		*Ocoee*	70'4"	W. S. Milne	(to23p185)
			Pamona		Paul O. Richmond	(28p223)
			Berto		Walter M. Hort	(35p60)
			Onawa	70'4"	Winthrop P. Moore	(39p322)
		(1941)	*Onawa*		Coppage Holding Co.	(47p325)
133	1923/223197		*Mycelma III*	56'	A. W. Atkinson	(28p203)
		(1935)	*Anjolee*	(49'11")	Clarence Leigh Moyer	(41p46)
			Anjolee		Harry S. Willey	(47p44to50)
134	1923/223445		*Bilma III*	70'	W. G. Selby	

Contract Number	Year Built/ Documentation Number	1st in Lloyd's	Original & Subsequent Boat Names	Length	Original & Subsequent Owner(s)	Lloyd's Register Reference
			Querida		Edward F. Bishop	(28p236)
			Pamela II		Harold A. Clark	
			Helma			
			Veneck B			
			Querida II			
			Morada		L. E. Searles	(39p296)
			Miyo III		Dr. Walter M. Yost	(41p305)
		(1947)	*Kay-Bob*		Kloeppel Hotel	(64p320)
		(1967)	*Lady Fair*		Arledge Real Estate Corp.	(75p281)
			Ebenezer II		Ebenezer II Limited, Dave Camlier & Tom Ward	1985
135	1923/223476		*Mariposa*	80'	Dr. George D. Rosengarten	(to30p216)
			Charlotte			
		(1933)	*Olivette*		Mark C. Honeywell	(41p338)
			Cintra		Sydney E. Hutchinson	(47p102)
		(1950)	*Sea Deller*		Aruther W. Hamm	(54p454)
		(1955)	*A-PAC-O*		Atlanta Paper Co.	(56p54)
			Nadia		John F. Mason & Irwin Frantz	(60p403)
			Safari		J. Mason & E. Fraatz	(62p510)
		(1964)	*Safari*		Larry S. Beck	(69p597)
			Francis Fayard		Fayard Moving & Transport	Doc. 1981
136	1924/223788		*Conowingo*	65'11"	G. W. Fleming	
			Priscilla		G. R. Hemenridge	(28p234)
			Rosecliff II		Clifford G. Ludvigh	(35p295)
137	1924/223960		*Mariska*	65'	F. D. Owsley, Greenwood VA	
			Hiawatha			
		(1928)	*Elise*		Clyde T. Bailey Est.	(41p146)
			Tahoma			
			Raymar			
			Traveler		Mrs. Clara May Downey	(47p444)

Contract Number	Year Built/ Documentation Number	1st in Lloyd's	Original & Subsequent Boat Names	Length	Original & Subsequent Owner(s)	Lloyd's Register Reference
		(1950)	*Lucy II*		A. R. & Lucille W. Lindsley	(75p305)
138	1924		*Acomes*	35'9"	A. C. Middleton	
		(1946)	*Blue Heron*	Yawl, converted	A. E. McKinley, Jr.	(55p87)
		(1960)	*Blue Heron*	sloop	Dr. G. Jay Anyon	(78p60)
139	1924/224168		*Coconut*	85'	William J. Matheson	(to28p90)
		(1935)	*Coconut*		George A. Dobyne	(47p104)
			Tumbler		M. B. Dickinson	(50p491)
			Virginia J.			
		(1954)	*Virginian*		Victor Tracy	(62p647)
140	1924/224073		*Sequoia*	85'	Richard M. Cadwalader	
			Serenia		P. J. Morgan	(28p262)
		(1935)	*Serenia*		Charles U. Bay	(41p409)
		(1947)	*Serenia*		B. Adelbert Barstow	(54p467)
		(1955)	*Serenia*		P. T. Cox	(60p525)
			Serenia			(62p547)
141	1924/224223		*Zenithia*	85'	Albert J. Fay, Lowell MA	(to41p510)
			Zenithia		Richard K. LeBlond	(28p321 to35p392)
		(1947)	*Heavy Moon*		John S. Sensenbrenner	(50p211)
		(1954)	*Sylvia*		Sidney Weinberg	(56p517)
			Intrepid		William G. Reynolds	(60p281
		(1962)	*Intrepid*		Commodore Inc.	(64p293)
??	1924		USN YP38	75'	Converted to yacht	1948
		(1950)	*Grayling*		Loyd R. & Edith O. Gray	(55p221)
		(1956)	*Grayling*		Janis R. Sedgley	(60p245)
142–156	1924		C.G. 100–114	75' Patrol Boats	U.S. Coast Guard (15 boats)	
157	1925/224699		*Alscotia*	98'	Dr. Sticker Coles	(to28p52)
			Triad			
			Arab		C. Willard Young	(35p44)
			Sirena		S. F. Briggs	(39p398)

Contract Number	Year Built/ Documentation Number	1st in Lloyd's	Original & Subsequent Boat Names	Length	Original & Subsequent Owner(s)	Lloyd's Register Reference
			Sirena	(Lengthened to 103'6" 1942)	Sherburn M. Becker	(41p419)
		(1947)	*Sirena*		Brig. Gen. Robert W. Johnson	(54p478)
		(1955)	*Sirena*		Christopher S. Jenkins	(56p487)
		(1960)	*Sirena*		F. L. Fraser	(71p627)
158–160	1925		C.G. 278–280 (3 of 15 boats)	75' Patrol Boats	U.S. Coast Guard	
161	1925/232737		C.G. 281(1 of 15 boats) *Ethyl Ruth*	75' Patrol Boat (71'1")	U.S. Coast Guard John D. Shibe	(35p129)
162–172	1925		C.G. 282–292 (11 of 15 boats)	75' Patrol Boats	U.S. Coast Guard	
??	1925		*Ebenezer* *She Tiger*	71.7'	Maria Delsart Shutt converted Coast Guard cutter	(84p661) Lloyd's '84
173	1925/225101		*Samuri*	99'	Earl Dodge, Tams & King, N.A.	
			Eleanor IV		A. Hamilton Rice	(28p113)
			Sydney		Sydney R. Hutchinson	(35p339)
			Sea Play		George W. Codrington	(39p383)
			Helma		Bruce Dodson	(41p198)
			Helma		Sylvia Corp.	(47p192)
			Helma		Macabi, Inc.	(50p213)
174	1925/225115		*Sequoia II*	104'	Richard Cadwalader, Jr.	(to28p262)
			Sequoia		William F. Dunning	1928
			Sequoia		Dept. of Commerce	1931
			Sequoia		Presidential Yacht	1933 to 1977
			Sequoia		Thomas A. Malloy	5/18/77
			Sequoia		Norman F. Pulliam, (22 limited partners)	10/77
			Sequoia		John C. Grant Ocean Learning Inst. of PB	April 1980
			Sequoia		Presidential Yacht Trust	Jan. 12, 1981

Contract Number	Year Built/ Documentation Number	1st in Lloyd's	Original & Subsequent Boat Names	Length	Original & Subsequent Owner(s)	Lloyd's Register Reference
			Sequoia		Presidential Yacht	11/15/88
			Sequoia		Repo Norfolk Ship & Dry Dock	~1991
175	1925/225227		*Thalia*	92'	Thomas M. Howell	(to28p287)
			Yowana	(94'8")		
		(1935)	*Marion*		Robert P. Hooper	(41p279)
		(1947)	*Shiawassee V*		C. P. Bentley	(64p564)
			Shiawassee V		Warren M. & W. Lonton Atkinson	(67p617)
		(1971)	*Golden Greek*		Alex Gregory	(75p207)
			Private Dancer		Ginsborg	
			Private Dancer		Joseph Ducato	Doc. 1989
176	1925/225226		*Troubadour*	92'	Webb Jay	(to28p293)
		(1935)	*Ilderim*		Sabine Towing & Trans. Co.	(71p320)
177	1926/225498		*Riposo*	92'	Dr. H. B. Baruch	(to28p242)
			Minoco		Mills Novelty Co.	(30p228)
			Worthwyle			
			North Star		Mathis Yacht Building Co.	(33p267)
			North Star		Stanton Griffis	(35p258)
			North Star		Charles Coryell	(39p317)
			North Star		D. Spencer Berger	(41p333)
			North Star		Joseph H. Hines	(47p319)
			North Star		Coastal Petroleum Co.	(50p347)
		(1954)	*North Star*		Stephen A. Lynch	(56p383)
			Margo II			
		(1960)	*Harmonell*		Harmon P. Elliott	(69p305)
178	1926/234153		*Burlington*	70'	Fish & Game Commission, NJ	
		(1939)	*H. J. Burlington*	(72')	S. C. Loveland Co.	(41p202)
179	1926/225758		*Pilgrim II*	92'	William E. Elkins	(to41p356)
		(1947)	*Pilgrim II*	(92'5")	John W. Vessels	(50p371)

Contract Number	Year Built/ Documentation Number	1st in Lloyd's	Original & Subsequent Boat Names	Length	Original & Subsequent Owner(s)	Lloyd's Register Reference
		(1954)	*Pilgrim II*		Marie Geneau	(55p399)
		(1956)	*Pilgrim II.*		J. Ray McDermott & Co.	(64p476)
		(1967)	*Pilgrim II*		George Sanders	(79p386)
			Pilgrim II	(84.4')	Pilgrim Leasing Corp.	Doc. 1990
			Pilgrim II		W. Louise Davis	
180	1926/225966		*Trail*	92'	William Wallace, Jr.	(to28p291)
		(1935)	*Trail*		Henry Hemmerdinger	(41p460)
		(1955)	*Trail*		James L. Oakes, Jr., & Mary Sue McCulloch Oakes	(56p541)
		(1960)	*Southern Trail*		Castro Convertible Corp.	(77p445)
			Southern Trail		Ken Kreisler	Summer 1991
			Reported sunk in Detroit, raised and taken to Toronto			1992-93
181	1926/225797		*Freedom*	103'	A. G. Fay	(to28p127)
		(1935)	*Freedom*		Mrs. J. P. Donahue	(39p166)
			Sunset		S. A. Lynch	(41p439)
			Sunset		Herbert M. Plimpton	(47p422)
			Sunset		Hollis W. Plimpton	(50p463)
		(1954)	*Sunset*		Yachts, Inc. Ashley E. Howes, Jr.	(71p662)
182	1927/226118		*Summer Girl*	93'	J. G. Roberts	(to28p278)
			Ranora III		Frank C. Munson	(33p294)
			Dormar		Margaret W. Love	(35p113)
			Americana			
		(1939)	*Heavy Moon*		John S. Sensenbrener	(47p190)
183	1927/226170		*Truant*	104'	Truman H. Newberry	(to28p293)
			Nancy IV		Parry D. Saylor	(33p255)
		(1935)	*Shiawassee III*		Calvin P. Bentley	(41p414)
		(1947)	*Shiawassee III*		Junaita James	(50p435)
184	1927/226186		*Eala*	93'	Judge Robert W. Bingham	(to35p117)

Contract Number	Year Built/ Documentation Number	1st in Lloyd's	Original & Subsequent Boat Names	Length	Original & Subsequent Owner(s)	Lloyd's Register Reference
		(1939)	*Maroc*		Robert Busby	(41p283)
		(226186)	*For 'Evansake II*		R. S. Evans Boats, Inc.	(47p162)
		(1950)	*For 'Evansake II*		Advance Co.	(60p218)
185	1927/226991		*Mariska*	93'	F. D. Owsley	
		(1935)	*Truelove*		Fred W. Weller	(37p396)
			Heigh-Ho			
			Dolphin		Howard Bonbright	(39p127)
			Josephine		Allen P. Green	(41p227)
			Windswept		Nelson M. Davis	(47p482)
		(1950)	*Helma*	(97')	Bruce Dodson	(69p312)
		(1971)	*Helma*		Edward S. Dodson	(77p196)
			Lady Mary			
186	1927/226578		*Dixie Belle*	94'	Jacob Aron	(to35p109)
		(1939)	*Marybelle*		W. E. Ferguson	(41p286)
		(1947)	*Marybelle*		John & Louise Hawes	(50p304)
187	1927/226527		*Dream*	78' Cruiser	F. L. DuBosque	(to28p109)
			Impulse	(79'6")		
			Jedge II		B. W. Lamson	(35p177)
		(1939)	*Luneta II*		Sherman Flint	(41p263)
			Luneta II		Andrew J. Flatten	(47p252)
			Luneta II		Arthur R. Cannon	(50p282)
		(1954)	*Rover*		Chandler Hovey	(71p565)
		(1973)	*Rover*		Raymond T. Bell	(75p437)
188	1927		*Bilma IV*	46'	W. G. Selby	
189	1927/227135		*Nicoya*	95'	Fred B. Lovejoy	
			Nicoya		H. Rodney Sharp	(35p252)
		(1939)	*Nicoya*		Albert W. Johnson	(41p326)
		(1947)	*Nicoya*		Howard Gould	(50p340)
			Nicoya		Richard P. Herzfeld	(54p367)
		(1955)	*Nicoya.*		Nepenthe Charter Co.	(60p413)

Contract Number	Year Built/ Documentation Number	1st in Lloyd's	Original & Subsequent Boat Names	Length	Original & Subsequent Owner(s)	Lloyd's Register Reference
190	1927/227642		*Daydream*	126'	W. H. Reynolds	
		(1935)	*Daydream*		Walter S. Gubelmann	(39p120)
			Niagara		Howard Gould	(41p236)
			Niagara		Baker Foundation, Inc.	(50p339)
		(1954)	*Niagara*		Cia Indus. Univ. de Mexico S.A.	(56p375)
		(1960)	*Niagara*		R. P. Haupt	(71p477)
			Sunk at Stillsville, off Miami, to be called Bimini Club			early 1960
191	1927/227582		*Frolic III*	75' Cruiser	Walter P. Chrysler	(to41p173)
			Explorer		W. Gordon Wing	(56p185)
		(1960)	*Explorer*		Clarence Y. Martin	(73p199)
192	1928/227581		*Waleda II*	125'	Walter H. Lippincott	(to35p372)
193	1928/227907		*Elsie Fenimore*	81'	E. R. F. Johnson	
			Ericka			
194	1927/228024		*Lanai*	85'	Arthur Curtiss James	(to41p245)
			Lanai		Mrs. A. C. James	(35p194)
			Who Cares			
		(1947)	*Undine*	(85'1")	George W. Gibbs	(50p494)
		(1954)	*Vergemere*		Ogden Phipps	(60p617)
		(1962)	*Vanity Fair*		Northern Flying & Marine Ser	(67p716)
		(1969)	*The Midas Touch*		Louise F. Roberts	(73p621)
		(1975)	*Golden Lion*		Robert McManus, Grand Prize, Inc.	(79p192)
			Lady Mary		Sundream Yacht Charter	
195	1928/228063		*Mariposa*	98'	Dr. George D. Rosengarten	
		(1935)	*Mariposa*	(101', stern lengthened 3')	Frank Miller Gould	(41p280)
196	1928/228294		*Luneta*	98'	Col. S. L. H. Slocum	(to35p206)
			Jedge			
			Carolyn		Carolyn Dashiell	(39p92)

Contract Number	Year Built/ Documentation Number	1st in Lloyd's	Original & Subsequent Boat Names	Length	Original & Subsequent Owner(s)	Lloyd's Register Reference
		(1941)	*Carolyn*		Herman W. Folk	(47p90)
			Carolyn		Rhodes Perdue	(50p97)
			Carolyn		E. A. Stephens	(54p108)
		(1955)	*Genie*		Colby M. Chester	(71p271)
			Lady Esther		Dwight Moyer	
197	1928/228120		*Saunterer*	98'	Jeremiah Milbank	(to41p394)
			Saunterer		J. T. Kingsley	(46p29)
		(1935)	*Saunterer*		Jeremiah Milbank	(39p374)
			Saunterer		Miami Insular Transport Corp.	(47p377)
			Saunterer		Verna S. Lance	(50p412)
??	1928	(1935)	*Sea Call II*	44' Aux. Sch.	John Trumpy	(39p378)
			Sea Call II		Dr. Irving R. Deibert	(41p397)
		(1947)	*Sea Call II*		Dr. F. A. Slack, Jr.	(67p588)
			Sea Call II		James Griffith	(69p619)
			Sea Call II			(71p591)
198	1929/228292		*Viator*	106'	Dr. Maitland Alexander	(to41p478)
199	1929/228643		*Maemere*	110'	Dewitt Page	(to39p254)
			Maemere		Mrs. Dewitt Page	(41p266)
			Big Pebble		Edward S. Moore	(47p68)
		(1950)	*Big Pebble*		Mrs. Edward S. Moore	(56p82)
		(1960)	*Sea Panther*		Oscar F. Holcombe	(62p537)
		(1964)	*Sea Panther*		John J. Atwater, Jr.	(67p600)
		(1969)	*Sea Panther*		Richard Wallace	(71p602)
			High Spirits		Arnold & Sons	(73p265)
			High Spirits		James T. Bell	(75p229)
			High Spirits		Charles Cauthen	(84p307)
			High Spirits		Mr. Bright, Vernon S&L	~1985
			High Spirits		U.S. Government, repossessed	
			High Spirits		Horn Blower Yachts	
			High Spirits		William D. Lench,	Doc. 1989,

Contract Number	Year Built/ Documentation Number	1st in Lloyd's	Original & Subsequent Boat Names	Length	Original & Subsequent Owner(s)	Lloyd's Register Reference
					California Charters	1990
200	1929/228805		*Dream Girl*	101'	J. G. Roberts	
			Dream Girl		Reamy Eugene Field	(35p115)
			Dream Girl		Mrs. E. Widener Dixon	(39p133)
			Big Pebble		Mrs. Edward S. Moore	(41p72)
201	1929/229211		*Memory*	101'	F. E. Kingston	
			West Wind		Frank O. Sherrill	(35p378)
		(1939)	*Lela*		Mrs. Ogden M. Edwards, Jr.	(41p250)
202	1929/229090		*Sahlou*	80'	Dr. C. Sahler Hornbeck	
			Doreta		D. F. Wheeler	(35p112)
			Florence		L. W. Hench	(39p161)
			Bangalore		Lowell P. Weiker	(41p64)
??	1929		U.S.N. YP57	75'		
		(1950)	*Yipee*		Jack Thiers	(64p696)
		(1969)	*Yipee*		Clifford Harmes	(71p772)
203	1930/229497		*Silver Moon II*	101'	John E. Zimmerman	(to35p321)
		(1939)	*Masquerader*		John Charles Thomas	(41p289)
			Masquerader		Lee & Ruby Johns	(47p280)
		(1950)	*Aras*		Hugh J. Chisholm	(56p56)
			Aras		Estate of Hugh J. Chisholm	(60p60)
		(1960)	*Aras*		Sara C. Chisholm	(64p58)
			Fransu		Daniel E. Taylor	(67p252)
		(1969)	*Governors Lady*		Robert L. Jackson	(75p209)
		(1977)	*Governors Lady*		Governors Club, Inc.	(78p204)
			Lost at sea (sunk)			1985

Contract Number	Year Built/ Documentation Number	1st in Lloyd's	Original & Subsequent Boat Names	Length	Original & Subsequent Owner(s)	Lloyd's Register Reference
204	1930/229886		*All Alone*	80'	George W. Codrington	
			Anahita		Demund C. Lynch	(35p39)
		(1939)	*Anahita*		Alfred Epstein	(41p44)
205	1930/229498		*Tech, Jr.*	85'	F. V. duPont	(to35p344)
		(1939)	*Tech*		F. V. duPont	(41p449)
			Admiral Charles H. Lyman		U.S. Naval Sea Cadet Corps	(84p7)
206	1930/229930		*Lanakila*	103'	Frederick B. Lovejoy	
		(1935)	*Ellenar*		C. J. Root	(41p147)
207	1930/229790		*Truant*	120'	Truman H. Newberry,	(to35p354)

Contract Number	Year Built/ Documentation Number	1st in Lloyd's	Original & Subsequent Boat Names	Length	Original & Subsequent Owner(s)	Lloyd's Register Reference
					Detroit YHB-9	
			Idyl		Walter P. Murphy	(37p185)
		(1939)	*Carnan*		Louis J. Kolb	(41p94)
			Muriel	(121'3")	Walter P. Chrysler, Jr.	(47p301)
			North Wales		Walter P. Chrysler	(50p347)
		(1954)	*Carola*		Col. Leon Mandel	(64p123)
			Manatee		Advertising Agency Assoc.	(84p430)
			Broken up at Jones Boat Yard late 1980		Pilothouse at Nautical Antiques, Ft. Lauderdale, FL	
208	1930/229872		*Mono*	106'	George K. Morrow	
			Carita		Edward E. Bishop	(35p79)
		(1939)	*Carita*		Lillian H. & Edward E. Bishop	(41p94)
		(1947)	*Carita*	(105'7")	R. W. Sawyer	(50p95)
209	1930/229834		*Arminia*	110' Steel	Gen. W. W. Atterbury	(to35p48)
			Stella Polaris		Livingston L. Short	(39p411)
			Stella Polaris		Vincent R. Trabucco	(50p458)
		(1954)	*Stella Polaris*		Sprout & Davis Inc.	(55p496)
			Stella Polaris		John P. McNabb	(56p506)
			Stella Polaris		Hal Roach Studies	(60p558)
		(1962)	*Stella Polaris*		M. B. & Ruth F. Tuxhorn	(64p594)
		(1967)	*Stella Polaris*		E. L. Reitz	(69p684)
		(1971)	*Stella Polaris*		North Star Marine Sales Inc.	(75p510)
210	1930/230414		*Minoco.*	108'	Mills Novelty Co.	(39p286)
			Idyl		Walter P. Murphy	(41p209)
211	1931/230897		*Captiva*	111'	Mrs. Helen Hay Whitney	(35p78)
			Captiva		Mrs. Payne Whitney	
			Captiva		Lee & Ruby Johns	(47p87)
			Captiva			(50p94)
		(1954)	*Captiva*		Joseph A. Martino	(62p120)
			Captiva		University of Miami, Institute	(64p119)

Contract Number	Year Built/ Documentation Number	1st in Lloyd's	Original & Subsequent Boat Names	Length	Original & Subsequent Owner(s)	Lloyd's Register Reference
					of Marine Sciences	
		(1967)	*Captiva*		Frank O. Sherrill	(73p101)
			Captiva			(75p90)
	231651	(1975)	*Babe Rainbow*		Fred A. McKechnie	(79p35)
			Columbia			
212	1931/230681		*Virago*	98'	Thomas N. McCarter	(to35p367)
		(1939)	*Virago*		George F. Getz, Jr., Globe Corporation	(41p480)
213	not issued					
214	1931/231388		*Alamo*	148' Steel	William F. Ladd, Tams & King N.A.	
			Alamo		Lucius B. Manning	(35p28)
			Alamo		Alamo Inc., W. F. Ladd, Pres.	(37p28)
			Relimpa			
			Ranley		Guernsey Curran	(39p353)
			Ronaele		Mrs. E. Widener Dixon	(41p382)
		(1954)	*Alamo*		C. S. Smith	(60p37)
			Fiesta II		Enrique Braun	(62p217)
215	1932/231671		*Veruselle*	107'	John R. Hopkins	(to35p366)
			Hielander			
		(1939)	*Alcedo*	(108'7")	George W. C. Drexel	(41p32)
216	1933/232258		*Seagoin'*	48' Aux. Sch.	William K. Barclay, Jr.	(to47p384)
		(1950)	*Rambler II*		George B. Howell	(54p415)
		(1955)	*Rambler II*		John S. McCourtney	(62p488)
217	1933/232280		*Minel*	50' Schooner	Ritner K. Walling	(to35p232)
			Minel	(49'11")	L. J. Goldbach, M.D.	(39p285)
			Margot		Ward Wheelock	(41p276)
		(1947)	*Pipe Dream II*		William Wikoff Smith	(50p372)
			Liat		Holland Potter	(54p292)
			Linda		F. H. Eddy	(56p303)

Contract Number	Year Built/ Documentation Number	1st in Lloyd's	Original & Subsequent Boat Names	Length	Original & Subsequent Owner(s)	Lloyd's Register Reference
218	1933		*Lodsen*	30' Cutter	Franklin M. Doan	(to41p258)
			Dipper		Edward D. Payne	(47p122)
		(1954)	*Dipper*		Robert Franzblau	(56p153)
			Pavanne		Valentine A. Hofmann	(60p440)
			Pavanne		Richard Carr	(62p457)
219	1934/233593		*Elsie Fenimore*	87' Aux. Ketch	E. R. Fenimore Johnson	(to56p176)
			John M. Howard		Boy Scouts of America	(60p295)
		(1962)	*Earl of Desmond*		The Geraldines, Ltd.	(71p211)
		(1973)	*Earl of Desmond*		James W. Fitzgerald	(75p153)
			Northern Light			
220	1935/233947		*Edrus*	46'6"	Russell L. Heverling	(to35p119)
		(1935)	*Olive IV*	(Len. 9'6" 1938)	Mrs. Boake Carter	(39p321)
		(1941)	*Olive IV*		Bernard F. Diamond	(47p324)
		(1954)	*Allegro*		Howard F. Isham	(59p36)
		(1960)	*Allegro*		Janet E. Dieterle	(71p44)
		(1973)	*Allegro*	(56')	Alex Thompson	(75p16)
221	1935/233946		*Alelnansr*	57' Aux. Yawl	Sayre M. Ramsdell	(to35p30)
		(1939)	*Malihini*		H. Gregory Wait	(41p270)
			Malihini		Dr. A. J. L. Moritz	(47p261)
			Malihini		Cornelius Rathborne	(50p288)
222	1935		Stock boat	30' Cutter		
223	1935/538196		Stock boat	30' Aux. Cutter		
		(1937)	*Rip-Tide*	(30.5')	Joseph J. Summerill, Jr.	(55p426)
		1954	*Rip-Tide*		Leonard H. Grantland	
		1987	*Rip-Tide*		Ches. Bay Maritime Museum	
		1989	*Rip-Tide*		Asher Tourison	
224??	1936		*Eugenia*	30' Aux. Cutter		
			Eugenia	30'6"	W. Lynn Hendrickson	(39p152)
			Eugenia		S. Roger Gale	(41p155)
		(1947)	*Eugenia*		Roger W. Buntin	(50p163)

Contract Number	Year Built/ Documentation Number	1st in Lloyd's	Original & Subsequent Boat Names	Length	Original & Subsequent Owner(s)	Lloyd's Register Reference
		(1954)	*Spray*		H. L. Gruehn	(64p588)
225	1935		Stock boat	30' Cutter		
226	1935/234212		*Florence V*	80'	William J. McCahan, III & Mrs. Thomas C. McCahan	(to41p166)
		(1946)	*Florence V*	(79'2")	USCG AUX 4 Nav. Dist. Foun.	(56p196)
		(1960)	*Florence V*		Florence V Foundation	(69p257)
			Florence V		Howard B. Thorne	(71p250)
		(1973)	*Florence V*		Helen G. Thorne, Florence V, Inc.	(79p169)
			Contessa		Mal Nevel	Doc. 1993
227	1935		*Deepwater*	36' Cutter	Charles Welsh	
			Saracen		C. Egerton Warburton	(37p339)
			Deep Water		Benjamin F. Bunn	(39p121)
			Deep Water		John Hertz, Jr.	(47p119)
		(1954)	*Deep Water*		George Wauchope	(64p168)
		(1967)	*Deep Water*		State University of N.Y. Maritime College	(69p193)
			Deep Water		Peter-Thor Watson	(71p188)

Contract Number	Year Built/ Documentation Number	1st in Lloyd's	Original & Subsequent Boat Names	Length	Original & Subsequent Owner(s)	Lloyd's Register Reference

Contract Number	Year Built/ Documentation Number	1st in Lloyd's	Original & Subsequent Boat Names	Length	Original & Subsequent Owner(s)	Lloyd's Register Reference
228	1935/234490		*Innisfail*	85'	Joseph M. Cudahy	
			Sea Call		Joseph B. Dunbaugh	(39p378)
			Sea Call		A. Arnold	(41p397)
			Wadu			
		(1947)	*Variety*	(84'11")	Elton Hoyt, II	(50p500)

Contract Number	Year Built/ Documentation Number	1st in Lloyd's	Original & Subsequent Boat Names	Length	Original & Subsequent Owner(s)	Lloyd's Register Reference
		(1954)	*Variety*		Don F. Rayburn	(56p554)
		(1960)	*Variety*		Bill Allen Investment Co.	(75p568)
			Reported bought in 1952 changed name to *Minerva*			1974
		(1977)	*Minerva*		Bill Allen Investment Co.	(78p339)
			Enticer		Paul Zimmer	
			Enticer		Milton Sender	March 1980
229	1936		*Suitsus*	36'6"	F. V. duPont	
		(1939)	*Muja III*		E. F. Darrell Estate	(41p312)
		(1947)	*Muja III*		A. J. Flatten	(47p300to50)
230	1936/234913		*Consort IV*	90'	T. Munroe Dobbins	(to41p112)
			Consort IV		Gerald W. Ford	(46p14)
			Consort IV		Albert E. Schwabacher	(47p107)
			Pez Espada IV		Albert E. Schwabacher	(47p338)
		(1950)	*Jagua*		Dr. Santiago Claret	(62p296)
231	1937/236529		*Tritona*	61'	John H. Ballantine	
		(1939)	*Tritona*		William O'Neil	(41p462)
		(1947)	*Mako*		Thorne Donnelley	(50p286)
			Jasuva		Lois S. & W. A. Rinehart	(54p255)
			Jasuva		J. C. Herbert Bryant	(55p258)
			Margo		J. C. Herbert Bryant	(56p328)
		(1960)	*Otsego*		Harold S. Smith	(64p456)
		(1967)	*Tranquill II*		Dr. Robert G. Randall	(69p735)
232	1937/236204		*We Three*	61'	Dr. Leon Levy	(39p466)
			Ro		Stanley M. Rumbough	(41p379)
			Random		Random Trips, Inc.	(47p353)
		(1950)	*Natamor*		M. Forgash	(54p362)
		(1955)	*Dorick*		Richard C. Kettles	(56p159)
		(1960)	*B-Way*		Sidney P. Lipkins	(67p120)
		(1969)	*Mizpal*		John E. Richards	(71p455)
			Princess Holly		J. O. Hice	(75p411)

Contract Number	Year Built/ Documentation Number	1st in Lloyd's	Original & Subsequent Boat Names	Length	Original & Subsequent Owner(s)	Lloyd's Register Reference
233	1937/236691		*Blue Heaven*	61'	W. W. Trimpi	
			Inspector		Dept. of Health, N.J.	11/9/38
					Yacht Sales & Service	4/25/50
					Fred Geiger	
			Blue Heaven		John J. Hill, Jr.	1/17/51
		(1973)	*Flying Lady*.	(62'6")	Citizens & Southern National Bank. Rebuilt 1988-89.	8/8/61
			Flying Lady		Donated to Georgia So. Univ.	May 1, 1993
234	1937/236861		*Arev*	45'	Harold Payne Whitmore	(to41p52)
			Pendula			
			Shearwater		Charles E. Dunlap	(47p396)
			Arev		Charles E. Dunlap	(50p434)
235	1938/236970		*Helma*	61'6"	Bruce Dodson	(39p193)
			Siren			
			Mariana III		Allen R. Joslin	(41p276)
		(1947)	*Sea Tabby*		Charles A. Karagheusian	~'44 (78p485)
			Sea Tabby		Donated (College in FL)	~1977
			Sea Tabby		J. Britten Stokes	(79p459)
			Sea Tabby		Stodder	1981
			Sea Tabby		Addison Pratt & Robert Libby	Feb.1982
236	1938/237423		*Abadab*	61'6"	Max H. Thurnauer	(50p25)
		(1954)	*Mariah*		Charles P. Ryan	(56p328)
		(1960)	*Mariah*		H. Gregg Danby	(67p413)
		(1971)	*Mariah*		F. Christian Berg	(73p371)
			Mariah		Danniel family	
			Mariah		The Citadel, Charleston, SC	
			Getana (Panama flag, running tourists in Cuba)		Narcello Perrone	Jan. 1995
237	1938		*Egret*	46'	Charles Porter Schutt	(to41p142)
238	1938/237648		*Far Cry*	47'4" Sloop	Col. Edwin M. Chance	(to41p161)

Contract Number	Year Built/ Documentation Number	1st in Lloyd's	Original & Subsequent Boat Names	Length	Original & Subsequent Owner(s)	Lloyd's Register Reference
			Far Cry		F. C. Anderson	(50p168)
239	1938/238027		*Morning Star*	85' Ketch	Eugene E. duPont	(to41p311)
			Pez Espada III		Albert E. Schwabacher	(47p338)
			Pez Espada IV		Albert E. Schwabacher	(50p368)
		(1954)	*Pez Espada IV*		Paul Mantz	(56p405)
			Pez Espada IV		Ray C. Sparling	(60p445)
		(1962)	*Pez Espada IV*		Mrs. Elizabeth S. Floyd	(64p473)
		(1967)	*Pez Espada IV*		Leslie Cook	(69p540)
		(1971)	*Pez Espada IV*		Oliver W. Beaulieu	(73p462)
			Turning Point	(80.5')	Ronald C. Pouliot	Doc. 1990
240	1939/238567		*Halaia*	61'6" Cruiser	A. J. Drexel Paul	(to41p190)
			Alice B. IV			
			Helene		Charles E. Sorensen	(47p191)
			Sea Dream		John M. L. Rutherfurd	(50p417)
			Sea Dream		John P. Porter	(54p453)
		(1955)	*White Wing*		Roscoe S. Miller	(62p667)
		(1967)	*Curlu*		Curtis F. & Lulu Bryan	(73p143)
			The Lady		Skip Mauer at Mystic, CT	5/91
241	1939/238675		*Nameni*	55'	L. Rodman Paige	(to41p317)
			Nameni		Robert Leslie Taylor	(47p305)
242	1939/239004		*Innisfail*	91'	Joseph M. Cudahy	(to41p211)
			Ora B			
			YP 354		U.S. Navy	1942
			Innisfail		Col. W. T. Baughn	1947
		(1964)	*Innisfail*		Ralph W. Burger	(71p323)
			Innisfail		Florida. Institute of Technology	(73p280)
			El Presidente		Florida. Institute of Technology	(73p184)
			Innisfail		L. J. Mercer & S. L. Tricater	(75p242)

Contract Number	Year Built/ Documentation Number	1st in Lloyd's	Original & Subsequent Boat Names	Length	Original & Subsequent Owner(s)	Lloyd's Register Reference
			El Presidente		Florida. Institute of Technology	(75p161)
		(1978)	*El Presidente*		Leonard J. Mercer	(77p139)
			Innisfail		Leonard J. Mercer & Stanton L. Tricater	(79p225)
			El Presidente		Leonard J. Mercer	(79p147)
			El Presidente	(96')	El Presidente, Inc.	Doc. 1981
			El Presidente		Mirabel Marine Charters	(84p207)
			El Presidente		Roger S. Kolasinski	Doc. 1989
			Reported sold, winter 1995			
243	1939/240167		*Martha*	71'	William M. Davey	(to41p284)
			Mystic V		Philip R. Mallory	(47p303) 1942 to 1957
		(1954)	*Mystic V*		Adolph M. Dick	(50p330)
			Vita		So. Builders of Houston	(56p564)
			Vita		Hughes Tool Co.	(60p622) 1957 to 1961
			Agrion		Ralph W. Burger	(62p36) 1961 to 1963
		(1964)	*Agrion*		Daytona Marine Supplies	(67p34) 1963 to 1967
		(1969)	*Marben*		Bennett C. O'Boyle	(71p417) 1967 to 1980
		(1973)	*Marben*		Margery K. O'Boyle	(79p301)
			Joint Venture		John E. & Voss C. Milloway	1980 to 1989
			Joint Venture		Dr. John Kilgore	8/89
			Barchrisda		Frederick L. & Barbara J. DeRatto	Doc. 1990
244	1939/239627		*Drifter*	76'	Frank O. Sherrill	(to41p136)
			Charmarie			

Contract Number	Year Built/ Documentation Number	1st in Lloyd's	Original & Subsequent Boat Names	Length	Original & Subsequent Owner(s)	Lloyd's Register Reference
		(1947)	*Nautilus*		Frederick L. Regnery	(50p336)
			Minerva		William R. Allen	(54p343)
			Minerva		F. W. Ayers	(55p345)
		(1960)	*Minerva*		Carl & Leo Rosen	(64p408)
		(1967)	*Leonie*		Homer J. Moore	(71p382)
		(1971)	*Lady Mary*		John E. Willis	(73p326)
		(1969)	*Leonie*		Homer J. Moore	(75p293)
			Maryann			
			Martha Ann			
245	1939/239767		*Jinia III*	69'	Arthur M. Stoner	(to41p223)
			Mojo		Gregory S. McIntosh	(47p298)
			Mojo		Gaudin Motor Co.	(50p323)
		(1954)	*Mojo*		Frank Muller	(75p347)
		(1977)	*Phyllis II*		Thomas Ballard	(79p385)
			Renown	(65.4')	Ronald Lee Bailey	Doc. 1981
			Renown		Classic Yacht Charterers	Doc. 1989, 1990
246	1939/239687		*Tech, Jr.*	45' Cruiser	F. V. duPont	
		(1947)	*Tech, Jr.*		Herbert M. Laford	(64p616)
??	1939		*Samari*	55'		
			Kate III		Reeve Schley	(50p247)
			Cher A Mar		Roland M. Lagueux	(64p135)
247	1940/240262		*Alcy*	64'10"	Howard A. Perkins	
		(1947)	*Mystic*		Robert & Fay Glendinning	(75p355)
??	1940/139641	(1941)	*Sea Call III*	36'3" Aux. Cut.	John Trumpy	(41p397
			Bonny		Malcolm Matheson	(50p83)
		(1954)	*Bonny*		Roy N. Livingston	(75p75)
248	1940/240724		*Chanticleer*	65'	Samuel S. Sanford	(to41p99)
			Coastal Patrol Boat		U.S. Government	
			Chanticleer		Irwin Corp.	(47p94)

Contract Number	Year Built/ Documentation Number	1st in Lloyd's	Original & Subsequent Boat Names	Length	Original & Subsequent Owner(s)	Lloyd's Register Reference
			Chanticleer		Warren MacPherson	(50p103)
			Chanticleer		C.B.C. Corp	(60p129)
		(1954)	*Elizabeth*		Howard K. Teague	(62p195)
		(1964)	*Elizabeth*		Gordon Hurd	(71p219)
249–278	1940-42		SC 507, 508, 524–529, 630–635, 1023–1028, 1067–1076 (total 30 boats)	110' Sub Chaser	U.S. Navy, (Sparkman & Stephens)	

End of yachts built by Mathis Yacht Building Co., Camden, NJ. Mathis Yacht Building Company moves to Gloucester City, NJ, July 1, 1942.. Company name changed to John Trumpy & Sons, Inc., January 28, 1943.

Contract Number	Year Built/ Documentation Number	1st in Lloyd's	Original & Subsequent Boat Names	Length	Original & Subsequent Owner(s)	Lloyd's Register Reference
279–282	1942–1946		YTB 225–228 (total 4 boats)	110' Harbor Tug	U.S. Navy, Cox & Stephens	
283–312	1942–1946		PTC 37–66 (total 30 boats)	63' Sub Chaser	U.S. Navy, Miami Shipbuilding Corporation	
??	1943		*Aurelia*	111'6" Cruiser	Lyman A. Whitney	(50p57)
		(1954)	*Aurelia*		Harold Earll	(56p64)
??	1943/262197		*Cajun Queen*	107.2	James Mock	Doc. 1990
313	not used					
314	1947/249213		*Aurora*	55' Pilot model	John Trumpy (started 1945)	
			Kay-Bob			
			Helma		Bruce Dodson	(47p192)
			Janirv III			
			Jimijo V		F. A. McGuire	(50p238)
		(1954)	*Thelmar*		Frank M. Smith	(56p529)
			B'way Lady			
			Estelle G.		Gelman Eng. Co.	(60p198)
			Celadon		J. P. Wade Levering	(62p130)
		(1964)	*Celadon*		Hermann Sebold	(75p98)
		(1975)	*Sea Princess*		Princess House Inc.	(79p456)
			Sea Princess	(52.4')	Sunny So. Yacht & Chart	Doc. 1981
			Sea Prince		Sea Prince Trust	Doc. 1989
			Sea Prince		Stephen N. Cucci	Doc. 1993

Contract Number	Year Built/ Documentation Number	1st in Lloyd's	Original & Subsequent Boat Names	Length	Original & Subsequent Owner(s)	Lloyd's Register Reference
315	1946/285227		*Sylvia IV*	55'	Samuel S. Bell, Jr.	(55p506)
			Ingress II		Joseph L. Eastwick	(56p253)
			Treasure		Theodore Pratt	(60p599)
		(1962)	*Nenemoosha*		Lyman F. Hewins	(71p474)
			Sanderling		at Sagman Marina, NY	
316	1946/284432		*Marion II*	55'	R. F. Bain	(to47p271)
		(1950)	*Clare H. IV*		Harold C. & Clara Heermann	(56p128)
			Lo-Ha		Harold H. & Louise Wardle	(60p339)
			Wailana			
		(1962)	*Sunrise*		Andrew DeGraff Berkey	(64p601)
		(1967)	*Sunrise*		James R. Anthony, Jr.	(79p494)
			Sunrise		Hal Jones	1978/79
			Andrea		Demoustes, Inc.	Doc. 1981, 93
317	1947/269767		*One Forty Four II*	55'	A. R. Gross	
			Vita			
		(1954)	*Electra*		Porter B. Chase	(55p170)
		(1956)	*Frances T*		Charter Craft Corp.	(60p221)
		(1964)	*Sinbad*		Fred H. Gordon, Jr.	(69p655)
		(1971)	*Snowbird*		Harold F. Falk	(77p440)
			Snowbird	(52.3')	Laurence C. Moman, Jr.	Doc. 1981, 1989, 1993
318–320			Stock boats not built	55'		
321	1946/250099		*Makaira*	65'	R. W. Johnson	
			Mak aira		Charles F. Johnson	(47p258)
		(1950)	*Makaira*	Len. 5', '53 (70')	Lester M. & Ruth P. Sears	(64p372)
		(1967)	*Makaira*		Y. & S. Investment Co.	(69p425)
			Stranger II		Leslie Taylor, Jr.	
			Stranger II			
			Sea Level II	(61.1')	West India Fruit & Steamship	Doc. 1981 (84p635)

Contract Number	Year Built/ Documentation Number	1st in Lloyd's	Original & Subsequent Boat Names	Length	Original & Subsequent Owner(s)	Lloyd's Register Reference
			Sea Level II	(71.1')	Jerry Lacouture	Doc. 1989
			Twin-Dee		Irvin Devilnd & Dinburg	
			Reported sunk 1985 as *Sea Level II* or *Twin-Dee*		Seen 1993 as *Sea Level II*	
322	1942–45		Plane Personnel Rescue Boats (96 boats total)	24'	U.S. Navy	
323	1946/250631		*Carol Anne*	60'	R. Foster Reynolds	(50p96)
		(1954)	*Bolou*		Edward N. Rich, Jr.	(62p104)
			Patrician			
		(1964)	*Supremus*		Falconi Leasing Co.	(69p694)
		(1971)	*Vixen*	(57.1')	Arthur L. Sauerberg	Doc. 1981
						(79p553)
			Vixen		T. A. McCord, Jr.	Doc. 1989, 93
324	1946/251106		*Malova V*	61'6"	J. Rodman McCoy	(to50)
		(1955)	*The McCoy*		J. Rodman McCoy	(56p530)
		(1960)	*The McCoy*		Vernon S. Dallman	(77p485)
			Alicia	(58.0')	John Pellarin	Doc. 1981
			Vida Mia		Fred M. Korber	Doc. 1993
325	1947/285378		*Curlew*	45'	R. Snowden Andrews	(64p159)
		(1967)	*Curlew*		F. K. Thayer, Jr.	(69p182)
			Sea Plow			
326	1947/503136		*Jinofor*	45'	Edward H. Ellis	(to54)
		(1955)	*Chevron*		Miss Katherine W. Foster	(56p122)
		(1960)	*Marian C.*		Lincoln Clark	(64p381)
			Flying M.		Robert B. Walker	(67p246)
		(1969)	*Flying M*		Earl B. Stearns	(75p186)
			Corn Husker		Clarence D. Wilson	Doc. 1993
327	1946/251399		*Silver Swan*	71'	Arthur W. Conley	(to47p400)
			Melmar		Dr. Mathew T. Mellon	(50p310)
			Marycia			
			Virginian			

Contract Number	Year Built/ Documentation Number	1st in Lloyd's	Original & Subsequent Boat Names	Length	Original & Subsequent Owner(s)	Lloyd's Register Reference
			Bettina			
		(1954)	*Masquerader*		Nolan Brown Motors, Inc.	(79p311)
					Conner Brown	
			Masquerader		United Yacht Brokers	
			Cadillac Lady		Dr. William Schwartz	~2 to3 years
			Capricorn Lady		Dan & Judy Gilman	1980, Doc. 93
328	1947/253965		*Seaplay*	80'	Diesel Towing Co.,	(55p460)
					George W. Codrington	
		(1956)	*Natamor II*		Transport & Charter Corp.	(64p431)
		(1967)	*Natamor II*		Overland Merchandise Corp.	(75p360)
		(1977)	*Seaway*		Odecca Terminal Co.	(79p459)
			Seaway		Inter. Ocengr (sic) Corp.	
			Beau Rivage		Dr. William Cirksena	
			Beau Rivage		Tamara Charters, Ltd.	Doc. 1993
329	1947/252222		*Marylin*	80' Houseboat	Col. Frederick Pope	(to47p279)
			Random		Random Trips, Inc.	(50p385)
			Tarmarac		Arthur E. Wheeler	(54p509)
		(1955)	*Budgit*		Albert L. Gustin, Jr.	(71p121)
			Sinbar		Edwin M. Belcher	
			Mauretania		David Banta,	
					Dee & David (Henry) Mancini	
			Mauretania		Charter Concepts	
			Mauretania		John T. Boyt	
			Mauretania	(76.4')	Mauretania Assoc.	Doc. 1989, 1993
330	1947/253445		*Tomadge*	60' Houseboat	Thomas T. Keane	
			Southern			
			Tomadge III			
			Commander		Consolidated Motor & Finance Co.	(50p116)

Contract Number	Year Built/ Documentation Number	1st in Lloyd's	Original & Subsequent Boat Names	Length	Original & Subsequent Owner(s)	Lloyd's Register Reference
		(1954)	*Commander*		Jacob Meyerhoff	(56p132)
			Jenirve V		Irving J. Reuter	(60p288)
		(1962)	*Paradise*		Joseph H. Eisenberg	(69p527)
			Paradise		"Kings Point"	(71p505)
			Miss Elaneous		Elaine Hall	3 years
			Rusty Su	(57.1')	Bibrab Trading Co.	(84p603) Doc. 1989, 1993
331	1947/253074		*Gretchen III*	60' Houseboat	Roland H. & Gertrude Zinn	(to47p182)
		(1950)	*Gretchen III*		William. A. DeLaney	(55p222)
		(1956)	*Sun Shower*		Vernon G. Cardy	(60p565)
			White Cloud		Florence H. Maxwell	(64p680)
		(1967)	*El-Lin III*		Eleanor R. Walsh	(71p220)
					Hopbrener	
					Davis	
			Shenacock		William Barr	1981
			Shenacock		Samuel Jack Lanahan	Doc. 1993
332	1947/260277		*Aurora II*	61' Houseboat	John Trumpy & Sons	
			(*Aurora II* was started in Gloucester City, NJ, and finished in Annapolis, MD.)			
		(1950)	*Sheila VI*		W. P. & Elizabeth McIntosh	(56p481)
		(1960)	*Thelmar*		Frank M. Smith	(67p523)
		(1962)	*Polaris*		E. Boykin Hartley	(73p470)
		(1978)	*Veritas*	(57.8')	Dan P. S. Paul	Doc. 1981 (84p778)
333	1947		PT 811	94' PT Boat	U.S. Navy (Destroyed in Vietnam 1969-1970)	
			(Completed for Annapolis Yacht Yard)			
334	1948		*Tech, Jr.* (First keel laid by John Trumpy & Sons in Annapolis)	60'	Francis V. duPont	(62p604)
			Counterpoint.		Coleman duPont	(71p172)
			Counterpoint.		Donated to Maryland Militia	1967
	(664867)		*Counterpoint.*		Pointer, Inc.	Doc. 1993

Contract Number	Year Built/ Documentation Number	1st in Lloyd's	Original & Subsequent Boat Names	Length	Original & Subsequent Owner(s)	Lloyd's Register Reference
335	1948/255666		*Seaholm*	61'	Alfred V. duPont	(to56p466)
		(1960)	*Jimp*		Ivor R. Pardee	(73p296)
			Seaprobe			
			Pattyscake			
			Doris M			
		(1975)	*Seaholm*		J. Bates Harcum	(79p451)
			Seaholm		Mr. Jean Newbold	
			Seaholm	(58.2')	Carl W. Vesper	(1988) Doc. 1989, 1993
336	1948/256986		*Mikaro*	72'	G. M. Stull	(64p406)
			Exact		J. Burr Bartram	(67p230)
		(1969)	*Heather V*		Ken G. MacCart	(71p298)
		(1973)	*Gemini*		Samuel F. & Joanne J. duPont	(79p185)
			Sank or burned-Johan Trumpy			
337	1949/282626		*Florence VI*	61'	William J. McCahan, III	(62p222)
		(1964)	*Hie Seas*		George Boza	(67p298)
338	1949/258074		*Alva*	60'	E. E. Dickenson, Sparkman & Stephens, designer	(69p48)
			Alva		William J. Irwin, Jr.	(71p48)
		(1977)	*Midnight Sun*		Edwin T. Boyle	(78p336)
			Midnight Sun	(57.8')	Voorhis Lane, Inc.	Doc. 1981
			Midnight Sun		Edwin T. Boyle	Doc. 1993
339	1949/280154		*Rumak II*	60'	M. & M. William McKelvy	(to 1955)
		(1956)	*Natelva*		Clyde E. Speer	(60p408)
		(1962)	*Sylvia IV*		T. S. Walker	(64p607)
		(1967)	*Road Runner*		Merrill B. John, Jr.	(75p433)
340	1950/281452		*Sea Call IV*	40' Aux. Sloop	John Trumpy	(54p451)
		(1954)	*Lyra*		Richard Rachals	(56p316)
		(1960)	*Staral*		Johnson Stoddard	(64p593)
		(1967)	*Melita*	(34.6')	M. A. Wight, Jr.	(77p290)

Contract Number	Year Built/ Documentation Number	1st in Lloyd's	Original & Subsequent Boat Names	Length	Original & Subsequent Owner(s)	Lloyd's Register Reference
						Doc. 1989
341	1950/281711		*Co-Ed II*	55'	E. R. Fuller	
			Aurora III		John Trumpy & Sons	(54p62)
		(1955)	*Gramma Jo*		F. P. Asher	(56p223)
			Windsong II		Frederick G. Higham	(60p648)
		(1962)	*Windsong II*		George Garvin Brown	(64p689)
			Dibbie Dear		Edward A. Bacon	(67p188)
		(1969)	*Manatee*		Manatee Corp.	(79p298)
			Manatee		Seamora Corp.	(84p431)
			Manatee		Chuck Montares	
			Manatee		Seamora Corp.	Doc. 1993
342	1950		*One Forty Four*	50'	A. R. Gross	
??	1950/541418		*Rowdy*	50'		
		(1954)	*Elsanbil VI*		Wm. Price	(69p228)
			Trumpy Five-O		William P. Angel, Jr.	Doc. 1993
			(Not positive)			
343–349	1951		MSB 5–9	57' Minesweepers	U.S. Navy, Design Contract, Central Procurement	
350	1952		*Sea Call V*	36' Sloop	John Trumpy	(69p619)
			Sea Call V		John Trumpy, Jr.	1963
			Sea Call V		Johan Trumpy	~1965
			Sea Call		Last known owner kept boat in Maine	
351–355	1952–53		MSB 25–29	57' Minesweepers	U.S. Navy	
356–361	1952–1954		Total 6 boats	50' Utility Boats	U.S. Navy	
362	1953		Total 2 boats	'Skiffs'	U.S. Navy, Sparkman & Stephens, designer	
363	1953		*Makaira* (Rebuild)	See #321	Lester M. Sears	
364	1953		MSB Stowage Chocks		U.S. Navy	
365	1953		NOBS 55480		U.S. Navy	

Contract Number	Year Built/ Documentation Number	1st in Lloyd's	Original & Subsequent Boat Names	Length	Original & Subsequent Owner(s)	Lloyd's Register Reference
366	1954/285759		*Aurora IV*	67'6" Houseboat	John Trumpy & Sons	(to56p65)
		(1960)	*Nedell IV*		Ned Dunn	(64p433)
			Janirve VI		Irving Reuter	
			Don Quixote		Stanley Vineberg	(1962 to 64)
			Yorel V		Caddell Dry Dock & Repair Co.	(73p702)
		(1975)	*Adventurer*		Col. & Mrs. Lizz Whitney	(84p8) Doc.
			(Bottom rebuilt, 1985)		Tippett	1981, 1989
			Glory		Wilcox Crittendon Co.	1990
			Entire boat put back in like new condition			1990
			Glory		Binnie Foley Limited	~1991Doc93
367	1954/274696		*Jinofor II*	53' Fish. Cr.	Edward H. Ellis	(to56p266)
			Camelot			
			Nedell		Ned Dunn	(58p389)
			Heather III (IV)		Kenneth G. MacCart	
			Tritona V		John H. Ballantine	
			Milmar		Martin Slifka	(60p387)
		(1962)	*Josephine M IV*		Harry Liebeck	(64p312)
			Tautog		William C. Albertson	(71p678)
		(1973)	*Karanda*		James T. Leftwich	(77p231)
		(1978)	*The Lady*		E. R. Pipping, Jr.	(79p517)
			Norsaga		Gordon McCarthy	Feb/Apr1991
			Norsaga		Charles A. & Janet Maase	Doc. 1993
368	1954/280797		*Sereno III*	67'6" Cruiser	L. M. Miller	
		(1962)	*Treasure IV*		Theodore Pratt	(67p700)
		(1969)	*Imps III*		Col. James C. Smoot	(71p321)
		(1973)	*Mambo*		Charles P. Martyn	(79p297)
						Doc. 1981
			Mambo		Charles F. Chapman School (donation)	

Contract Number	Year Built/ Documentation Number	1st in Lloyd's	Original & Subsequent Boat Names	Length	Original & Subsequent Owner(s)	Lloyd's Register Reference
			Lucky Seven			
			Orion		Louis Knox Newton	
			Manuela		Austin Lynwood Cox	1987
			Liberty		Gary Brink	
			Liberty		Roderick G. Cary	Doc. 1993
369	1954		MSB 29	82' Minesweeper	U.S. Navy	
370	1955/269582		*Willit*	55' Fish. Cr.	Lammot duPont	(64p684)
			Princess Pat.		A. Winston Edwards	(67p530)
		(1969)	*Edwinna IV*		A. Winston Edwards	(to 3/89)
			Edwinna			
			Wings		Teresita Miguel	Doc. 1993
371	1955/284377		*Shelly Kay V*	55' Fish.Cr	J. B. Rich	
			Gay Head		Bohnfalk	
			Four Square		Eli M. Lippman, M.D.	(79p175)
			Four Square			
			Tashtego		John L. Baringer	(84p732)
			Capricorn Mistress		Dan & Judy Gilman	1985
			Summer Place			~1987
			Dixonia		Robert Henkal	
			Dixonia		Dixonia, Inc.	Doc. 1993
372	1955/270489		*Rumak III*	79' Cruiser	William McKelvy	(60p487)
		(1962)	*Bettco*		Clinton Realty Co., Mrs. Bettis	(67p92)
		(1969)	*Windsong II*		George Garvin Brown	(73p692)
			Windsong II		William Weyms	
			Windsong II		Nova Univ. (donation)	
		(1975)	*Windsong II*		Dr. Albert W. Auld	(77p544)
			Windsong II		Warren Atkinson	
			Entre Deux Mers		Jerald Van Brynke	
			Iliana		Edward Young	

Contract Number	Year Built/ Documentation Number	1st in Lloyd's	Original & Subsequent Boat Names	Length	Original & Subsequent Owner(s)	Lloyd's Register Reference
			La Contessa		Jerold Van Brynke	
			Oz		Frank Caruth	~1989
					Major rebuild, Miami River	July, 1990
					U.S. Government	Feb. 1992
			Oshea		Avlake Properties, Inc.	Doc. 1993
373	1955/277448		*Silver Mist.*	67'6" Cruiser	Herbert W. Stone	
			Silver Mist		York Hoover Corp.	(56p485)
		(1960)	*Greetings IV*		Fred Pollak	(67p278)
		(1969)	*B'Way*		Sidney P. Lipkins	(77p69)
		(1977)	*Minerva II*		Bill Allen Invest. Co.	(78p339)
			By Design		Roy Sklarin	
			L'Etoile		Charter Concepts	
			Zimbroda		Michael Silverman	April, 1987
			L'Etoile		L'Etoile, Inc.	Doc. 1993
374	1956/271379		<u>*Bunky*</u>	55' Cruiser	Stephen Paine	(60p184)
			Sea Sack		Alice H. Prager	(62p539)
			Jubilee III		Mrs. Dorthy G. Koar	(64p313)
		(1967)	*Harmony*		Harlowe R. Zinn	(73p254)
		(1975)	*Stargazer III*		Mr. & Mrs. Russell D. Hay	(78p509)
			Stargazer III		John Geany	
			Stargazer III		Robert W. Bernard	sold 1982
			Stargazer III		Kenridge Co., Inc.	Doc. 1993
375	1956		Total 10 boats	40' Patrol Boats	R.C.A. (Sparkman & Stephens, designer)	
376	1956		Design only, not built	80' Cruiser	G. W. Codrington	
377	1957/273995	(1960)	*Aquarius*	66' Cruiser (72'4")	John M. Dimick	(64p56)
			Big D			(69p98)
			Joy III		Bennett S. Chapple, Jr.	(71p345)
		(1973)	*Joy III*		Fla. Ocean Sci. Institute	(75p261)

Contract Number	Year Built/ Documentation Number	1st in Lloyd's	Original & Subsequent Boat Names	Length	Original & Subsequent Owner(s)	Lloyd's Register Reference
			Burned			
378	1957		*Vael*	55' Cruiser	Allison F. Fleitas	
			George III			
		(1967)	*Wyandanch*		Palmer K. Leberman	(71p768)
			Pintail		David Wagstaff, Jr.	(73p466)
			Sanbar V		Sam Paul	
379	1957/274967		*Amie*	59'6" Cruiser	Edward K. Warren	(64p47)
			Gypsy			
		(1969)	*Helenrose III*		Helenrose S. Ullman	(79p209)
			Chesapeak		Robert W. Bernard	
			Chesapeak		Austin Linwood Cox	1985
			Chesapeak		Charles K. Osborne	1988
			Chesapeak		Chesapeak Corp., Inc.	Doc. 1989
			Sea Barron III		Manfred (Dutch) Von Ehrenfried	~1989, Doc. 1993

*71' Houseboat **Litchfield Lady**, #380 (ex- **Aurora**) in St. Michaels, Maryland, 1995*

Contract Number	Year Built/ Documentation Number	1st in Lloyd's	Original & Subsequent Boat Names	Length	Original & Subsequent Owner(s)	Lloyd's Register Reference

— DECK PLAN —

— CABIN PLAN —

380	1958/282271		*Aurora*	71'5" Houseboat	John Trumpy	
		(1960)	*Marcoo*		Mrs. J. S. Denham	(62p373)
		(1964)	*Prima Donna*		John R. Sheppard, Jr.	(73p475)
		(1975)	*Daril-X*		Allen C. Polivy	(77p112)
			Sylvia			
			Aurora		Payte	
			Aurora		Dennis O'Neil	83 to Fall 88
			Litchfield Lady		A. (Tony) Foster McKissick	July, 1988

Contract Number	Year Built/ Documentation Number	1st in Lloyd's	Original & Subsequent Boat Names	Length	Original & Subsequent Owner(s)	Lloyd's Register Reference
			Litchfield Lady		Clay Brittain	Sep., 1990
			Litchfield Lady		Tony McKissick	May, 1992
			Rebuilt bottom, Summer 1993 Woofried Cove Marina, R.I.		Lady Ltd.	Doc. 1993
381	1957/275249		*April Showers*	55' Cruiser	George Senn	(64p56)
			Lady Anne		W. Bladen Lowndes	(67p359)
		(1969)	*Carousel*		Edwin R. Broden	(71p137)
		(1973)	*Carousel*		Price Howell	(79p81)
			Carousel		Marshal Coyne	
			Carousel		The Madison Hotel	Doc. 1993
382	1958/276204		*Tonda*	57' Cruiser	Howell van Gerbig	to 1960
		(1960)	*El-G-El*		Lynn G. Lindsay	(64p196)
		(1967)	*Wilwat*		Watkins Motor Lines	(69p790)
		(1971)	*Panorama*		Frederic Meyer	(75p387)
			Panorama		Charles Maase	
			Freedom	(53.9')	Yacht Freedom, Inc.	Doc. 1981
			Freedom		Joseph M. Hovland	
			Freedom		Hap Hall	
			Freedom		Benjamin W. Rawlins, Jr.	Doc. 1989
383	1958/276864		*Valor*	57' Cruiser	Frank Michaux	(60p611)
			Valor		Herbert Palestine	(62p637)
		(1964)	*Lady Birchfield*		Herbert Palestine	(69p380)
			Arnal			
			Moonspinner	(53.9')	Dunbar Marine Sales, Inc.	Doc. 1981
			Moonspinner		Mr. Dennis	
			Overdraft		Carley Captal	
			Molly Ann		Gary Koch	~1989
			Molly Ann		Molly Ann Ventures	Doc. 1993
384	1958/277351		*Eskimo III*	67' Houseboat	John Kimberly	(60p197)
			Mary Ellen			
		(1962)	*Pleione II*		Joseph V. Santry	(75p405)

Contract Number	Year Built/ Documentation Number	1st in Lloyd's	Original & Subsequent Boat Names	Length	Original & Subsequent Owner(s)	Lloyd's Register Reference
			Minerva		William Allen	
			Allison		Steve Nichols	
			Big Float		William Benson	
			Moonshine		Adler, Adler, Cay, & Post	Oct, 1987
385	1958/280464		*Shelly Kay VI*	53' Cruiser	John B. Rich	
		(1960)	*Seaholm*		Alfred V. duPont	(62p533)
		(1964)	*Blue Chip*		Fred S. Durham	(73p75)
			Blue Chip		Lee Bench	
			Broadview		Martin Vogel, Jr.	(77p67)
			Aquilon		Donald Martin	(84p38) Doc. 1993
386	1959/278589		*Sanban*	47' Ketch	George F. Johnson	(60p495)
			Sanban		Raymond H. George	(62p516)
			Sanban		David W. & Carla H. Barbour	(64p526)
			Sanban		Mr. Thomas A. McGraw	(67p574)
			Magic			
		(1969)	*Tranquilizer II*		Herman Wenzel	(71p704)
			Tranquilizer II		The Crown Yacht Corp.	(73p637)
		(1975)	*Farewell*		Charles L. Peet	(77p154)
		(1978)	*Ibis*		Robin Hill	(79p221)
387	1959/287055		*Fin V*	53' Cruiser	Dwight P. Allen	
		(1962)	*Dee Dee*		William B. Griscom, Jr.	(71p188)
	(667736)		*Tralee*		Thomas D. Bowes, Sr.	Doc. 1993
388	1959/278643		*Irene C.*	57' Cruiser	Lester Finkelstein	
			Irene C.		SW Steel Rolling Mill	(60p282)
		(1962)	*Irene C.*		Richard D. Bokum, II	(69p338)
			Four Queens	(53.9')	George M. Palmer	Doc. 1981, 89
			Four Queens		Annabell M. Palmer	Doc. 1993
389	1959/279792		*Beatrice*	75' Cruiser	Jack Meyerhoff	(62p83)
			Dormal		Malcolm Voldenberg	

Contract Number	Year Built/ Documentation Number	1st in Lloyd's	Original & Subsequent Boat Names	Length	Original & Subsequent Owner(s)	Lloyd's Register Reference
		(1964)	*Tomador*		Thomas E. Raffington	(77p495)
			Tomador			
			Sunk off Hillsboro Inlet, ca. 1978			
390			Navy reconditioning		U.S. Navy	
391	1959/280119		*Clara*	57' Cruiser	Harold F. Pitcairn	(60p138)
		(1962)	*Sally Forth*		Dorys Hall Faile	(64p524)
		(1967)	*Sally Forth*		H. P. .J. & Dorys McConnell Duberg	(78p455)
			Independence	(53.9')	Tyler Grove	Doc. 1981
			Independence		Myton Ireland	
			Independence		Meir K. Florenz	Doc. 1989, 93
392	1960/282249		*Claybeth*	80' Cruiser	E. Clayton Gengras	(62p144)
		(1964)	*Baleen*		Gerald C. Holbrook	(69p79)
		(1971)	*Wayfarer*		Winthrop W. Aldrich	(73p673)
			Wayfarer		Univ. of Miami (donation)	
			Birchminster II		Vincent Rogeo (sic)	
			Wayfarer		F. Eugene Dixon, Jr.	(77p527)
			Sunrise		Charles Creighton	April 1977
			Sunrise	(77.2')	James F. Keenan	Doc. 1981
			Trianon		James Keenan	
			Sandestin		Peter Boss	1985
			Charisma		Steve Watchmaker & Paul Goodrich	1987, Doc. 1993
			Karisma		John Concel (sic)	Winter, 1995
393	1960/281634		*Wind IV*	57' Cruiser	Ralph Atlass	(71p758)
			Miss Cincy			
			Fairlee		James G. Foreman	
			Fairlee		Richard Van den Bosch	
			Fairlee		Walter McCrory	
			Fairlee		Fairlee Marine Corp.	Doc. 1993

Contract Number	Year Built/ Documentation Number	1st in Lloyd's	Original & Subsequent Boat Names	Length	Original & Subsequent Owner(s)	Lloyd's Register Reference
394	1960/283544		*Tonda*	67'6" Cruiser	Howell van Gerbig	(to 1964)
			Makaira II		Lester M. & Ruth Sears	(67p403)
		(1973)	*Makaira II*		Dana Corp.	(75p313)
			Mon Amie		George A. Johnson	
			Mon Amie		Frank Harms	
			Tonda		Warren Tolmar	1987
395	1960/285149		*Little Aurora*	46' Cruiser	Stock boat	
			Little Kitten			
		(1977)	*Medallion*		Milton J. Ackerman	(79p314)
			Baboulina		(in Greece)	
396	1961/285177		*Exchange II*	57' Cruiser	R. W. Bartram, Jr.	(69p242)
			Cinque Ports		Merrill Stubbs	(71p156)
			Excite		Joe Bartram	
	Burned at dock, Greenwich, mid-70's. Fire started on *Flaming Hearth*, which also burned.					
397	1961/293779		*Jubilee*	57' Cruiser	Edward Kraus	1964
		(1964)	*Red Wing*		Bruce A. Norris	(73p493)
		(1975)	*Carillon*		Edgar P. Williamson, II	(79p78)
			Carillon		Edgar P. Williamson, III	(to 1989)
398	1961/286159		*Queen L.*	46' Cruiser	F. P. Asher	
			Old Die Hard		Fred B. Engert	(~14 years)
			Cristal		Jack Cuddire	June, 1993
399	1961/286472		*Martha P IV*	46' Cruiser	William N. S. Pugh	(to79p308)
			Scorpio		Dick Ross	
			Rowdy		Bud Schooley	
			Little Joe VII			
			Beachcomber II		William G. Major	(84p68)
			Beachcomber II		Ches. Research (donation)	July, 1989
			Beachcomber		George C. O'Brien	Doc. 1993
400	1961/287264	(1967)	*Eskimo*	84' Houseboat	John Kimberly	(71p230)
			Jardel		Jim Ryder	

Contract Number	Year Built/ Documentation Number	1st in Lloyd's	Original & Subsequent Boat Names	Length	Original & Subsequent Owner(s)	Lloyd's Register Reference
		(1973)	*Loulyfran*		Louis Wolfson, II	(79p287)
			Loulyfran		Univ. of Miami (donation)	
			Big Eagle		Bernie Little	
			Lovesong		Frank Loving	
			Dreamboat		Ed Bronstien	April, 1983
			Olde Guarde		George L. Horne, Olde Guarde Inc.	Doc. 1993
401	1962		*Fran-Mar*	46' Cruiser	F. P. Asher	
402	1962/288009		*Bunky*	46' Cruiser	Stephen Paine	(64p111)
			Millie		Frederic Meyer	(69p463)
		(1971)	*True Love V*		B. Leonard Polkosnik	(75p559)
			Sugan G		Richard F. Lankford	June, 1971
			Wick IV		James C. & Dorothy Lunn	June, 1973
			Wick IV		Gerald M. Voynick	Feb, 1983
			Aidenn		Rick Morris	Mar, 1984
403	1962/288049		*Privateer IV*	69' Cruiser	J. Glan Sample, Port Royal, Inc.	(71p534)
			Lad		Lee A. Doer	
			Antho M		William H. Combs	
			Mary Lynn		Hearne Christopher	
			Mary Lynn		Robert R. Green, Maryland. Port Administration	Doc. 1993
404	1962/288788		*Westerly*	57' Cruiser	J. W. West	(71p756)
			Palma			
			Palma		Barbara Singer & Lou Fromkin	
			Rapport		Donald G. Atha	
			Windrush II		Robert Bernard	~1986
			Windrush		William. J. Waskey	Jan. 1990
			Windrush		Dr. William. Burke,	Jan. 1993

Contract Number	Year Built/ Documentation Number	1st in Lloyd's	Original & Subsequent Boat Names	Length	Original & Subsequent Owner(s)	Lloyd's Register Reference
					J. V. Marine Corp.	Doc. 1993
405	1962/289397		*Martha P. V*	57' Cruiser	William N. S. Pugh	(78p325)
			Madeline		Russell P. Hoyt	~1979
			Carina B.		Robert Towse	~1984
			Carina B.		Robert Weeks	April, 1990
			Air Waves		Key Six Holding Corp.	Doc. 1993
406	1962/289991		*Aries*	53' Cruiser	Henry Gibson	(64p61)
		(1967)	*Idalia*		C. W. Middleton	(73p276)
			Flameless		Russel Firestone	
			Loulyfran		Lou Wolfson	
		(1971?)	*Thumper*		Carl D. Sherman	(73p624)
		(1975)	*Polaris*		E. Boykin Hartley	(77p356)
			Jenny Clark		Mrs. Helen Tinnerman	
			Jenny Clark		Jeanette L. Tinnerman	Doc. 1993
407	1963/291258		*Pintail*	84' Cruiser	Col. David Flagstaff	(64p477)
		(1964)	*Aras*		Sara C. Chisholm	(79p24)~1980
			Achastes		Bud Wellman	~1981
			Wishing Star		Michael Eagan, Alamo Rent-A-Car	~1984
			Wishing Star		I.D. Properties, Inc.	~1986
			Wishing Star		L & L Marine	~1988
			Failed survey		Bank seized	Nov, 1989
			Wishing Star		Bill Criswell, Crismark Corp.	April, 1990
			Rebuilt June, 1990			
					Tamarind Resort Assoc. in St. Thomas	Doc. 1993
408	1963/293280		*Oceanus*	48' Cutter	Charles Owen	
			Beguine			(67p486)
		(1964)	*Oceanus*		Oceanic Yachts	(67p486)
		(1969)	*Oceanus*		Charles Owen	(75p374)
			Oceanus	(36.9')	Brian M. Baldwin	Doc. 1981

Contract Number	Year Built/ Documentation Number	1st in Lloyd's	Original & Subsequent Boat Names	Length	Original & Subsequent Owner(s)	Lloyd's Register Reference
			Oceanus		John Mcateer	Doc. 1993
409	1963/291817		*Blue Hen*	67'6" Cruiser	Richard E. Riegel	(71p105)
			Blue Hen		Univ. of Miami (donation)	
			Gibson Girl		Gibson	
			Janal		Dr. William Benderski	
			Tayana II		Ralph Friedman	March, 1991
			Prime Plus Two		Robert Deison	1994
410	1963/292467		*Tireless*	67'6" Cruiser	Roger S. Firestone	(to79p526)
			Daril X		Allen C. Polivy	
			Moriah		Arthur Carter	
			Moriah		Univ. of Miami (donation)	
			Moriah		Perry Harris	1982–1983
			Principia		Jack Childs	1986–1987
			Principia		Darrell Ferguson	Aug, 1990
						Doc. 1993
411	1964/293779		*Matthanja*	67' Cruiser	Berge Bergensen	
		(1967)	*Kimari*		Edward A. & Angela Kilroy	(71p359)
			Wilwat		William Watkins	
		(1973)	*Red Wing*	Flybridge added	Bruce Norris	(79p412)
			B. B. Sea		Donald R. Wilborn	
412	1964/294959		*Sirius*	60' Cruiser	Henry C. Gibson	(69p656)
		(1971)	*Majorie*		Lewis P. MacAdams	(77p281)
			Petite Ruth		Roger Dean	1973
			Sirius		Carolyn Weaver	1976, Doc. 93
413	not used					
414	1964/296594		*Sea Dream VI*	60' Houseboat	Cdr. John Rutherfurd	
		(1967)	*Nicola*		George L. Todd	(75p365)
			Lin Jim			
			Ojai			
			Lazy Tiger		James Patton	

Contract Number	Year Built/ Documentation Number	1st in Lloyd's	Original & Subsequent Boat Names	Length	Original & Subsequent Owner(s)	Lloyd's Register Reference
			Dee Vocean		Joe (Dee) Dussich	Spring, 1990
			Liquid Asset		Van Stuart	April, 1992
			Le Petit Bac		Evelyn Weiser,	1993
					Zelda Charters	
415	1964/297160		*Polaris*	75'	Ben Tobin	(71p527)
		(1973)	*Jaru*		Jack Wasserman	(79p236)
			Jaru		Univ. of Miami (donation)	
			Jaru		Bill Bolling	
			Jaru		Bill Walker	
			Jaru		James Stamm	
			Perry Cabin		Walter Johnson	
			Fire aboard in Oxford, Md, Dec, 1989. Reported being rebuilt 1990 as *Celebration*			
416	1965/297543		*Eager Miss*	46' Fish	William Tutton	(75p152)
		(1969)	*Jayho*		Jayho Corp.	(71p335)
			Cygnet		Charles P. Irvin	
			Gold'n Wood			
			At Waves hauled out in very poor condition, Aug, 1989. Being rebuilt winter 1989/90. Moved to Ft. Laud. to finish interior '92.			
417	1965/297905		*Wavey II*	46'	John R. Kimberly	
		(1967)	*Miss Boots*		Bart B. Chamberlain, Jr.	(75p341)
			Tempest			
		(1977)	*Miss T.S.U.*		Troy State University	(78p344)
			Cliff Hanger		Clifton S. Forsythe	Doc. 1993
418	1965/294187		*Plateen*	47'	Joseph R. Pape	
					Jacqueline M.	
			Whirlaway		Edward Beers McNought	
			Barbara Ann			
			Barbara Ann	(43.9')	Miss Lisa, Inc	Doc. 1989, 1993
419	1965			Semi-submersible	U.S. Navy	
420	1965/500329		*Jimiana*	75' Houseboat	James L. Knight	

Contract Number	Year Built/ Documentation Number	1st in Lloyd's	Original & Subsequent Boat Names	Length	Original & Subsequent Owner(s)	Lloyd's Register Reference
		(1971)	*Cavalier II*		Frances F. Burden	(73p110)
			Sea Level II		Daniel Taylor	
		(1977)	*Yorel VI*		Caddell Dry Docks & Repair	(78p620)
			Patience II		Norman D. & Barbara C. Groh	(79p375)
			Patience II		Norman Groh & J. Halloran	
			Patience II		Bernie Little	
			Patience II		James Halloran	1980
			Patience II		Mrs. June McNelis	1987
421	1965/500788		*Georgejan*	67' Cruiser	George Wasserman	
			Georgejan		Robert & Janice Goldsten	
			Georgejan		Georges Radio & TV Co.	Doc. 1981
			Georgejan		AMI (donation)	Aug, 1991
			Georgejan		Associated Marine Institutes	Doc. 1993
		Stored at Crackerboy, W. Palm Beach, April, 1993–May, 1995				
			Georgejan		Kevin Lessing & Kevin Anglim	1995
422	1965/501583		*Megaera*	48' Cruiser	Henry Sears	(75p332)
		(1977)	*Passage*	(49'6")	James A. Russell	(79p374)
			Ariescor		Christian F. Richter	Doc. 1993
			Ariescor		John Timinsky & Lisa Mann	Aug, 1995
423	1966/501856		*Odyssey*	67' Cruiser	Wallace S. Whittaker	(69p511)
			Odyssey		Charles Coyer	(71p490)
			Don Quixote		Stanley Vineberg	
			Koala		John Farrel	
			Koala			
			Paragon		Randolph Topjun	1989
			Paragon		NCNB Bank	Sep, 1991

Contract Number	Year Built/ Documentation Number	1st in Lloyd's	Original & Subsequent Boat Names	Length	Original & Subsequent Owner(s)	Lloyd's Register Reference
			Paragon		James L. Chandler	Doc. 1993
424	1966/502552		*Minnow*	70' Cruiser	Phillip Miller	(78p339)
			Petite Ruth		Roger Dean	1977
			Doubloon		Robert Parrillo,	Sep, 1980
					Safeway Insurance Co.	Doc. 1993
425	1966/507552	(1969)	*Sea Dream VII*	54'	John M. Rutherfurd	(73p534)
			Marker			
			Frederica		Mr. Brown	
			Frederica IV		Mrs. Jean Williams	Spring, 1991
			Windrush		William J. Waskey	Doc. 1993
426	1965/508446		*Fin V*	60' Houseboat	Dwight P. Allen	(67sup.p4)
		(1969)	*Julie*		Henry C. Rexach	(73p302)
			Today We Live		Saul Walter	
			Today We Live	(60.4')	SSW Service Corp.	Doc. 1981
			Sumoria		Mrs. H.P. (Sue) Whitemore	1985–87
			Elegante		William J. Major,	Doc. 1989,
					W. M. Service Co.	1993
427	1965/506381	(1967)	*Admiral Blake*	64' Cruiser	John P. Blair	(to79p10)
			The Katherine			
			Trident		I.D. Properties; United Equity, Louis Ramundo; Overseas Corp., Lita Simpson (to bank)	1984–1985
			Trident			
			Trident		Alen Grives	March, 1990
			Liberty			
428	1967/508054		*Rebel II*	75' Houseboat	Mary Perry Alexander	(69p574)
		(1971)	*Miss Hollywood III*		Eleanor R. Hansberry	(78p343)
			Empty Pocket		Robert L. Lambert	Doc. 1981
			Petite Ruth		Roger Dean	1981
			Petite Ruth		P.B. Atlantic Univ. (donation)	Dec, 1985
			Oceania		Geoffrey Muller,	1986

Contract Number	Year Built/ Documentation Number	1st in Lloyd's	Original & Subsequent Boat Names	Length	Original & Subsequent Owner(s)	Lloyd's Register Reference
					Oceanic Adventures	
					Japanese owner	1990
429–434	1967–68		PTF 17–22	80' Patrol boat	Dept. of Defense	
PTF 17 survives at the Naval and Serviceman's Park, Buffalo, NY, along with several other warships.						
435	1969/519823		*Aurora V*	58' Cruiser	John Trumpy & Sons	(71p74)
			Vega		C.W. Schooley	(75p569)
			Vega		George E. Ford	(79p546)
			Auf Wiedersehen VI		L.N. Weisser	(84p53)
			J.T.'s Aurora		Ray Giovanini	
			J.T.'s Aurora		Frank Winslow & James Reid	1986–1987
			(Bottom rebuilt Fall, 1989, at Ft. Laud. Yacht Basin)			
			Lauren Alexander		Mike Hogan,	Doc. 1993
					Lauren Alexander Inc.	
436	1969/523111		*Peaches*	58' Cruiser	Leonard Butscher	(71p510)
			Excite		Joseph Barr Bartram, Jr.	(73p198)
		(1973)	*Arundel*		A. Atwater Kent, Jr.	(79p29)
			Passage III		Passage Inc.	Doc. 1981
			Passage II		Yegen Marine (repos)	
			Cheerio		Jack L. Clayton	~2-3 years
			Seaport		Peter Rappaport	June, 1985
						Doc. 1993

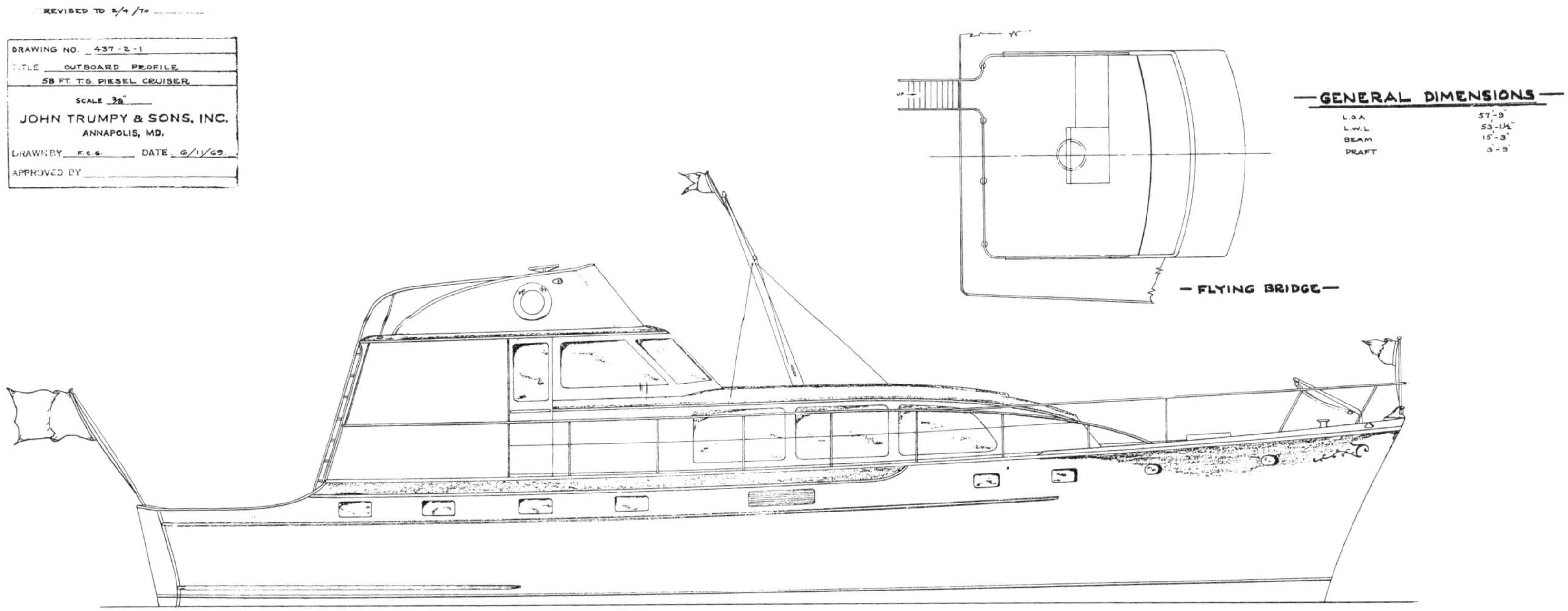

Contract Number	Year Built/ Documentation Number	1st in Lloyd's	Original & Subsequent Boat Names	Length	Original & Subsequent Owner(s)	Lloyd's Register Reference

REVISED TO 3/4/70

DRAWING NO. _437-2-1_
TITLE _OUTBOARD PROFILE_
58 FT. T.S. DIESEL CRUISER
SCALE _3/8"_
JOHN TRUMPY & SONS, INC.
ANNAPOLIS, MD.
DRAWN BY _F.C.C._ DATE _6/11/69_
APPROVED BY _____

— GENERAL DIMENSIONS —
L.O.A. 57'-3"
L.W.L. 53'-1½"
BEAM   15'-3"
DRAFT   3'-5"

— FLYING BRIDGE —

Contract Number	Year Built/ Documentation Number	1st in Lloyd's	Original & Subsequent Boat Names	Length	Original & Subsequent Owner(s)	Lloyd's Register Reference
437	1970/524974		*Target*	58' Cruiser	Ferdinand Eberstadt	(75p530)
		(1973)	*Target*		F. Eugene Dixon	(75p530)
			Spellbound		William J. Crocker	1974
			Scott Free		George R. Scott	9/78
			Steamer		Nick B. Stanley,	Oct, 1988
					Scott Free, Inc.	Doc. 1993
438	1970/527536		*Katuna V*	58'	Gilbert Verney	(71p353)
			Dalliance			
		(1975)	*Bal Versailles*		T. D. Burgess	(77p41)
		(1978)	*Bal Versailles*		Edgar P. Williamson, II	(84p60)
			Claudette		Phillip Redmon	Doc. 1993

Contract Number	Year Built/ Documentation Number	1st in Lloyd's	Original & Subsequent Boat Names	Length	Original & Subsequent Owner(s)	Lloyd's Register Reference
439	1970/522462		*Sinbad*	63'	Fred H. Gordon, Jr.	Doc. 1993

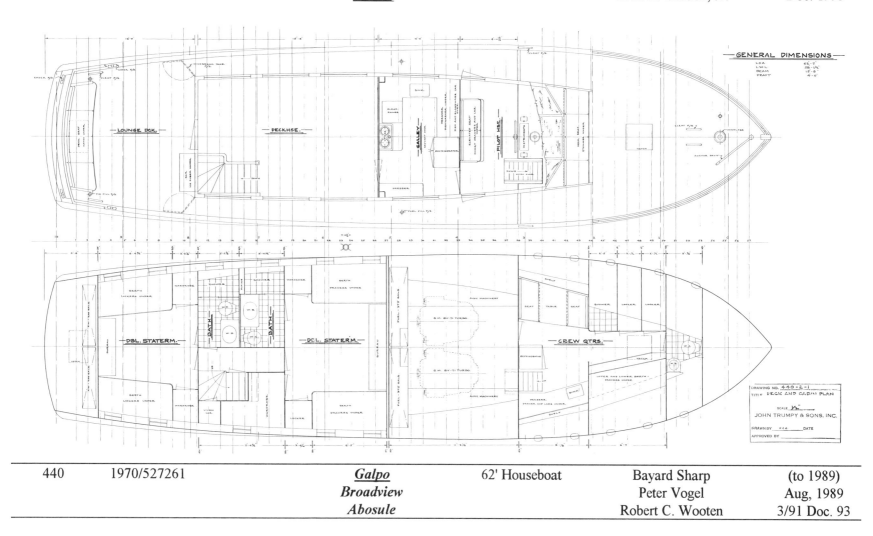

| 440 | 1970/527261 | | *Galpo* *Broadview* *Abosule* | 62' Houseboat | Bayard Sharp Peter Vogel Robert C. Wooten | (to 1989) Aug, 1989 3/91 Doc. 93 |

Contract Number	Year Built/ Documentation Number	1st in Lloyd's	Original & Subsequent Boat Names	Length	Original & Subsequent Owner(s)	Lloyd's Register Reference

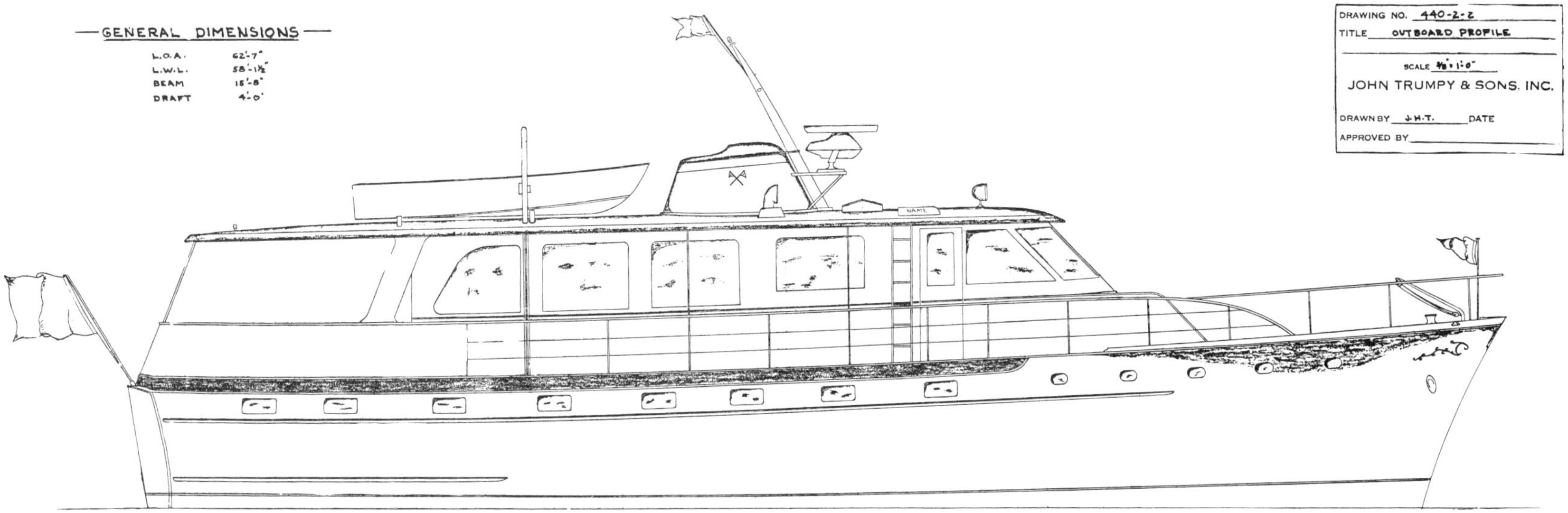

─ GENERAL DIMENSIONS ─

L.O.A.	62'-7"
L.W.L.	58'-1½"
BEAM	15'-8"
DRAFT	4'-0"

DRAWING NO. 440-2-2
TITLE OUTBOARD PROFILE
SCALE ⅜" = 1'-0"
JOHN TRUMPY & SONS. INC.
DRAWN BY J.H.T. DATE
APPROVED BY

Contract Number	Year Built/ Documentation Number	1st in Lloyd's	Original & Subsequent Boat Names	Length	Original & Subsequent Owner(s)	Lloyd's Register Reference

— GENERAL DIMENSIONS —

L.O.A. 57'-9"
L.W.L. 53'-1½"
BEAM   15'-3"
DRAFT   3'-9"

PRINTS ISSUED

	No.	DATE
SUPT. - F.A.	2	13/3/70
JOINER SHOP		
PLUMBING SHOP		
MACHINE SHOP		
ELECTRICAL SHOP		

DRAWING NO. 442-2-1
TITLE ____ OUTBOARD PROFILE
58 FT. T.S. DIESEL CRUISER
SCALE ⅜"
JOHN TRUMPY & SONS, INC.
ANNAPOLIS, MD.
DRAWN BY F.C.G. DATE OCT. 14. 1970
APPROVED BY ____

2¾ TEAK
ALL AROUND

Contract Number	Year Built/ Documentation Number	1st in Lloyd's	Original & Subsequent Boat Names	Length	Original & Subsequent Owner(s)	Lloyd's Register Reference
441	not built			58'		
442	1971/534276		*Spindle*	58' Cruiser	Gerrish H. Milliken, Jr. (Begun for Monroe Dreher, deceased)	(to1989) Doc. 1993
443	1971/531002	(1975)	*Little Sissie* *Dawn Patrol* *Hummingbird*	68' Houseboat (72'0")	John W. Koons, Sr. Donald M. Doyle George L. Richardson	(79p116) Jan, 1980 Doc. 1993
444	1971/536385		*Aurora V* *Aurora V* *Aurora V* *Aurora V* *Aurora V*	58'	John Trumpy & Sons Pierce L. Richard Maryland Port Authority Herbert Molz Elman & Bruce Gray	1981 1987 1987 1989, Doc. 93

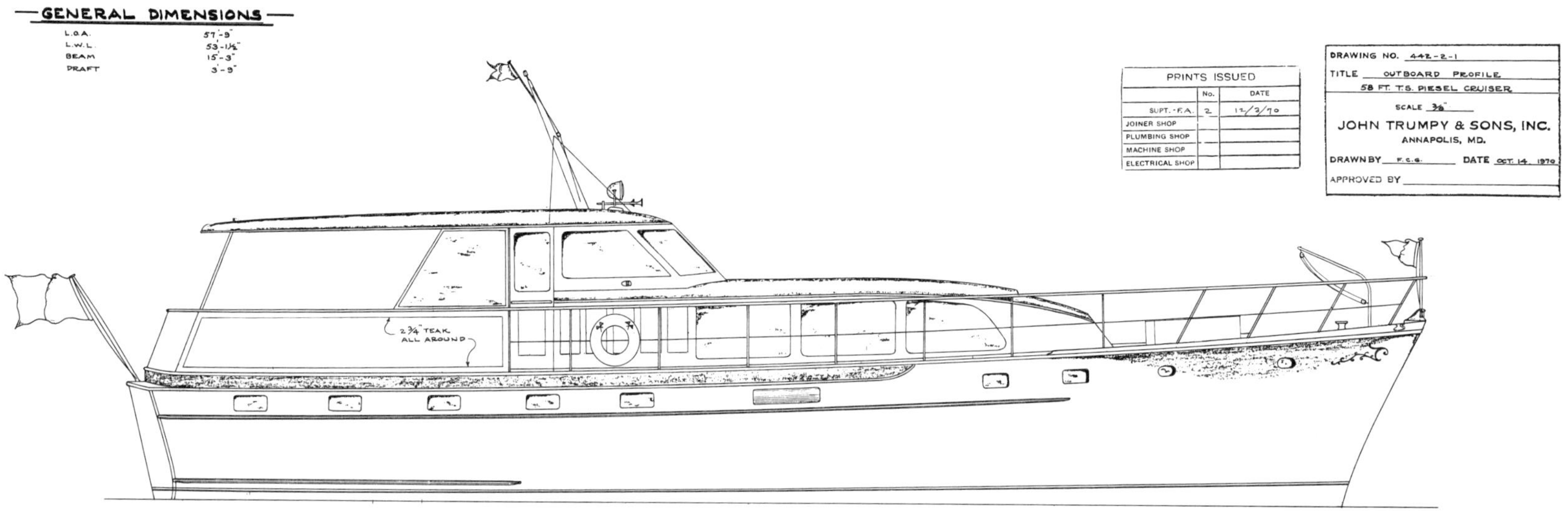

Contract Number	Year Built/ Documentation Number	1st in Lloyd's	Original & Subsequent Boat Names	Length	Original & Subsequent Owner(s)	Lloyd's Register Reference
445	not used					
446	1972/541288		*Gerifay*	72' Houseboat	Earle Cantor	
			Lady Q.		Reynold Q. Black	
			Hillary Jane		Mark Rubenstein	~1976 (84p308)
			Caronia		Carolyn Weaver	May, 1995
447	1972/542982		*Egret*	62' Sail	C. Porter Schutt	(79p142)
			Egret		I.O.F. Miami	
			Whistle Wind VI		Hasting Harcourt	Doc. 1981
448	1972/546770		*Sirius*	60' Cruiser	Henry C. Gibson	
			Skua			
			Burwat		Powell Watson	
			Broadway		Owner of Concordia Yachts	May, 1991
					Southern Environmental Ind	Doc. 1993
					Bill Steitz (Mr. Howlin)	

End of Yachts built by John Trumpy & Sons, Annapolis, MD.

*Drawing on following page shows 60' Houseboat **Sirius**, #448, last boat built by John Trumpy & Sons.*

Contract Number	Year Built/ Documentation Number	1st in Lloyd's	Original & Subsequent Boat Names	Length	Original & Subsequent Owner(s)	Lloyd's Register Reference

Contruction of some of the following boats were begun by the Annapolis Yacht Yard and completed by John Trumpy & Sons.

Contract Number	Year Built/ Documentation Number	1st in Lloyd's	Original & Subsequent Boat Names	Length	Original & Subsequent Owner(s)	Lloyd's Register Reference
	1947/252457		*Sally Forth*	59'9"	Charles J. Gibson	(62p514)
	1947		*Caroline*	47'0"		
			Mava			
		(1978)	*Mary B. III*		Dale L. Reistad	(79p309)

Contract Number	Year Built/ Documentation Number	1st in Lloyd's	Original & Subsequent Boat Names	Length	Original & Subsequent Owner(s)	Lloyd's Register Reference
	1947/252839		*Tamarack*	46'7"	Univ. of Rhode Island	(78p532)
	1947/252122		*Jennie Belle IV*	46'7"	Jules Gorliz	(47p4 Adden.)
			Tamaroa		Lewis S. Bellem, Jr.	(62p598)
			Tamaroa		Univ. of Rhode Island	(79p504)
	1947/252028		*The Bemyma*	46'9"	Ernest I. Schwarz Annapolis Yacht Yard	(47p435)
	1947/253906	(1950)	*Hurricane III*	54'	Allen B. DuMont	(64p286)
			Vixen II		(67p728)	
		(1969)	*Vixen II*		Joseph Brocia	(79p554)
	1947/252135		*Salar II*	54'2"	Eugene E. Wilson	(47p372)
			Merrie Mac			
			Festival			
			Serenata			
			Quandary			
			Bomar			
			Calypso II			
			Half Moon IV		Industrial Eng. Works, V. S. Grundy	(62p261)
	1947/252200		*Privateer*	46'9"	J. G. & Helen Sample	(47p347)
			Barbette IV			
			Jolly Val			
			Kay-Bee II			
			Pemco		Perkins Machinery Co.	(62p460)
		(1978)	*Prime Time*		Lawrence A. Reilly	(79p394)
	1947/254286		*Miss Mae III*	47'		
			Onlyus II		Wm. J. & Margaret J. White	(50p353)
		(1954)	*Makon*		Stepan Chemical Co.	(55p313)
			Vega		Verner Z. Reed, Jr.	(56p555)
			Vega		Kenneth McDonald	(60p613)

Contract Number	Year Built/ Documentation Number	1st in Lloyd's	Original & Subsequent Boat Names	Length	Original & Subsequent Owner(s)	Lloyd's Register Reference
		(1962)	*Fairlee III*		J. G. Foreman	(64p213)
		(1967)	*Aqua*		John Watters	(69p60)
			Tranquil Roamer III		Robert G. Randall	(71p704)
	1947/253477		*Wind II*	47'0"		
			Page Boy		Esterly C. Page	(62p450)
	1947/253086		*Walgert III*	54'3"	Walter D. Pacy	(47p466)
			Schaddar II			
			Fifty-Fifty		Edward C. Baltz	(62p217)
			Ensign D.			
			Bay Breeze		Albert E. Matlack, Jr.	(79p42)
	1947/252320		*Eniac*	59'11"	Yale Fabrics Corp.	(47p4)
			Yard		Cy Caine, Pres	
			Bettina			
			Three Rings			
			Dunreath			
			Kailua		John E. Myer	(62p312)
	1947/252173		*Ens'n Sam*	59'11"		
			Revmar			
			Tritona			
			Shelly Kay IV			
			Marcoo III			
			Helen F. V		F. J. Federighi	(62p269)
	1948/254438		*Do-Ho III*	60'0"		
			Black Horse			
			Starflite		Rasmussen Boating Co.	(62p580)
			Wind-A-Way			
			Chaisma		Jones Boat Yard	(78p93)
	1948		*Armisu II*	48'0"	Dr. Miguel A. Escoto	(62p65)

APPENDIX C
PATRONS OF THE ARTS

Name	Vessel	Year	Name	Vessel	Year
Alexander, R. C.	*Rebel II*	1967	Baruch, Sailing W.	*Donaldo*	1920
Alexander, Dr. Maitland	*Viator*	1929	Bell, S. S., Jr.	*Sylvia IV*	1942
Allen, Dwight P.	*Fin V*	1959	Bergensen, Berge	*Matthanja*	1964
Allen, D. P.	*Fin V*	1966	Bessey	*Palisades*	1915
Allison, T. C.	*Miakka*	1914	Betz, John F., III	*Sybilla II*	1910
Andrews, R. S.	*Curlew*	1947	Betz, J. F.	*Tender*	1911
Armour, A. W.	*Chieftan*	1916	Biddle, L. L.	*Adios*	1915
Aron, Jacob	*Dixie Belle*	1927	Bingham, Judge R. W.	*Eala*	1927
Asher, F. P.	*Queen L.*	1961	Black, Van Lear	*Palisades* (Rebuilt)	1919
Asher, F. P.	*Fran-Mar*	1962	Blair, J. P.	*Admiral Blake*	1966
Atkinson, A. W.	*Mycelma III*	1923	Bloch, Arthur	*Snug*	1922
Atlass, Ralph	*Wind IV*	1960	Bond, Robert M.	*Cyrene*	1921
Atterbury, Gen. W. W.	*Arminia*	1930	Bourne, Arthur K.	*Reverie*	1920
Bain, R. F.	*Marion II*	1942	Bower, F. B.	*Elise*	1922
Ballantine, John H.	*Tritona*	1937	Brigham, M. B.	*Caliph*	1909
Barclay, William K.	*Seagoin'*	1933	Burk, Louis	*Enchantress II*	1915
Bartram, R. W., Jr.	*Exchange II*	1961	Burk, Louis	*Enchantress III*	1921
Baruch, H. B.	*Riposo II*	1919	Butscher, Leonard	*Peaches*	1969
Baruch, H. B.	*Riposo*	1926	Cadwalader, Richard M.	*Sequoia*	1924
Baruch, H. N.	*Nahmeoka*	1911	Cadwalader, Richard M.	*Sequoia II*	1925
Baruch, H. N.	*Nahmeoka*	1913	Cantor, Earle	*Gerifay*	1972
Baruch, H. N.	*Nahmeoka*	1921	Carib Syndicate	*Equitorial*	1921

Name	Vessel	Year	Name	Vessel	Year
Carstairs, J. H.	*Ruffled Grouse*	1912	duPont, Eugene E.	*Morning Star*	1938
Carstairs, J. H. & J. D.	*Nadesah*	1919	duPont, F. V.	*Tech, Jr.*	1930
Chance, Col. Edwin M.	*Far Cry*	1938	duPont, F. V.	*Suitsus*	1936
Christie, F. F.	*Ibis*	1912	duPont, F. V.	*Tech, Jr.*	1939
Chrysler, Walter P.	*Frolic*	1927	duPont, F. V.	*Tech, Jr.*	1948
Clarke, S. H.	*Trinitaria*	1913	duPont, Lammot	*Willit*	1955
Codrington, George W.	*All Alone*	1930	Eastwood, John H.	*Scarus*	1919
Codrington, George W.	*Sea Play*	1948	Eastwood, John H	*Scarus*	1921
Coles, Dr. Sticker	*Alscotia*	1925	Eberstadt, Ferdinand	*Target*	1970
Conley, A. W.	*Silver Swan*	1947	Elkins, William	*Pilgrim*	1921
Cudahy, Joseph M.	*Innisfail*	1935	Elkins, William E.	*Pilgrim II*	1926
Cudahy, J. M.	*Innisfail*	1939	Ellis, E. H.	*Jinofor*	1947
Davey, William M.	*Martha*	1939	Ellis, Edward H.	*Jinofor II*	1954
Deering, James	*Nepenthe*	1916	Elverson, Col. James	*Inquirer*	1915
Dickenson, E. E.	*Alva*	1949	Fay, A. J.	*Zenithia*	1924
Dimick, John M.	*Aquarius*	1957	Fay, A. J.	*Freedom*	1926
Disston, A. H.	*Alela*	1913	Finkelstein, Lester	*Irene C.*	1959
Disston, William	*Cocopomelo*	1910	Firestone, Roger S.	*Tireless*	1963
Disston, William	*Pauline*	1911	Fish & Game Commission	*Burlington*	1926
Dixon, Glayton G.	*Osana*	1919	Flagstaff, Col. David	*Pintail*	1963
Doan, F. M.	*Lodsen*	1933	Fleitas, Allison F.	*Vael*	1957
Dobbins, T. Munroe	*Consort IV*	1936	Fleming, G. W.	*Conowingo*	1924
Dobson, Bruce	*Helma*	1938	Fuller, E. R.	*Co-Ed II*	1950
Dodge, Earl	*Samuri*	1925	Garcin, Edward H.	*Miramar*	1921
Drexel, G. W. C.	*Tender*	1911	Gengras, E. Clayton	*Claybeth*	1960
Drexel, G. W. C.	*Akbar*	1915	Gerbig, Howell van	*Tonda*	1958
Drexel, G. W. C.	*Ace*	1914	Gerbig, Howell van	*Tonda*	1960
DuBosque, F. L.	*Dream*	1927	Gibson, Henry	*Aries*	1962
duPont, Alfred	*Seaholm*	1948	Gibson, Henry C.	*Sirius*	1964

Name	Vessel	Year	Name	Vessel	Year
Gibson, Henry C.	*Sirius*	1972	Kraus, Edward	*Jubilee*	1961
Glass Bottom Co.	*Vipi*	1912	Ladd, William F.	*Alamo*	1931
Gordon, Fred H., Jr.	*Sinbad*	1970	Lennig, R. K.	*Chelwood*	1911
Greacen, E. J.	*Lodona*	1911	Levy, Dr. Leon	*We Three*	1937
Gross, A. R.	*One Forty Four II*	1942	Lippincott, Walter H.	*Waleda II*	1927
Gross, A. R.	*One Forty Four*	1950	Longstreth, Charles	*Zenith*	1916
Guggenheim, Murray	*Leonie*	1916	Lovejoy, Fred B.	*Nicoya*	1927
Hall-Seeley Motor Co.	*Lady Baltimore*	1915	Lovejoy, Frederick B.	*Lanakila*	1930
Heverling, R. L.	*Edrus*	1935	Martin, A. H.	*Vigilant*	1915
Hornbeck, Dr. C. Sahler	*Sahlou*	1929	Matheson, W. J.	*Calabash*	1912
Howell, Thomas M.	*Thalia*	1925	Matheson, W. J.	*Marpessa*	1915
Hubbel, V. B.	*Helen Louise*	1919	Matheson, W. J.	*Coconut*	1924
James, Arthur Curtis	*Lanai*	1911	McCahan, William J., III	*Florence V*	1935
James, Arthur Curtis	*Lanai*	1927	McCahan, William. J., III	*Florence VI*	1949
Jay, Webb	*Troubadour*	1925	McCarter, Thomas N.	*Virago*	1931
Johnson, E. R. F.	*Elsie Fenimore*	1927	McCoy, J. R.	*Malova V*	1946
Johnson, E. R. F.	*Elsie Fenimore*	1934	McHugh, John J.	*Mary C.*	1912
Johnson, George F.	*Sanban*	1959	McKelvy, William	*Rumak*	1949
Johnson, R. W.	*Makaira*	1942	McKelvy, William	*Rumak III*	1955
Keane, Thomas T.	*Tomadge*	1947	McNeely, G. H.	*Margo*	1913
Kemmerera	*Emeska*	1923	Megargee, M. B.	*Content*	1912
Kimberly, John	*Eskimo III*	1958	Mickley, E. J.	*Mascot*	1910
Kimberly, John	*Eskimo*	1961	Mickley, E. J.	*Abeona*	1914
Kimberly, John R.	*Wavey II*	1965	Michaux, Frank	*Valor*	1958
King, John C.	*Loaf Along*	1919	Middleton, Albert C.	*Tosca*	1919
King, E. L.	*Kingfisher*	1919	Middleton, A. C.	*Nedmac*	1922
Kingston, F. E.	*Memory*	1929	Middleton, A. C.	*Acomes*	1924
Knight, James L.	*Jimiana*	1965	Milbank, Jeremiah	*Saunterer*	1927
Koons, John W., Sr.	*Little Sissie*	1971	Miller, L. M.	*Sereno*	1954

Name	Vessel	Year	Name	Vessel	Year
Miller, Philip	*Minnow*	1966	Ramsdell	*Alelnansr*	1935
Milliken, Gerrish H., Jr.	*Spindle*	1971	Reynolds, R. F.	*Carol Anne*	1946
Mills Novelty Co.	*Minoco*	1930	Reynolds, W. H.	*Daydream*	1927
Milne, W. S.	*Ocoee*	1923	Rich, J. B.	*Shelly Kay V*	1955
Moore, Edward S.	*Zigan*	1919	Rich, John B.	*Shelly Kay VI*	1958
Morrow, George K.	*Mono*	1930	Riege, Archer G.	*Gleam*	1910
Meyerhoff, Jack	*Beatrice*	1959	Riegel, Richard E.	*Blue Hen*	1963
Newberry, Truman H.	*Truant*	1927	Riker, A. L.	*Ocoloqua*	1910
Newberry, Truman H.	*Truant*	1930	Riker, J. J.	*Dielta*	1910
Ordway, A. P.	*Jane VI*	1916	Roberts, J. G.	*Summer Girl*	1927
Owen, Charles	*Oceanus*	1963	Roberts, J. G.	*Dream Girl*	1929
Owsley, F. D.	*Mariska*	1924	Rosengarten, Dr. George D.	*Mariposa*	1923
Owsley, F. D.	*Mariska*	1927	Rosengarten, Dr. George D.	*Mariposa*	1927
Page, Dewitt	*Maemere*	1929	Rutherford, Commander	*Sea Dream VI*	1964
Paige, L. Rodman	*Nameni*	1939	Rutherford, John M.	*Sea Dream VII*	1966
Paine, Stephen	*Bunky*	1956	Sample, J. Glan	*Privateer IV*	1962
Paine, Stephen	*Bunky*	1962	Sanford	*Chanticleer*	1940
Pape, Joseph R.	*Plateen*	1965	Sausage, M. W.	*Dorinda*	1915
Paul, A. D. J.	*Buzzer*	1919	Schoelkopf, Paul A.	*Minken*	1923
Paul, A. J. Drexel	*Halaia*	1939	Schutt, Porter	*Egret*	1938
Perkins	*Alcy*	1940	Schutt, C. Porter	*Egret*	1972
Pitcairn, Harold	*Clara*	1959	Sears, Henry	*Megaera*	1965
Pope, Col. Frederick	*Marylin*	1947	Sears, Lester M.	*Makaira*	1953
Prettyman, C. B.	*Amitie*	1921	Selby, W. G.	*Bilma II*	1919
Price & McLanahan	*Gondola*	1913	Selby, W. G.	*Bilma III*	1923
Proctor, F. F.	*Georgena*	1912	Selby, W. G.	*Bilma IV*	1927
Pugh, William N. S.	*Martha P. IV*	1961	Sellers, Alexander	*Black Duck*	1912
Pugh, William N. S.	*Martha P. V*	1962	Sellers, Alexander	*Ameera*	1915
Quackenbush, A. J.	*Lunaria*	1911	Senn, George	*April Showers*	1957

Name	Vessel	Year	Name	Vessel	Year
Sharp, Bayard	*Galpo*	1970	Trumpy, John & Sons	*Aurora V*	1971
Shelton, George G.	*Riette II*	1919	Tutton, William	*Eager Miss*	1965
Sherrill, Frank O.	*Drifter*	1939	Verney, Gilbert	*Katuna V*	1970
Slocum, Col. S. L. H.	*Luneta*	1921	Wall, Charles F.	*Agnes B*	1916
Slocum, Col. S. L. H.	*Luneta*	1927	Wallace, William, Jr.	*Trail*	1926
Smith, J. J.	*Alice*	1914	Walling, R. K.	*Minel*	1933
Stone, Herbert W.	*Silver Mist*	1955	Warren, Edward K.	*Amie*	1957
Stoner, A. M.	*Jinia III*	1939	Wasserman, George	*Georgejan*	1965
Stull, G. M.	*Mikaro*	1948	Welsh, Charles	*Deepwater*	1935
Thomas, George C., Jr.	*Ednada III*	1911	West, J. W.	*Westerly*	1962
Thurnauer, Max H.	*Abadab*	1938	Wheelock, Louis W.	*Seaway*	1921
Tobin, Ben	*Polaris*	1964	Whitmore, Harold Payne	*Arev*	1937
Trimpi, W. W.	*Blue Heaven*	1937	Whittaker, Wallace	*Odyssey*	1966
Trumpy, John	*Sea Call*	1950	Whitney, Mrs. Helen Hay	*Captiva*	1931
Trumpy, John	*Sea Call V*	1952	Wolstenholme, Robert	*Lazy Lady*	1922
Trumpy, John & Sons	*Aurora IV*	1954	Zimmerman, John E.	*Silver Moon II*	1930
Trumpy, John & Sons	*Aurora V*	1969	Zinn, Roland H.	*Gretchen III*	1947

BIBLIOGRAPHY

Albion, Robert G. **The Rise of New York Port 1815–1860**, New York, Scribners and Sons, 1939.

Baruch, Bernard M. **Baruch, My Own Story**, New York, Henry Holt, 1957.

Bergens, Sjøfartsmuseum. **Må hell og lykke følge deg, Bergen: 1982** (printed on the occasion of the museum exhibit on wooden shipbuilding in Bergen on the 150th anniversary of Annanias Dekke's birth).

Bergens, Tidende. **Husker du Bergen**, Bergen, 1975.

Bray, Maynard and Pinheiro, Carlton. **Herreshoff of Bristol**, Brooklin, Maine, Woodenboat Publication, 1989.

Brosing, Gustav, **Bergen Vår By**, Bergen, J. W. Eides, 1959.

Cagle, Malcolm W. and Manson, Frank A. **The Sea War in Korea**, Annapolis, United States Naval Institute, 1957.

Chapelle, Howard I. **The History of American Sailing Ships**, New York, Bonanza Books, 1982 (originally published in 1935).

Davis, Charles G. **American Sailing Ships: Their Plans and History,** New York, Dover, 1984 (originally published in 1929).

Det Hanseatiske Museums Skrifter Nr. 24, **Bryggen The Hanseatic Settlement in Bergen**, Bergen, 1982.

Dunlap, Orrin E. Jr. **Marconi: The Man and His Wireless**, New York, Arno Press and the *New York Times*, 1971.

Eaton, Charles Aubrey. "Delaware River Shipyards–A Modern Miracle," American Review of Reviews, July 1918, pp. 53-63.

Eisenhower, Julie Nixon. **Pat Nixon: The Untold Story**, New York, Simon and Schuster, 1986.

Fossen, Anders Bjarne. **Bergen Havn Gjennom 900 År**, Bergen, 1985.

Freidman, Norman. **U.S. Combatants**, Annapolis, Naval Institue Press, 1987.

Gallagher, Hugh Gregory. **FDR's Splendid Deception**, New York, Dodd, Mead, 1985.

Gannon, Michael. **Operation Drumbeat**, New York, Harper & Collins, 1990.

Gjerset, Knut. **Norwegian Sailors in American Waters: A Study in the History of Maritime Activity on the Eastern Seaboard**, Northfield, Norwegian-American Historical Association, 1933.

Grant, Robert M. **U-Boats Destroyed: The Effect of Anti-Submarine Warfare 1914–1918**, London, Putnam, 1964.

Grant, Robert M. **U-Boat Intelligence, 1914–1918**, London, C. Tindling & Co., Ltd., 1969.

Harwood, Kathryn Chapman. **The Lives of Vizcaya**, Miami, Banyan Books, 1985.

Hasslof, Olof. **The Management and Structure of Swedish Shipping in the Late 19th and Early 20th Century**, Maritime Monographs and Reports No. 5–1972. National Maritime Museum, Greenwich, London, 1972.

Hunt, Albert Bradlee, Editor. **Houseboats and Houseboating**, New York, Forest and Stream Publishing Company, 1905.

Jane's Fighting Aircraft of World War I, New York, Military Press, 1990.

Johnson, Robert Erwin. **Guardians of the Seas: History of the United States Coast Guard, 1915 to the Present**, Annapolis, Naval Institute Press, 1987.

Jolly, W. P. **Marconi**, New York, Stein and Day, 1972.

Kelly, Roy Willmarth and Allen, Frederick J. **The Shipbuilding Industry**, Boston, New York, Houghton Mifflin, 1918.

Lambert, John and Ross, Al. **Allied Coastal Forces of World War I, Vol. I: Fairmile Designs and U.S. Submarine Chasers; Vol. II: Vosper MTBs and U.S. ELCOs**, Annapolis, Naval Institute Press, 1993 & 1994.

Littlefield, Doris Bayley. **Vizcaya**, Italy, Martori Enterprises II, 1984.

Marconi, Degna. **My Father Marconi**, New York, McGraw-Hill, 1962.

McCullough, David. **Truman**, New York, Simon and Schuster, 1992.

McKay, Richard C. **South Street: A Maritime History of New York**, New York, Putnam and Sons, 1939.

Melia, Tamara Moser. "Damn the Torpedoes," a short history of U.S. Naval mine countermeasures, Washington, D.C., Naval Historical Center, 1991.

Midgaard, John. **A Brief History of Norway**, Oslo, 1986.

Morrison, John Harrison. **History of New York Ship Yards**, New York, William F. Samotz & Co., 1909.

National Maritime Museum. **Problems of Ship Management and Operation 1870–1900**, Maritime Monographs and Reports No. 5–1972, Greenwich, London, 1972.

Nelson, O. N., Editor. **History of the Scandinavians and Successful Scandinavians in the United States**, Vols. I & II, New York, Haskell House, 1969 (originally published in 1904).

New York Shipbuilding Corporation. **50 Years, New York Shipbuilding Corporation**, Camden, NJ, 1949.

Pettersen, Lauritz. **Bergen og Sjøfarten, Volume III, Fra Kjøpmannsrederi til selvstendig næring 1860--1914**, Bergen, 1981.

Preston, Anthony. **Strike Craft**, Greenwich, Bison Books, 1982.

Riesenberg, Felix. **Under Sail**, New York, Macmillan, 1918.

Rousmaniere, John. **The Luxury Yachts**, Alexandria, Time-Life Books, 1944.

Schildhauer, Johannes. **The Hansa History and Culture**, German Democratic Republic, Dorset, 1988.

Stafford, Edward P. **Subchaser**, Annapolis, Naval Institute Press, 1988.

Susanne, Everett. **World War I, An Illustrated History**, Chicago, New York, San Francisco, Rand McNally, 1980.

Thue, Johannes B. **Bergen og Sjøfarten, Volume II, Skipsfart og Kjøpmannskap, 1800–1860**, Bergen, 1980.

Truman, Harry S. **Memoirs**, two volumes, New York, Doubleday, 1956.

Ward, Geoffrey C. **Closest Companion**, New York, Houghton Mifflin, 1995.

Wallace, William N. **The Macmillan Book of Boating**, New York, Macmillan, 1964.

Willoughby, Malcolm F. **Rum War at Sea**, Washington, D.C., U.S. Treasury Dept., 1964.

Works Progress Administration. **A Maritime History of New York**, New York, Haskell House, 1973 (originally published in 1941).

Index

Marine artist Robert Picardat was born in Petersburg, Virginia and is a graduate of the Richmond Professional Institute of the College of William and Mary. His varied background in architecture, advertising and commercial art led to his distinctive style painting

seascapes and portraits of many of the most prestigious yachts in the world, commissioned by international and domestic yacht brokers as well as private owners. He is a member of the American Society of Marine Artists.

Chicago native and Harvard graduate with a Ph.D. in history from the University of Rochester, Robert Tolf is the author of more than 40 books and guides on a variety of subjects ranging from Russian history to restaurants, Columbus to country inns and sketch-books on Chicago, Paris and architect Addison Mizner. His Russian Rockefellers

won a Thomas Newcomen Award in 1980 as one of the best three books on business history published in the U.S. during the preceding three years. His award-winning documentary videos on Christopher Columbus can be seen on the Discovery Channel, PBS and the National Instructional Satellite System.

PHOTO CREDITS:

Barge House Museum, Eastport, MD:
   Bond Bros. photos on p. 6, 11 & 12.
   Edwin Levick photos on p.72 (reproduced by permission from The Levick Collection, The Mariner's Museum, Newport News, VA.)
   Parrish & Read photos on 70 & 108.
   Joseph N. Pearce photos on 2, 4, 30, 41, 42, 47, 48, 54, 65, 66 & 146
   Unidentified photos on pages 66 (lower right - probably Pearce), 92 & 93

Chesapeake Bay Maritime Museum, St. Michaels, Maryland:
   Unidentified photo on page 95.

Photo page 85 courtesy of John Howell.

Photos page 194 courtesy of Jay Benford.

DRAWINGS:

Chesapeake Bay Maritime Museum:
   End papers, 79, 80, 86, 96, 140, 178, 195, 207, 208, 209, 210 & 212.

Barge House Museum:
   Pages 1 & 116.

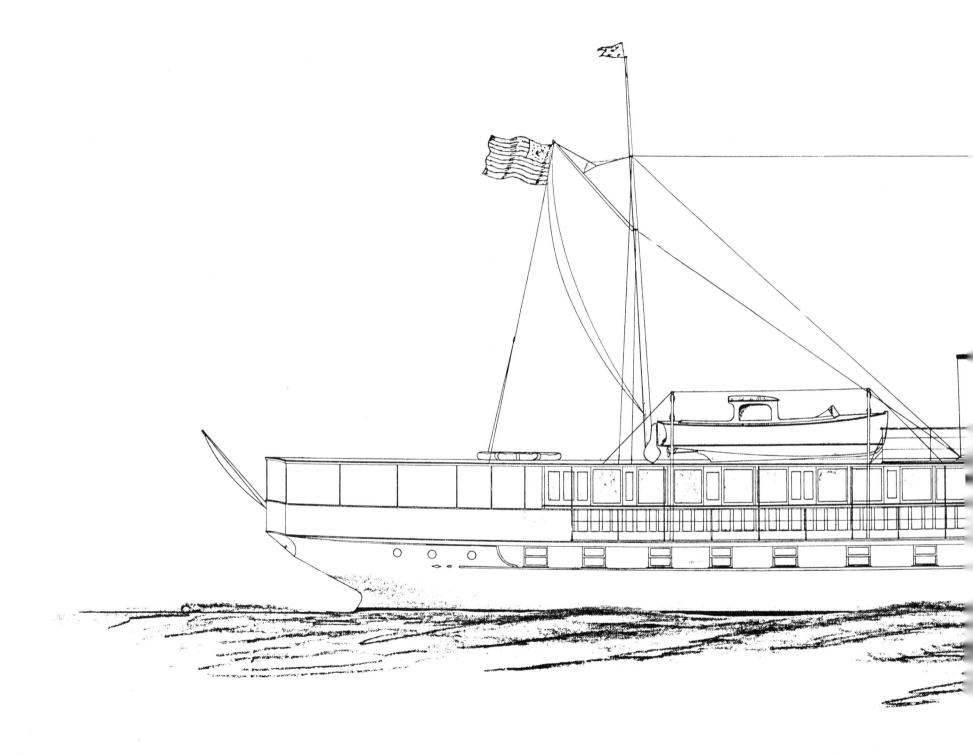